T0320272

AGRARIAN DISTRESS AND FARMER SUICIDES IN NORTH INDIA

This volume provides a comprehensive and detailed socio-economic overview of agrarian distress in India which has manifested in the suicides of farmers and agricultural labourers. Using empirical research and field data from rural India, especially Punjab, this book examines the underlying causes of farmer suicide and steps which can mitigate the crisis.

Covering nearly 1,400 rural households, the research in this volume identifies the various dimensions of the deepening crisis in agriculture and farming. It categorises the factors of the problem across different regions and estimates its extent and magnitude. In this updated edition the authors focus on instances of political mobilization and collective movements by farmers struggling to bring the issue of agrarian distress to attention. The book also discusses the implementation of state-waivered loans and compensations and their effect on the farming community.

Topical, comprehensive and rich in data, this book will be valuable to scholars and researchers of political economy, agricultural economics, South Asian politics, political sociology and public policy.

Lakhwinder Singh is a Professor at the Department of Economics and Coordinator at the Centre for Development Economics and Innovation Studies, Punjabi University, India. He has been a Visiting Fellow at Yale University, USA, and Seoul National University, South Korea. He is also the founding editor of *Millennial Asia: An International Journal of Asian Studies*. He has contributed more than 60 research articles in peer-reviewed journals and edited books, and has eight authored and edited books to his credit. One of his recent books is *Agriculture Innovation Systems in Asia: Towards Inclusive Rural Development* (2019).

Kesar Singh Bhangoo is a Professor of Economics at the Centre for Research in Economic Change, Department of Economics, Punjabi University, India. He specializes in labour economics, especially industrial relations, trade unionism and other labour issues. His book *Dynamics of Industrial Relations* (1995) discusses industrial disputes, trade unions and the working and welfare conditions in the cotton textile industry.

Rakesh Sharma is an Assistant Professor of Economics at Sachdeva Girls College, Gharuan, Mohali, India. Prior to this, he was an Indian Council of Social Science Research doctoral fellow at the Department of Economics, Punjabi University, India. He specializes in the areas of national agricultural innovation systems and has handled several projects related to agrarian distress and rural economic development.

'The research explores the roots and the various dimensions of Punjab's agrarian crisis through extensive empirical research in Punjab. While the work will be of particular interest to specialists in Punjab, the findings from this research will also be relevant for social scientists and economists exploring agrarian crisis in other parts of India and the developing world.'

—Nadia Singh, *Economic and Political Weekly*

'This book will help those (economists, sociologists, policy makers) who are interested in understanding the nature, gravity and causes of the agrarian crisis in the agriculturally developed state of Punjab.'

—Prabhjot Kaur, *Millennial Asia:*
An International Journal of Asian Studies

'A noteworthy study that provides much-needed insights into the nature and severity of the farm crisis in Punjab.'

—Sukhpal Singh, *Frontline*

AGRARIAN DISTRESS AND FARMER SUICIDES IN NORTH INDIA

Second Edition

*Lakhwinder Singh,
Kesar Singh Bhangoo
and Rakesh Sharma*

LONDON AND NEW YORK

Second edition published 2020
by Routledge
2 Park Square, Milton Park, Abingdon, Oxon, OX14 4RN

and by Routledge
52 Vanderbilt Avenue, New York, NY 10017

Routledge is an imprint of the Taylor & Francis Group, an informa business

© 2020 Lakhwinder Singh, Kesar Singh Bhangoo and Rakesh Sharma

First edition published by Routledge 2016

British Library Cataloguing-in-Publication Data
A catalogue record for this book is available from the British Library

Library of Congress Cataloging-in-Publication Data
Names: Singh, Lakhwinder, author. | Bhangoo, Kesar Singh, author. |
   Sharma, Rakesh, author.
Title: Agrarian distress and farmer suicides in North India / Lakhwinder Singh,
   Kesar Singh Bhangoo, Rakesh Sharma.
Description: Second edition. | New York, NY : Routledge, 2019. | Includes
   bibliographical references and index.
Subjects: LCSH: Farmers—Suicidal behavior—India, North. | Agriculture—
   Economic aspects—India, North. | Agricultural laborers—India, North.—
   Economic conditions. | Agricultural laborers—India, North.—Social
   conditions.
Classification: LCC HV6545.35 .S54 2019 (print) | LCC HV6545.35 (ebook) |
   DDC 362.28088/6309541—dc23
LC record available at https://lccn.loc.gov/2019028945
LC ebook record available at https://lccn.loc.gov/2019028946

ISBN: 978-0-367-22071-6 (hbk)
ISBN: 978-0-367-22078-5 (pbk)
ISBN: 978-0-429-27062-8 (ebk)

Typeset in Bembo
by Apex CoVantage, LLC

CONTENTS

FIGURES

TABLES

FOREWORD

The state of Punjab has a special place in India. It is the only state with a Sikh majority population. It was also the cradle of India's Green Revolution and has been a major contributor to India's self-sufficiency in crucial food grains like wheat. Punjab's flourishing agricultural economy helped to make it the country's highest-income major state. More recently, however, the picture has been less bright. Punjab went through a long period of violent conflict, has fallen in per capita output rankings, and now suffers from societal problems such as drug and alcohol addiction, as well as environmental degradation that imperils its agricultural base. In this context, the study of agrarian distress in Punjab, by Lakhwinder Singh, Kesar Singh Bhangoo and Rakesh Sharma, is an important contribution to understanding some of the dimensions and causes of Punjab's current problems.

The current monograph focuses on farmer suicides. This is a problem in many parts of India, as evidenced by the public suicide of a farmer from Rajasthan at a political rally in the national capital, just a few days before this writing (April 2015). Even without such cases, the issue is extremely emotive, as one would expect. Thus, the study in this book makes a significant contribution to understanding a national problem. In this respect, the analysis here stands out in using a large amount of unique primary data, collected through detailed surveys and collated with secondary data that provides important context for the phenomenon being analysed. Hence, this work represents a significant contribution in multiple dimensions.

For me, however, the focus on Punjab is the most important source of value of this study. In the realm of work on economic development in India, the state of Punjab tends to be relatively neglected, because it is perceived as better off or more advanced, compared to many other parts of the country. The relative income status of Punjab is certainly accurate (it is still seventh in the rankings), but, in my view, the current problems of the state point to looming disaster. It is admirable, therefore, that the authors have tackled their topic, using farmer suicides, to lead into a more general discussion of the causes of agrarian distress in the state.

There are many facets of the analysis in this book that deserve recognition. In addition to the large-scale primary survey, the use of treatment and control groups (households with and without suicides), separate consideration of farmers and labourers, the focus on districts where suicide rates are the highest, careful analysis at the sub-district level and combining the survey data with existing secondary data are all positive features of the study. My understanding of the results of the analysis is, briefly, as follows. The authors find that smaller and more marginal farmers are more likely to commit suicide. Greater indebtedness, as well as greater reliance on non-institutional sources of credit, is associated with a greater risk of suicide. On the other hand, religion and caste do not seem to matter for suicide propensities. Importantly, lack of access to reliable irrigation, including farmers who are at the tail ends of canal irrigation systems, is associated with greater chances of suicide.

The results are not causally definitive, but they are consistent with a causal story, where inefficiencies and inequalities in access to water and to credit are contributors to agrarian distress. The authors step back from the specifics of their data to draw on their broader knowledge of Punjab economy and trace out the broader story of Punjab's increasingly dysfunctional agrarian economy. They discuss the problems with interlinked credit and output markets, the dire fiscal position of the state and the potentially disastrous situation with respect to agricultural water use. Their policy recommendations include fixing these problems, as well as actions to diversify agriculture and, even more important, steps to change the long-run structure of the economy. As they point out, the lack of alternative economic opportunities contributes to lock-in within agriculture for marginal farmers, and their persistent vulnerability.

Whether politicians and policymakers in Punjab will pay attention to this study, and learn from its analysis, is difficult to predict. They certainly ought to read it, and understand what it says, as well as the broader implications of the authors' analysis. Undoubtedly, the deeper problems of Punjab, uncovered as the authors drill down in detail to look at farmer suicides and agrarian distress, are serious. One can only hope that this significant monograph will spur discussion, as well as further research on the economic problems of Punjab, and possible solutions. The authors deserve to be congratulated for their effort.

Nirvikar Singh
Distinguished Professor of Economics
University of California, Santa Cruz

PREFACE

Punjab economy has remained one of the most prosperous states of the Indian Union since the ushering in of the green revolution till the 1990s. The green revolution flourished in the mid-1960s in Punjab, and it has made India food self-sufficient. Agricultural growth of Punjab not only ensured the much-desired food security of the nation but also due to direct and indirect linkages with other sectors of the state's economy initiated the process of overall economic development. Consequently, poverty reduction occurred dramatically in a short span of time. This process gave the status of Punjab economy the role model of capitalist economic development. In fact, it was suggested that the economic development experience of Punjab is worth emulating in other states of India as well as in other developing economies.

Agrarian transformation dramatically increased capital intensity during the maturity stage of green revolution. Punjab farmers have intensively used increasingly made available biological and mechanical innovations that required huge amounts of new investment on the one hand and reduced the role of family labour in agricultural activities on the other hand. Therefore, Punjab agriculture turned highly market oriented and heavily dependent on borrowed finances. The agricultural output market arrangements are heavily dependent on intermediary agencies called 'commission agents', since the commission agents have long-term dealings with the farmers and know well the history of the client farmers. Keeping in view the needs of the client farmers, the commission agents turn out to be the major source of finance for their client farmers. Formal financial institutions with a high degree of cumbersome procedures that involve high transactions costs pushed the farmers to the clutches of the informal lenders. Due to exorbitant rate of interest charged by the informal lenders and interlinked agrarian credit markets turned out to be highly exploitative. This has increased the cost of cultivation multiple times. Falling returns and increasing cost of cultivation are well-known realities of Punjab agriculture. As a result of it, indebtedness increased multiple times. The small- and marginal-sized holdings started turning non-viable. The economic reforms process initiated in July 1991 resulted in the increase in prices of industrial products which were mainly used as an input in agricultural production, and recovery from services such as education and health care hit hard the already fragile economy of a large number of small and marginal farmers. The paradigm shift of economic policy dramatically reduced public investment in agriculture in general and rural economy in particular. This has increased agrarian distress in Indian agriculture in general but more intensely in Punjab.

Punjab also suffered from sociopolitical turmoil in the 1980s and early 1990s. During the period of this turmoil, Punjab state governance and institutional structure remained almost disrupted. The fiscal policy of Punjab since then continues to remain dysfunctional. Consequently, the public investment in agriculture reached to the lowest ebb. Precisely because of this reason, agriculture of the state has suffered heavily but it has hit hard the small and marginal farmers and agricultural labourers. The suicides of farmers and agricultural labourers were reported from all parts of Punjab. However, it was surprising that agrarian distress was widespread but the farmers and agricultural labourers in the particular area of Malwa region of Punjab were severely affected. A number of similarly positioned farmers and agricultural labourers have been surviving.

Therefore, this study was undertaken to investigate why some of the farmers and agricultural labourers committed suicides and why others are still surviving. This study, based on primary survey covering 1,392 rural households from three districts of Malwa region of Punjab, has examined why farmers and agriculture labourers committed suicides. A new Chapter 4 related to Farmer and Agriculture Labourer Suicides in Punjab is based on the census survey conducted by the Govt. of Punjab through three universities is added in this updated edition. This study is unique and first of its kind that examines the factors that have allowed some to survive and others to commit suicides. The policy lessons that have emerged from this study are useful both for Punjab and other agrarian-distressed states of India.

This study would not have been possible without the active support of several individuals and organizations. The Indian Council for Social Science Research (ICSSR), New Delhi, supported this study while financing the project 'Agrarian Distress in Punjab – A Study of Farmers and Agriculture Labourers'. The financial support of ICSSR is gratefully acknowledged and appreciated.

The authors gratefully acknowledge the intellectual input received from well-known scholars in this specialized area of research and their participation in agrarian distress one-day workshop on 31 August 2013 organized by the Centre for Development Economics and Innovation Studies (CDEIS), Punjabi University. The prominent scholars among them who participated in the workshop were late professor G. K. Chadha, Professors K. N. Nair, H. S. Shergill, Sucha Singh Gill, Rajinder Singh Sidhu, M. S. Sidhu, Kamal Vatta, J. S. Sidhu, A. S. Bhullar, Neelma Deshmukh, Inderjeet Singh, Anita Gill, Sukhwinder Singh, J. S. Brar, Deepak Kumar, Umrao Singh, Kewal Krishan and Parmod Aggarwal. Several representatives of farmer organizations also participated and contributed their viewpoints based on grassroots realities faced by them. We benefited immensely during discussions with all of them. The authors are grateful to all of them without implicating them for the views expressed in this study. The earlier version of the book was reviewed by Prominent Scholars such as Professor Sukhpal Singh, Professor Satish Verma, Dr. Nadia Singh and Dr. Prabhjot Kaur. The points raised by the reviewers and others helped us immensely to revised the earlier version of the book.

We also express thanks to our respondent farmers, agricultural labourers and their family members for providing relevant information and support during the survey of the villages of three districts. We would also like to thank the team members, research assistants and research investigators, for doing tremendous work for the project. Several libraries and their staff including Bhai Kahan Singh Nabha library and Department of Economics library of the Punjabi University, Rattan Tata Library, Delhi School of Economics, University of Delhi and the library of the Jawaharlal Nehru University helped us in providing the relevant research material. Their assistance and cooperation is gratefully acknowledged.

The comments and suggestions of an anonymous referee on an earlier draft of the book immensely helped the authors in refining the text. The authors are thankful to the anonymous referee for strategic support. Routledge team, both commissioning and publishing, in New Delhi office deserve our deep appreciation for their help at every stage and also bringing out the book in a short span of time.

We express our thanks to the supporting staff of the Department of Economics, the CDEIS, and Accounts Branch of Punjabi University for cooperation and assistance in completing this study and Mr. Baltej Singh Bhathal for typing several drafts of the manuscript. However, any errors and omissions that remain are the sole responsibility of the authors.

Lakhwinder Singh
Kesar Singh Bhangoo
Rakesh Sharma

ABBREVIATIONS

AFDR	Association for Democratic Rights
ESO	Economic and Statistical Organization
GFCF	gross fixed capital formation
GSDP	gross state domestic product
IDC	Institute for Development and Communication
KALIA	Krushak Assistance for Livelihood and Income Augmentation
LPG	liberalization privatization globalization
MSP	Minimum Support Price
NCRB	National Crimes Record Bureau
NSDP	net state domestic product
NSSO	National Sample Survey Organization
NYAY	Nyuntam Aay Yojana
OBCs	other backward castes
PM-KISAN	Pradhan Mantri KIsan SAmman Nidhi
PSFC	Punjab State Farmers Commission
Rythu Bandhu	Agriculture Investment Support Scheme
SCs	schedule castes
SDP	state domestic product
WTO	World Trade Organization

1
INTRODUCTION TO THE SECOND EDITION

When India embarked on the era of planned economic development with the first five-year plan in 1950–51, it faced shortages of food supplies due to low productivity and traditional methods of production applied in agriculture. To overcome these food shortages, India attempted several institutional changes, such as land reforms and consolidating landholdings. It also created basic infrastructure, such as a modern irrigation system, a research and extension system and the right mix of input and output markets. The strategies of the green revolution were a success in the state of Punjab – with the productivity of food grains rising many times, especially wheat and rice. This increase happened mainly because of the forward-looking entrepreneurial skills of Punjabis, who were ready to take risks for making investments into agriculture and who were supported by the state while enacting the right kind of institutions and infrastructural facilities.

The ushering in of the green revolution in Punjab initiated multidimensional rural economic development and an agrarian transformation. At the early stage of the agrarian transformation, engineered by technological breakthroughs, the agricultural progress benefited the rural society of Punjab across castes and classes (Bhalla and Chadha 1983). The relative egalitarian impact of agrarian transformation lies in the nature of technological progress that was scale-neutral and labour absorbing. This raised the wage rate and availability of work in agriculture and allied activities (Dhesi and Singh 2008). The state government of Punjab, apart from providing agriculture-related institutional and infrastructural support also opened up educational facilities in each village and health care system. Each village was connected with metalled roads, and Punjab ranked first in providing universal electrification to the villages. These developmental initiatives of the state government made the rural economy of Punjab a model of economic development and symbol of economic prosperity. Punjab has emerged as the state with the highest per capita income and the lowest population below the poverty line among the Indian states and is thus projected as a model of modern rural economic development worth emulating in other parts of India and in other developing countries.

The agricultural progress-based economic prosperity started showing signs of stagnation in returns in the late 1970s and early 1980s and deceleration in returns in the 1990s. Scholars who had examined the economic development process of Punjab had given warning signals with regard to nature of agricultural progress that had specialized in food production without essential linkages with the industrial development of the state (Bhalla and Chadha 1983; Johl 1986; Gill 1988). The agriculture specializing in food grain production using mechanical and chemical innovations reduced the labour demand, but due to diseconomies of scale, small farm production made small and marginal farmers non-viable. Due to the unavailability of the remunerative gainful employment opportunities to both educated and illiterate workforce, turmoil ensued in the rural economy of Punjab. The political leadership successfully converted the economic transition question into a religious one, and consequently, the crisis fell into the hands of the fundamentalist religious leadership. The political instability and turmoil lasted more than a decade and a half (1980–95), and during this period, the existing supportive and developmental institutional arrangements turned dysfunctional. Even afterwards, the restoration of the democratic system could not restore the required institutional arrangements that could have taken Punjab from a predominantly agrarian to an industrialized economy. The liberalization, privatization and globalization phases introduced increasing interventions of market, which has further disrupted the fragile economy of the small and marginal farmers and agricultural labourers. The reduction of the required number of days for agriculture production and the unavailability of work other than agriculture hit hard the household economy of the agricultural labour and made small-scale farming not viable. Therefore, it is important to understand the process of agrarian crisis and its impact on farm labour and small land holders. This chapter is organized into eight sections. The origin of agrarian distress is laid out in the first section. The response of public policy is examined in the second section. The objectives of the study and methodology are laid out in the third and fourth sections, respectively. The procedure of sample selection and scope of the study are outlined in the fifth and sixth sections, respectively. The outline of the book and the limitations of the study are presented in the seventh and eighth sections, respectively.

Origin of agrarian distress

Agrarian crisis and distress among farmers and agricultural labourers are very much linked to agrarian transition and other unresolved agrarian questions. Agrarian transition entails transforming the rural and agrarian economy, for the sake of the overall economic development of the economy, with a capitalistic mode of production and on the basis of a national social formation (Byres 1986). The historically observed pattern of economic transformation shows a shift in income-generating sectors from agriculture to industry. The workforce also received a similar movement of transformation with some time lag. These changes were engineered by techno-logical innovations, which entail conducive institutional, ideological, cultural and societal transformation. If any roadblocks occurred over this course of economic transformation, the state played an important role, even enacting suitable legisla-tion to smoothly transition towards and on the path of modern economic growth (Kuznets 1966). However, the undergoing economic transformation in developing countries, except those in East Asia, is largely confined to sectoral income trans-formation, and the workforce continues to depend on the agricultural sector of its respective economies. The lack of industrial sector dynamics and non–absorption of surplus workforce of the agricultural sector is the major feature of the character of capitalist path adopted by the developing economies in general and India in particular.

As capitalist development in different social and political formations takes place, the range of substantive diversity has been seen to widen. To understand agrarian distress and rural economic backwardness, the prerequisites are to grasp the nitty-gritty of the agrarian transition and agrarian issues. Therefore, alleviating and eradicating agrarian distress and rural economic backwardness require following a consistent and firm idea about the intricacies of distress and economic back-wardness. Although agrarian distress has been the expression of multiple causes, indebtedness and indebtedness-related factors were considered as the most vital manifestation of rural distress and precursor of farmer and agricultural labourer suicides. Indian agriculture has undergone some major structural changes over the period of time (1991–2017), which has enhanced market-induced vulner-ability across rural households. The most significant among them are agricultural labour and small-scale and marginal farmers. There has been a dramatic decline in the labour use in the crop sector, that is a 21.4 per cent decline by the turn of the century, as compared with the late 1980s (Sidhu, Bhullar and Joshi 2005). This fall of labour use in the crop sector mainly affected hired labour. The avail-ability of work in the non-agricultural sector has also remained negligible. This is mainly due to the low skill base of the workforce. This is indicative of the fact that 89.68 per cent of the labour households do not have anyone with college-level education (Ghuman, Singh and Singh 2007). Not only did the structural changes in the agrarian economy of Punjab reduce employment opportunities, but low household income also forced them to borrow at a high interest rate, and hence, labour households became indebted. The growing incidence of indebted-ness and shrinking opportunities for the labourers led farmers to die by suicide. The growing instability induced by the market forces impacts social fabric of the rural society. As a consequence, the agricultural sector has been progressively acquiring the small farm character,[1] which affected the income and expenditure of the cultivators. Agricultural labourers mainly derive their livelihood from wage employment in agriculture. They constitute about 20 per cent of India's popula-tion and 25 per cent of the rural population. Economically, socially and politically, they are the marginalized, overworked, underprivileged and underpaid section of the Indian population, but they are indispensable to agriculture operations. The growth in the numerical strength of this class is mainly due to the failures of small owner-peasant farming caused by crop failures, sickness, or family misfortunes, loss of land through usurious debts, subdivisions among and fragmentation in land holdings through inheritance and the flow of displaced peasants and artisan workers into the ranks of hired agricultural labour as a result of the decline of handicraft industries.

The agricultural operations are increasingly becoming more and more capital intensive.[2] The adoption of biological and mechanical innovations has been considered as a necessity for raising output and productivity of the crops sown. The application of these innovations has reduced the use of labour in the production process of agriculture, and availability of work for labour, except during the peak season, has declined substantially. On the one hand, the availability of work for the agricultural workforce has declined in general, and on the other hand, it has increased the financial needs of conducting agricultural operations. Due to the unavailability of regular work for agricultural labourers and growing financial costs in agriculture, this in fact has increased the dependence of the rural workforce on borrowing financial resources. In the near absence of availability of institutional finance, the agricultural labour and small and marginal farmers usually resort to borrowing from non-institutional sources, which usually comes with a high rate of interest and sometimes undervaluing the labour, agricultural goods and assets. Above all, the borrowings require collateral and surety. There is a growing tendency of interlinking agrarian markets, which is exploitative (Gill 2006). This process culminates in increasing the burden of debt in the absence of the capacity to repay loans. This is how agrarian distress originates and deepens over time, especially among small and marginal farmers and agricultural labourers.

Various studies conducted on Punjab show that Punjab farmers remained highly indebted, which is clear from the widely publicized remark 'a Punjab peasant is born in debt, lives in debt and dies in debt' (Darling 1925). This was subsequently confirmed by the rural indebtedness survey conducted by the National Sample Survey Organisation, India's national data collection agency (NSSO 1956). During the green revolution, institutional finance increased substantially, which has given some reprieve to the farmers from indebtedness, but in the 1990s, due to slowdown in the access to institutional credit, farmers again depended on informal lenders and indebtedness. This time, agrarian distress and the rising influence of the informal lenders who have developed large political clout started confiscating the most prized asset of the farmers: the land. This is popularly called as the process of land 'grabbing'. When the small and marginal farmers faced the threat of losing their only source of livelihood and were rebuked in public by the politically influential and highly organized informal lenders, in the absence of any formal institutional and informal social institutional support, the small and marginal farmers and landless agricultural labourers started dying by suicide. During this period of severe agrarian distress, the large number of farmers of Punjab left agriculture and accelerated the process of depeasantization in the state (Singh, Singh and Kingra 2009).

Agrarian distress: public policy and response

The agrarian crisis surfaced during the mid 1980s in Punjab. It was a manifestation of the stagnation of agriculture, along with falling rate of productivity, rising costs, diminishing family labour in agriculture and rising indebtedness across farming households. These processes of agricultural stagnation more severely impacted small and marginal farmers. Furthermore, it has deepened at a fast pace with the introduction of neo-liberal policies during the early 1990s (Reddy and Mishra 2009a). In the era of the liberalization, privatization and globalization (LPG) policy regime, the policies relating to agriculture have turned against the poor small and marginal farmers, though a handful of resourceful farmers have harnessed opportunities. Neo-liberal policies resulted in decline in public investment in agriculture; freezing of minimum support price of wheat and rice under the guise of food price stability led to a decline in returns and an increase in the number of small and marginal farmers; high borrowing costs for both formal and informal sources of credit and the neglect of agriculture due to the changing agrarian political economy compounded the agrarian distress in the countryside. Distress sale of paddy in the late 1990s and the long wait in grain markets due to non-lifting of paddy by the government procurement agencies, which was done with the objective of encouraging privatization of grain trade and sale, in fact added fuel to the fire to deepen the agrarian distress and triggered farmer suicides. Furthermore, successive failure/damage to crops, especially cotton; price instability of cotton; and increased borrowings by farmer in the hope of revival have landed the farmers, especially small and marginal one, in a debt trap. All these factors pushed the agrarian sector to the wall, and as a result, many farmers and agricultural labourers died by suicide, abandoned agriculture or joined the ranks of labour and other menial workers in rural/urban areas (Nair and Singh 2014). This was the consequence of the exclusionary nature of the neo-liberal economic policy regime. The widespread distress that emerged in the countryside has reflected through growing agitations across the board by the farmers' and agricultural workers' organizations. The focus of the farmers' organizations had remained on the assured purchase of agricultural produce, remunerative prices for their produce and subsidies to ensure the sustainability of the farm sector. However, agricultural workers' organizations have been asking for better agricultural wages and access to village common resources, which had shrunk tremendously during the LPG period. The focus of the agitation of farmers' organizations has been on the problems related to relatively well-to-do farmers: medium- and large-scale farmers. These groups have captured the leadership and predominantly been the ones to participate in these organizations. Several reports from voluntary organizations and committees appointed by the government through the National Commission on Farmers gauged the gravity of the situation and recommended steps for alleviating agrarian distress (National Commission on Farmers [NCF] 2006).

The events started going in a positive direction after 2004–05, mainly due to some policy interventions in the wake of pressure from stakeholders throughout the country. Marginal increases have been restored in minimum support prices of agricultural produce, especially wheat and rice. The state also made some improvements in the credit delivery system for agriculture; by cutting the cost of credit by providing 3 per cent subsidy on crop loans as it reduced from 7 per cent to 4 per cent; and by increasing the limit on the amount that can be borrowed with the given level of collateral. During 2008–09, the government also introduced and provided a loan waiver for farmers, especially small and marginal farmers (Gill 2014). There were also some improvements in public investment in agriculture during this period. It was also noticed and observed that due to farmer organizations' concerted opposition to forcible recovery of debt and, in lieu of debt return, land 'grabbing' by the commission agents, the morale of the indebted farmers was raised, which led to a slowdown in the incidence of suicides. This rise in the consciousness among the farmers not to borrow from the informal lenders has reduced the burden of debt, especially from informal sources, and rescheduling loans and interest has also contributed to reducing the incidence of farmer suicides. The rural employment guarantee for providing stipulated days of work under the Mahatma Gandhi National Rural Employment Guarantee Act programme has given gainful work to rural and agricultural labourers. All these factors brought some temporary respite from agrarian distress.

The temporary and short-term public policy has given respite, as was expected, but the incidence of suicides is back. A report stated that two brothers of Mansa district attempted suicide together by consuming poison; one died and the other was battling with death in hospital (*Tribune* 2014). Their father, 13 years ago, died by suicide arguably due to non payment of his loans and his mounting debt burden. One week later, another report, on 23 May 2014, stated that two farmers in the Bathinda district of Punjab died by suicide due to high debt burden (*Hindustan Times* 2014). More than 32 farmers died by suicide from two districts alone, namely Mansa and Bathinda, in the first four months of 2014. There is a spurt in the incidence of farmers dying by suicide, as evident from 900 farmers who died by suicide during March 2017 to January 2019 (Chaba 2019). The government of Punjab has undertaken affirmative measures to compensate the left-behind family members of the deceased farmers by paying Rs. 2 lakh. This compensation was disbursed for the first time in 2016. The coverage of this scheme began with farmers dying by suicide during 2000–2013. Thereafter, the government of Punjab authorized the deputy commissioner of the district to immediately compensate a farmer's family who died by suicide after verifying the cause of suicide as indebtedness. Another measure to give immediate relief to the indebted small and marginal farmers of the state was the crop loan waiver, of up to Rs. 2 lakh, which was started in June 2017. Such loan waivers were also given by various other states in India, like Uttar Pradesh, Maharashtra, Karnataka, Madhya Pradesh, Rajasthan, Chhattisgarh and Kerala.

The farmer organizations formed the All India Kisan Sangarsh Coordination Committee (AIKSCC) in June 2017, which is an alliance of more than 200 farm organizations, to bring the agrarian crisis to the centre stage of public policymaking at the national level. The AIKSCC organized several protests in New Delhi, the capital city of India, and demanded remunerative prices for the various crops and freedom from indebtedness. The political elite, gauging the gravity of the mobilization and its impact on elections, and the Union government of India in its interim budget in 2019–20 announced an income support scheme, named Pradhan Mantry Kisan Samman Nidhi Income Support Scheme (PM-KISAN), to provide Rs. 6000 per annum in three equal instalments. The government of Odisha started a comprehensive income support scheme, named Krushak Assistance for Livelihood and Income Augmentation (KALIA), in December 2018. The KALIA has covered financial cultivation support, livelihood, a reduction in interest rates from 1 per cent to 0 per cent and insurance support. The most significant part of this scheme was that it provides livelihood support to landless households. Similarly, the government of Telegana also initiated an agriculture investment support scheme, named Rythu Bandhu, in May 2018. Despite all this, there is an increasing incidence of farmer suicides in India in general, and Punjab in particular, which signals that some concrete policy interventions/steps at the grassroots level are urgently needed, which should combine short- and medium-term strategies with the long-term strategies to rescue agriculture from an increasingly deepening crisis.

The manifestation of agrarian distress is stressful behaviour arising out of social, economic and psychological factors, and overwhelmingly, the common result of this stress can be seen in indebtedness-led economic distress (Johl 1986) and farm suicides across the country (Bhangoo 2006; Reddy and Mishra 2009). Other contributing factors of the agrarian crisis and farmers' and agricultural labourers' distress have been identified: crop failures on many counts; consistently lower prices of agricultural produce disproportionate to the prices of farm inputs; unavailability and inferior quality of inputs; failure of public research and extension services; mounting indebtedness from both the institutional and informal sources of lending (resulting in a debt trap); the exploitation of farmers, especially small and marginal by informal lenders; and interlocked input-output product markets (Gill 2004).

In due course, experts have recommended a number of remedial measures to revive Indian agriculture and make it a profitable occupation. The various identified policy initiatives to alleviate the agrarian distress are raising farm productivity and production besides good prices for agricultural produce; improving and developing agricultural infrastructure; managing human-made and natural risks; institutional reforms; strengthening social support systems; generating non-farm employment; and making improvements in the social sector (Sirohi and Barah 2011).

The highly distressed village *panchayats* and social workers managed to pass resolutions in their respective villages for reducing burdensome expenditures on traditions such as serving food to the whole village at the time of death and marriage. Social response and other measures of public policy are highly inadequate and ad hoc compared with the intensity and nature of the persistence of the agrarian crisis faced by the rural population of Punjab.[3] Therefore, in such a state of affairs, it is of overriding importance to look into the causes for persistent agrarian distress and farmer and agricultural labourer suicides and to suggest policy initiatives to alleviate rural distress. Most of the literature has analysed the issue at the macrolevel, relying mainly on secondary sources of information. Besides, they are state-specific, and hence, their findings may not be relevant for Punjab, where the agro-climatic and socio-cultural features are altogether different. Further, most of the studies were confined to farmer suicides and did not include a comparison of the socio-economic conditions and activities of the deceased farmers and agricultural labourers with that of the farmers and agricultural labourers, who continued to bear the brunt of agrarian distress without turning to suicide.

Objectives of the study

The fundamental question investigated in this study is why some of the farmers and labourers died by suicide and why others continue to survive. This unique and first-of-its-kind study has examined the factors that have allowed some to survive while have died by suicide. The main objectives of the study are as follows:

1   To ascertain the causes of the prevailing agrarian crisis in Punjab agriculture and distress among farmers and agricultural labourers.
2   To examine the purpose of and the pattern of using agricultural credit.
3   To identify factors precipitating indebtedness and suicides in Punjab.
4   To draw comparisons between the deceased group and the on-the-brink/control group.
5   To suggest remedial policy measures and policy changes that would mitigate these serious problems.

Methodology

The quality of the primary survey is based on the procedure followed in the sample selection. The three districts in the Malwa region of Punjab – Mansa, Bathinda and Sangrur – where incidence of suicide is the highest were chosen to conduct a primary survey during 2010–11. In this study, the following procedure of sample selection was adopted:

1   We have identified deceased farmers and labourers from a census of all the farmer households and agricultural labourer households of Mansa district. From this census, a sample of 139 deceased farmers and 57 deceased labourers has been selected for in-depth analysis. And an equal number of 139 farm households and 57 agricultural labour households who were the on-the-brink/control group have also been selected for the study.
2   For Bathinda and Sangrur districts, the required sample was drawn from the census survey conducted by Punjab Agriculture University, Ludhiana, on behalf of the government of Punjab (PAU 2009). From this census survey, 172 deceased farmers and 60 deceased agricultural labourers have been selected from Bathinda district. And 199 deceased farmers and 69 deceased agricultural labourers have been taken up for in-depth analysis from Sangrur district. Further, an

equal number of farm households and agricultural labour households have also been selected from the control group of farmers and agricultural labourers.

3   Five structured interview schedules (see Appendix I) have been prepared: one each for suicide-victim farmers, farmers with the same conditions as victims (the control group), suicide-victim labourers and labourers with the same conditions as victim labourers (the control group) have been used to collect the relevant data and information. One questionnaire was developed for conducting the census study of the Harkishanpura village of Bathinda district. This village was not only severely under distress but also put on sale by the village *panchayat.*

4   Secondary information and data have been collected and used for the study at the district level and state level from the concerned offices and organizations.

5   The collected data and information have been processed and analysed by using simple statistical techniques.

Database and sample design

To reach a fruitful and meaningful analysis of the problem, an attempt has been made to include all the developmental blocks of the three districts. Furthermore, an attempt has also been made to provide more representation in the sample to highly distressed villages (see Appendix II) and blocks with a high incidence of farmer suicides. Details of the sample of farmers in the on-the-brink/control group, deceased farmers, agricultural labourers in the on-the-brink/control group and deceased agricultural labourers have been presented in Table 1.1.

TABLE 1.1 Block- and district-wise classifications and distributions of the sample

District	Block	Farmers			Labourers		
		Deceased	Control group	Total	Deceased	Control group	Total
Sangrur	1. Sunam	38	38	76	12	12	24
	2. Malerkotla I	18	18	36	8	8	16
	3. Malerkotla II	14	14	28	4	4	8
	4. Sherpur	17	17	34	6	6	12
	5. Dhuri	12	12	24	6	6	12
	6. Bhawanigarh	21	21	42	5	5	10
	7. Andana	23	23	46	9	9	18
	8. Lehra Gaga	46	46	92	16	16	32
	9. Sangrur	10	10	20	3	3	6
	Total	**199**	**199**	**398**	**69**	**69**	**138**

(*Continued*)

TABLE 1.1 (Continued)

District	Block	Farmers			Labourers		
		Deceased	Control group	Total	Deceased	Control group	Total
Bathinda	1. Bathinda	29	29	58	7	7	14
	2. Sangat	15	15	30	12	12	24
	3. Nathana	14	14	28	6	6	12
	4. Bhagta Bhai Ka	14	14	28	4	4	8
	5. Phool	18	18	36	6	6	12
	6 Talwandi Sabo	17	17	34	12	12	24
	7. Maur	25	25	50	4	4	8
	8. Rampura	40	40	80	9	9	18
	Total	**172**	**172**	**344**	**60**	**60**	**120**
Mansa	1. Mansa	24	24	48	9	9	18
	2. Bhikhi	14	14	28	9	9	18
	3. Sardulgarh	21	21	42	8	8	16
	4. Jhunir	29	29	58	11	11	22
	5. Budhladha	51	51	102	20	20	40
	Total	**139**	**139**	**278**	**57**	**57**	**114**
Overall	**Grand Total**	**510**	**510**	**1020**	**186**	**186**	**372**

Source: Field Survey

In all, 1020 farmers – 510 deceased farmers and 510 control group farmers on the brink – and 372 agricultural labourers – 186 deceased and 186 control group farmers on the brink – have been included in this study.

Scope of the study

To capture the recent and real issues looming large on the agrarian and rural scene of Punjab, the present endeavour has not been confined to study the deceased cases of farmers and agricultural labourers during 2010–11. But this endeavour also analysed the plight of the control group of farmers and agricultural labourers by including them in the study. To understand the rural and agrarian distress in the state, an in-depth analysis of the most affected Harkishanpura village of the worst-affected Bathinda district has also been carried out. Thus, this study, in comparison to earlier studies on the subject in the state, is much wider in scope and context.

Scheme of the study

The study is organized into eight chapters. Chapter 1 is devoted to providing a world view of the political economy of agrarian distress and also outlines the problem at hand, along with the objectives of the study, methodology, sample design and limitations of the study. An empirical and theoretical perspective based on the relevant review of literature on the various aspects of agrarian distress in Punjab is presented in Chapter 2. The relationship between economic development and agrarian distress in the context of the Punjab economy is examined and presented in Chapter 3. An attempt is also made to analyse the issues of agrarian distress at the macrolevel, and it provides the genesis, causes and policy of the state regarding agrarian issues. The analysis of farmer and labourer suicides based on a census survey of villages of Punjab is presented in Chapter 4. The causes of suicides of farmers and labourers are discussed while enlarging the scope of the study at district level. The socioeconomic characteristics of the respondents, based on a primary survey, are analysed to gauge differences and similarities between the deceased and the control group of farmers and agricultural labourers, which are presented in Chapter 5. The magnitude of the agrarian distress among the farmer and labourer households and determinants of distress based on primary survey of three districts of Punjab are analysed and presented in Chapter 6. In this chapter, an attempt is also made to examine the brutal manifestation of the distress in terms of rural suicides and plight of the farmers and agricultural labourers of the control group. An in-depth study of a highly distressed village – Harkishanpura of Bathinda district – is made in Chapter 7 to capture the minutiae of the agrarian crisis. In fact, the *panchayat* of the village put a notice at the entry points of the village stating 'village on sale', which reflects the apathy of the state government and other institutional agencies to the utter neglect and abandonment of the villagers who are facing severe economic crisis. A summary, conclusions and policy suggestions are presented in Chapter 8.

Limitations of the study

During the completion of this study, the research team encountered numerous problems and limitations: importantly, the unenthusiastic responses of some of the respondents due to different problems they faced, since many of them were hopeless about the role of the government to redress their miseries. Another limitation that the researchers have faced was the ignorance of the respondents regarding the quantum of debt, income and expenditure during the survey period. Some difficulties have also been faced while converting the verbal responses into numbers and other limitations associated with primary survey and data collection. In spite of the problems and limitations, a candid attempt has been made to present a scientific analysis of the deep-rooted, complex and multidimensional problem of agrarian and rural distress in Punjab.

Notes

1 There is an increasing tendency towards a division of landholdings. The proportion of small and marginal operational holdings has risen from 30.8 per cent in 1971–72 to 77.5 per cent in 2002–03. However, the proportion of the area operated has increased from 8.6 per cent in 1971–72 to 19 per cent in 2002–03. This clearly reveals that the number of small and marginal farmers in Punjab and area operated by them has increased. However, there is a growing tendency towards the concentration of land in the hands of medium

and large farms. The Gini coefficient has gone up from 0.717 in 1961–62 to 0.800 in 2002–03 (Nair and Banerjee 2011). There was substantial rise in the proportion of small and marginal operational holdings and area operated at the all-India level. The average area operated has gone down from 2.63 hectares in 1960–61 to 1.06 hectares in 2003. Thus, across the board, the scale of agricultural production has decreased (Reddy and Mishra 2009a).

2 The capital intensity of Punjab agriculture has increased many times over, over the past four decades. This is indicative of the rise in the number of tractors, tube wells/pump sets, threshers, harvesting combines and implements. As per Punjab government estimates, there are 77,000 tractors, 13.84 lakh tube wells, 6.24 lakh threshers and 13,000 harvesting combines owned by the farmers of Punjab (Government of Punjab 2013). Furthermore, capital intensity has also increased in the small and marginal farmers, because the small and marginal farmers have also mechanized their farms. Approximately 13 per cent of marginal farmers and 31 per cent of small farmers, respectively, operate their farms with their own tractors (Singh and Bhoghal 2014).

3 The issue of suitable public policy has been widely discussed and debated among the economists in Punjab. Two significant policy directions emerged from the public policy debate for the Punjab economy. First, the agricultural development of the Punjab state alone cannot sustain the long-term economic development process and economic prosperity. Therefore, it is suggested that Punjab should go for full-fledged industrialization while integrating agriculture with industry. Industrialization should be an engine of growth and future economic transformation. Second, some economists favoured agricultural diversification from low-value-added to high-value-added agriculture. They suggested that Punjab agriculture needs to shift from food grain production to other high-value-added crops. This strategy remained quite dominant, and state government has also implemented it to some extent. However, both schools of thought recommended state intervention, but the latter view tilted towards dependence on the market economy (for a detailed discussion, see Singh, Singh and Singh 2014).

2

PERSPECTIVES ON AGRARIAN
DISTRESS AND RURAL SUICIDES

The issue of agrarian crisis and rural suicides has been hitting the headlines of the media during the late 1980s and early 1990s, and also attracted the attention of scholars, researchers, governments and the concerned. This frightening and scaring phenomenon without any sign of abatement has turned out to be the most distressing, as every seventh suicide in the country was by a farmer during 1997–2006 (Nagraj 2008). Understanding, analysing and reviewing the viewpoints of the researchers and scholars who have attempted to investigate and explain agrarian distress and farmers' and agricultural labourers' suicides are really useful and will be helpful in further probing the different dimensions of the agrarian distress and farmers' and agricultural labourers' suicides. Literature on the agrarian distress and farmers' and agricultural labourers' suicides, that is the rural suicides of India during the past two decades, highlights the agrarian situation and ways and means to address it. Agrarian crisis surfaced on the agrarian scene of India as early as the 1980s; the 'crisis' of Punjab agriculture was already evident by the early 1980s and had become a political issue in the state. Johl Committee (Johl 1986) pointed out declining yields and farm incomes, stagnating productivity levels and deteriorating environment due to the cropping pattern dominated by wheat–paddy rotation, and suggested crop diversification as a remedy. Along with this, the structural transformation of the economy has also witnessed a decline in the share of agriculture in the gross domestic product, and the formation of WTO and its subsequent policies added to the woes of farmers as this had prematurely pushed the farming community to compete with the farmers of developed countries enjoying state support without a level-playing field.

Most of the literature on the issue discussed and concluded that the causes for the prevailing distress were capitalist model of economic development inherited from colonial past, agrarian transformation, neo-liberal policies adopted by the state and changing political conjunction and agrarian political economy of the country

(Vasavi 2012). This has resulted in marginalization of agrarian sector of the state as well as hitting the economy of farmers, especially of marginal and small and agricultural labourers, very hard. Therefore, in such a situation, it is of paramount importance to probe the relevant literature with the objective to explore origin and causes of agrarian crisis, agriculture credit, indebtedness and causes, consequences and manifestations of agrarian distress in the form of agrarian suicides.

In this analysis, an attempt has been made to cover almost all aspects of the problem with the objective to present the realistic and holistic perspectives of the agrarian distress and its manifestations. Analysis of studies conducted in the specific states which had witnessed the higher rate of rural suicides of the Indian Union especially during the post-reforms period reveals that the agrarian and rural sector is facing a tough and difficult time, and this has been accepted and acknowledged by almost all the stakeholders. In this light, this discussion and analysis is divided into four sections. In the first section, the origin and causes of agrarian crisis from the macroeconomic perspective based on earlier studies are developed. The analysis of studies related to agricultural credit and indebtedness is taken up in the second section. The third section is devoted to the literature on the causes, consequences and manifestations of agrarian distress in the form of suicides by farmers and agricultural labourers. Concluding remarks and identification of researchable gaps are presented in the final section.

Origin and causes of agrarian crisis

National Commission of Farmers (Swaminathan 2006) commented on the agrarian crisis in India and opined that something very serious and terribly wrong is happening in the countryside. This fact has been admitted and acknowledged by various studies, reports and all the stakeholders, and was also corroborated by the dismal performance of agriculture as the annual agricultural growth rate fell to an all-time low to 0.6 per cent during 1994–95 to 2004–05. As a consequence of it, the usurious moneylenders and other informal sources of credit re-emerged in the rural areas (Lerche 2011). Agrarian crisis created by several factors has pushed the small and marginal farmers into distress, and the distress has deepened due to structural changes taking place in agriculture. Importantly, increasing pressure of population on agriculture and land resources, continuous decline in the share of agriculture in gross domestic product, rigidity in shifting of the workforce away from agriculture and increased process/phenomenon of marginalization of the small and marginal farmers have taken place. Further, agriculture has undergone some major structural changes which have enhanced the market-induced vulnerability of the small and marginal farmers, especially opening up of Indian agriculture for foreign competition without any level-playing field, and agriculture has been progressively acquiring the small farm character, which affected the income and expenditure of the cultivators and landless agricultural labourers (Vyas 2004; Reddy and Mishra 2009b). Furthermore, the number of landholdings falls into marginal farmers' category owning less than 1 hectare of land, which has increased from 39 per cent in

1960–61 to nearly 75 per cent in 2009–10, and on the other hand, large farmers with 10 hectares of landholding squeezed from 5 per cent to 1 per cent during the same period (Lerche 2011).

Crop failure on many counts, consistently lower prices of agricultural produce disproportionate to the price level of inputs, non-availability and inferior quality of inputs, failure of research and extension services, mounting indebtedness resulting in a debt trap, exploitation of farmers especially the small and marginal farmers by informal lenders and interlocked input-output-product markets have deepened the misery and distress of farmers and caused severe agony and economic stress (Bhangoo 2006; Gill and Singh 2006; Deshpande 2009). Similarly, along with the slowdown of agricultural growth, the costs of farm inputs have increased faster as compared to farm produce prices, and also the costs of capital in the farm sector have increased substantially over the period. This turned agriculture into an unprofitable occupation and compelled the farmers, especially small and marginal, to borrow from costly informal sources of credit, which further deepened agrarian crisis and indebtedness (Singh 2009). During the era of liberalization, privatization and globalization policies, prices of wheat and rice, the two major crops of Punjab, remained stagnant at home but continuously declined in the international market, hitting hard at agriculture and making it nonviable and non-competitive for farmers. At the same time, agricultural input prices increased by 25 to 45 per cent, but the increase in agricultural output prices is only 9 to 9.5 per cent since 1967 (IDC 2006). The cost of cultivation of rice increased by 5 per cent from 44 per cent to 49 per cent during 2000–01 to 2005–06 over 1995–96 to 2000–01, and for wheat it increased by 8 per cent during the same period. The gross income was reduced by 33 per cent for rice and almost by 100 per cent for wheat from 1995–96 to 2000–01 to 2000–01 to 2005–06, respectively (IDC 2006). The cost of cotton cultivation increased 17 times and the income from cotton only 11 times during 1975–76 and 2001–02 (Narayanamoorthy 2006), and its continuous failure almost for a decade due to attack of American bollworm and water logging (Rangi and Sidhu 2000) has negatively affected the incomes of cotton growers.

Along with these, several social and structural factors are also responsible for agrarian and rural distress. Analysis clearly identified that the changed pattern of landholdings, that is increasing the number of landholdings and declining the size of average landholding; changed cropping pattern; neo-liberal policies; market vagaries; neglect of agriculture by the state and decline of public investment in agriculture were the other factors which aggravated the crisis (Suri 2006). Here, two important issues emerged over the period and were also highlighted in the relevant economic literature. First, the relatively agriculturally advanced and developed areas, especially green revolution belt, witnessed strong peasants' and farmers' movements. In these areas, the political leadership was dominated by the rural and farming community and was ruthlessly mesmerized in agrarian crisis. Second, it has also been repeatedly pointed out and observed in various studies that the farmers and agricultural labourers, that is rural people in the largest democracy of the world, are increasingly being politically and economically marginalized during the post-reform era against the set norms of the democracy (Suri 2006). The changing agrarian political economy during neo-liberal regime witnessed disjuncture in the interest of farmers and politicians, which eroded the strong political position of the farmers'/peasants' movement supported by politicians during the 1960s and 1970s, and presently politician are disinterested in politically supporting the farmers'/peasants' movement as the sources of their own incomes have shifted from agriculture to non-agriculture, such as business in transport, hotels and real estate. As a result of this, agriculture has been pushed to the margins and agrarian distress has deepened over time (Bhangoo 2014). As a consequence of it, the strength and bargaining power of peasants'/*kisan* (farmer) unions to protect the interests of the farming community and to raise/accept their demands for remunerative prices and other aspects/issues has declined during the post-reforms period as compared to the pre-reforms period (Mohanti 2005; Mishra 2007). The economic growth that has taken place during the neo-liberal regime has caused unbridled individualism and consumerism among the masses as well as among the rural people; this has weakened the position of small and marginal farmers and pushed them to the margins (Gill 2005; Mohanti 2005). Most of the experts and the stakeholders were of the view and in agreement that this has manifested in rural indebtedness, increasing family feuds, increasing indulgence in drugs in rural areas and ultimately rural suicides.

Indian agrarian political economy has transformed over the period of time, as commercialization of agriculture witnessed a shift from production for consumption to production for market and land started becoming a commodity during the colonial period. After independence, the development model adopted ignored agriculture, as it placed more emphasis on industrialization. However, during the 1970s and 1980s the farmers' unions launched agitations to put forward their demands, including remunerative prices, subsidies and loan waivers. The presence of elected and political representatives having an interest in agrarian economy lobbied for protecting the interest of farmers. Therefore, the farmers' movement succeeded in tilting the policy formulation in favour of agriculture. Again agrarian interests hit hard and marginalized during neo-liberal policy regime due to shift in economic policies led to stagnation in agriculture, and this also bankrupted farmers, especially the small and marginal ones (Posani 2009). Further, during the post-reforms period, the declining productivity in agriculture, due to declining public investment in agriculture, and increasing marginalization of peasantry (small and marginal farmers) along with high percentage of agricultural labour with much less productivities added to the agrarian distress (Sahay 2011).

The process of globalization, resulting shift in economic priorities and consequently weakening of the Indian state have played their role in making farmers' politics less effective and this added to the agony of already-distressed farmers (Jodhka 2006). Neo-liberal policy changes not only moved away from support system of subsidies for seeds, fertilizer, irrigation, energy, credit and so on, but also exposed farmers to compete in world market prematurely. This also stressed the resources and resulted in environmental and land degradation and receding water table. As a result, the major part of the income of the small and marginal farmers is from wages and subsidiary income from farming, and this class of farmers could be better understood as wage workers (Reddy and Mishra 2009). In such a situation, they confronted the difficulty in repaying the loans and in turn became indebted to the lenders (Mohanakumar and Sharma 2006).

The agrarian crisis and farmers' distress are closely linked to the neo-liberal policy regime; the worst affected are the small farmers, as they are more vulnerable to crop losses and a price fall. Agrarian distress further deepened because of steadily contracting area under agriculture and huge increase in the number of marginal and small landholders. Diminishing profitability and continuously declining real income of farmers has also been reflected in literature (Posani 2009) as farmers have faced rise in prices of major farm inputs, like diesel, seeds and fertilizers, without a corresponding compensatory rise in prices of farm produce. Agrarian distress aggravated in the wake of slowdown of agricultural exports (Government of India 2005), reduction in input subsidies (Acharya 2000; Acharya and Jogi 2004), uncertainty and volatile prices in domestic as well as in international markets, declining gross capital formation in agriculture (Chand 2009; Posani 2009) and decline in public investment in agricultural research and extension and irrigation (Balakrishnan, Golait and Kumar 2008). During the neo-liberal policy regime, under the guise of financial liberalization, closure of rural bank branches, a sharp decrease in the growth of credit flow to agriculture and increased marginalization and exclusion of small and marginal farmers from the institutional sources of credit have taken place on a large scale (Ramachandran and Swaminathan 2005; Shetty 2010). This added to the distress of small and marginal farmers, who have been compelled continuously to depend on unregulated sources of credit (Reddy and Mishra 2009). It has also been observed that enactments of land reforms 'acts' in most of the states and their implementation remained unfulfilled (Deshpande and Shah 2010); prematurely opening up the Indian agriculture for global competition without a level-playing field under neo-liberal policies, lack of proper irrigation facilities, shortcomings and problems with rural credit delivery system, lack of assured remunerative prices and marketing of agricultural produce along with adverse climatic factors were the leading causes of agrarian distress (Bhangoo 2005; Gill and Singh 2006; Suri 2006; Swaminathan 2006).

The studies from different states of the Indian Union with incidence of farmers' suicides and distress confirm the concentration of distress and suicides among the small and marginal farmers (Galab, Rewathi and Reddy 2009; Rao 2010). Literature also clearly pointed out that roots of agrarian distress, heavy accumulated burden of debt to multiple creditors and farmers' suicides were in low/negative returns due to successive crop failure/damage caused by natural and man-made factors. At the same time, due to the urge to move upwards and in the hope of revival, farmers persist in borrowing and investing, ultimately landing them into a debt trap (Rao 2010). Further, declining share of agriculture in gross domestic product, continuous dependency of a large proportion of population on agriculture and unfavourable policies and support system aggravated the agrarian crisis (Nair and Menon 2010).

Although, the rural and agrarian sectors of the economy have remained the bedrock and significantly contributed to the welfare of the rural economy, the crisis of this sector impinges heavily on the livelihood of the rural population (Vasavi 2012). Along with these macro issues, some local/micro issues like indebtedness, crop failure, deterioration of economic status, family feud and loss of social status due to continuous harassment by the lender in public also added to the crisis and caused vulnerability and triggered farmers' suicides (Bhangoo 2006; Mishra 2007). Moreover, in the case of Punjab, the issues and factors such as diversion of Punjab river waters to other states, unfavourable price structure of farm produce and inputs, inadequate availability of credit at affordable interest rates, lack of direct subsidy to needy farmers, reduction in public investment in agriculture and lack of crop insurance were identified as precipitators of agrarian crisis, indebtedness and agrarian suicides (Bhangoo 2005; Gill and Singh 2006; Sidhu and Jaijee 2011).

Discussion and analysis of the existing agrarian scenario and underlined causes clearly demonstrates that agriculture is facing a severe agrarian and rural distress, and its manifestation is very much clear from the increasing incidence of suicides among farmers and agricultural labourers. Also, it seems that Indian agriculture has lost its importance, as a provider of capital for industrialization, cheap raw material and food and market for industrial products (Lerche 2011). Further, it has also been observed that agrarian distress has social bearings and manifests in various non-economic factors such as family feud, drug addiction, impending marriages and feud with others, which were the underlying leading immediate provocations for suicides (Bhangoo 2006; Mishra 2007). The falling farm incomes and profitability, repeated crop failure due to natural and man-made causes, non-remunerative prices of agricultural produce, high costs of farm inputs and sharp rise in costs of cultivation have distressed the economy of the farmers and forced them to borrow heavily from institutional as well as non-institutional sources of credit in the hope of the revival of agriculture. This not only landed the farming community, especially small and marginal ones, into a debt trap but also led to rural suicides. In rural areas, the farmers and agricultural labourers have committed and continue to commit suicides mainly due to indebtedness and indebtedness-related factors (Bhangoo 2006; Gill and Singh 2006; Sidhu, Singh and Bhullar 2011).

Agricultural credit and indebtedness

The farmers need credit for fulfilling short-term requirements of working capital and long-term investment in capital goods for the farm sector. Further, the farming households require credit for a number of reasons, which include both productive purposes for income generation and unproductive purposes for non-income generation. In reality, most of the small and marginal farmers do not have enough access to the institutional sources of credit; this and other related issues have been discussed and highlighted in various studies (Rajeev, Vani and Bhattacgarjee 2011). Furthermore, it is observed that the policy interventions to increase the access of rural people, especially small and marginal farmers and landless agricultural labourers, to formal credit markets and regulation of non-institutional credit have not succeeded despite the best efforts of the policymakers. Still rural credit markets are dominated by informal credit sources such as commission agents (*arthiyas*) and money lenders, who are exploiting the rural people through malpractices and charging exorbitant rates of interest (Mohan 2006; Shah, Rao and Vijay Shankar 2007; Pradhan 2013).

Comparative analysis regarding the lack of access to institutional sources of credit shows that 30 per cent of the small and marginal farmers had access to formal credit as compared to 60 per cent in case of large farmers (NSSO 2005). For instance, per capita indebtedness among Punjab farmers is the highest in the country with the sizeable share of informal credit, which was delivered by the commission agents, and most of the credit supplied was interlocked with output market (Gill 2004). This denial and lack of access to institutional sources of credit for the poor and small farmers may be due to the absence of collateral, inability on the part of farmers to comply with complex and lengthy bureaucratic procedures, illiteracy among this class of farmers and other such factors (Gupta and Choudhuri 1997). The other main reason for the poor and inadequate performance of formal credit institutions is imperfect information of rural credit markets, poor understanding of functioning of rural credit markets, interlocking of rural input–output markets and monopolistic power and competition in the rural credit markets (Bell and Srinivasan 1989; Aleem 1990). The absence of any social security or other risk mitigation schemes, and with or no small savings of farmer households, especially the small and marginal ones, along with denial for institutional credit for unproductive purposes, forced/compelled these farmers to borrow from informal lenders who charge exorbitant rates of interest and exploit them by other means; as a consequence of this, these farm households are trapped in the vicious circle of indebtedness, and hence, suicides.

Thus, in this section, we propose to analyse the issues emerging from the literature on farmer indebtedness, concentrating in particular on the sources of credit, purpose and other aspects and relating them to the social and economic status of the farmers. In this background, the purpose of credit assumes significance – as consequences of indebtedness arising out of productive loan can be very different from that of the unproductive borrowings. Sources of credit provide important information regarding the burden of debt and stress on farmers. It is assumed that if the credit is taken from institutional sources like commercial banks, regional rural banks and cooperative institutions rather than from the private moneylenders, then the extent of indebtedness and stress on farmers will be comparatively less due to the differences in the rate of interest charged and also free from certain malpractices.

During the post-reforms policy regime, it has been pointed out that the number of indebted Indian farmers increased from 26 per cent in 1991 to 48.6 per cent in 2003 (NSSO 2005). Further, it is worrisome that the incidence of indebtedness was among the farmers of agriculturally developed states, and the intensity of indebtedness among the farm households belonging to scheduled castes, scheduled tribes and other backward castes was much higher (NSSO 2005). At all-India level 48.6 per cent farm households were reported to be indebted, led by Andhra Pradesh

(82 per cent) and followed by Tamil Nadu (74.5 per cent) and Punjab (65.4 per cent). Average outstanding loan per farm household at all-India level was Rs 12,585, and for the state of Punjab, it is Rs 41,576, which is highest among other states followed by Kerala, Haryana, Andhra Pradesh and Tamil Nadu (NSSO 2005). All the indicators of farmers' indebtedness highlighted in various studies (Shergill 1998, 2010; Bhangoo 2006; Punjab State Farmers Commission 2006; Satish 2006) have pointed out the grave/crisis/distress situation prevailing in the agrarian sector of Punjab economy. Punjab farm households are heavily indebted, but the amount of indebtedness was the heaviest in the southwestern region. In the cotton belt of Punjab, the average debt was Rs 112,636, out of which 60.5 per cent came from informal sources, and the marginal, small and semi-medium farm households were not in a position even to repay the interest due to the heavy burden of debt (Sidhu, Singh, Kaur and Goyal 2000). The increasing extent and magnitude of indebtedness among Punjab farmers has been noticed as the cause of agrarian distress, and it evidently emerged that this has trapped the small and marginal farmers deeper and deeper into indebtedness (NSSO 2005; Gill 2010).

The issue of indebtedness among farmers and use and purpose of borrowed funds has highlighted that with the increased rural prosperity during green revolution era, farmers' expenditure on house building, consumer durables and social ceremonies has also increased (Shergill 1998; Gill 2006). For this purpose, farmers have arranged finances and funds partly by using past savings, diverting/misusing institutional productive credit and borrowing from informal sources because of easy and flexible availability, especially commission agents and *arthiyas* (commission agents) (Shergill 1998, 2010; Punjab State Farmers Commission 2007). Due to contract of credit for unproductive purposes from informal sources and diversion and misuse of productive credit, it is pointed out that this phenomenon has led to non-payment of loan instalments, accumulation of debt and interest and vicious circle of indebtedness (Gill 2004; Punjab State Farmers Commission 2007). Literature also pointed out that this situation and phenomenon has been a cause of concern and should be resolved by initiating multi-pronged measures and strategy (NSSO 2005; Punjab State Farmers Commission 2007).

High incidence of suicides and indebtedness has been reported among agricultural labourers (Ghuman, Singh and Singh 2007; PAU 2009). Further, a very large majority of the agricultural labourers of Punjab belonged to scheduled castes and backward classes, the most socially and economically marginalized sections of the rural population (GoP 2010). The prevailing agrarian distress has impacted on real wages of agricultural labourers to stagnate along with squeezed employment opportunities in the farm sector, reduced man-days of farm work and increasing indebtedness among agricultural labourers, which has pushed them towards deprivation, impoverishment (immiserization) and pauperization (PAU 2009; Singh and Sangeet 2014).

Precarious and fragile economy of the farmers due to various factors such as uneconomic holdings, non-remunerative prices of agricultural produce, high cost of agricultural inputs and continuous crop failure pushed them into a debt trap (Gill 2005). Further, high rates of interest charged on loans by both the institutional and non-institutional sources of credit and sometimes misuse of loans for unproductive purposes also contributed to misery and indebtedness of farmers (Bhangoo 2006; Gill and Singh 2006). Another interesting dimension of rural indebtedness was that farmers were equally indebted to institutional and non-institutional sources of credit. However, the agricultural labourers were indebted to non-institutional sources only (Deshpande 2002; Bhangoo 2006; PSFC 2006). It is significant to note that the lack of institutional rural credit, even the diminished presence of institutional credit, in agriculture, pushed the rural people into the deadly trap of non-institutional credit (Menon 2001).

Landless agricultural labourers, especially belonging to scheduled castes, were the most vulnerable section of the rural population that mainly depend on low wages and to eke out living are forced to borrow from non-institutional sources and thus fall into a debt trap (Deshpande 2002). The credit facilities extended by the cooperative societies and other formal agencies in view of the rising cost of cultivation are inadequate. They hardly benefit the small farmers (Mohanty 1999).

The small-sized farm households on a per hectare basis were more heavily indebted than other farm-size categories. The marginal and small farmers with tractors were also heavily indebted, and they had a lower share of the institutional loans than the other large-sized farmers who owned tractors. The present situation of high indebtedness among Punjab farmers is a cause of concern for policymakers, politicians and academicians. Here, it is pertinent to mention that studies regarding indebtedness, especially of small and marginal farmers, have discussed and highlighted not only the heavy burden of debt but also three most disturbing dimensions of indebtedness. First, the higher share of informal credit among small and marginal farmers may be due to the policies of the state and lack of access to this class of farmers to formal credit sources. Second, the high share of unproductive debt against all farmer categories and especially among small and marginal farmers is due to diversion of borrowed finances for using it to meet social needs (Singh, Kaur and Kingra 2008). Third, the high costs of informal credit range between 24 per cent and 36 per cent much higher than that of formal credit and invariably with exploitation of the borrowers on one pretext or the other (Bhaduri 1984; Gill 2004). Furthermore, another important aspect of the informal debt discussed in economic literature, which has deepened the misery and distress among farmers especially small and marginal, has been the existence and prevalence of interlocked input-output-product markets (Gill 2004). It warrants multi-pronged strategies and measures for reducing indebtedness in the short run and increasing the incomes of farmers in the long run by generating employment and increasing productivity (Singh, Kaur and Kingra 2008).

Causes, consequences and manifestations of agrarian distress

The unabated phenomenon of farmers' and agricultural labourers' suicides in the agrarian sector is an extreme manifestation of prolonged agrarian distress and indebtedness in the country. During 1995–2006, the reported number of farm suicides reached 200,000. Farmers' suicides have witnessed a sharp spurt after 1998, and during 2002–06, annual average reported farmers' suicides remained between 17,000 and 18,000 (Sanchita 2009). These estimates appear to be conservative as the figure has been taken from police records based on stringent procedure. The Vidharbha region of Maharashtra; Telangana, Warangal and Rayalaseema of Andhra Pradesh; and parts of Karnataka, parts of Kerala and Malwa region of Punjab were the most suicide-affected and distressed parts of India. Analysis of the process of globalization, agrarian crisis and farmers suicides has highlighted that the main reasons of suicides were indebtedness, borrowing from money lenders, shift towards new technology, commercialization, crop failure due to spurious seeds and other inputs, increased cost of production, overexploitation of natural resources, absence of safety nets and collapse of villages institutions (Deshpande and Shah 2010; Iyer and Arora 2010). It has also been found that agrarian distress has manifested in rural suicides, as during the period of new policy regime, literature pointed out and highlighted the increasing proportion of suicides among farmers and agricultural labourers in rural areas (Deshpande and Shah 2010; Singh and Sangeet 2014).

Suicides among the farming community of Punjab, especially in the cotton belt of Malwa region, have been hitting the headlines for the past couple of years. This frightening and scaring phenomenon continues and has been increasing over time (Institute of Development and Communication [IDC] 2006) without any sign of abatement. This reveals the plight of the victims and survivors who are on the brink and still alive, but their condition is critical and resembles that of the victims (Punjab State Farmers Commission [PSFC] 2007). Punjab government initially ignored and tried to sweep the issue under the carpet till it blew up into huge proportions and was seen as repercussions of neo-liberal policy regime pursued since 1991 (Mohanakumar and Sharma 2006). But later on, the government of Punjab admitted that the farmers of the state are committing suicides due to economic distress and indebtedness. However, it did very little or nothing to resolve the crisis and indebtedness faced by the small and marginal farmers. Reports of the spate of unabated farmers' and agricultural labourers' suicides signify an alarming and disturbing development in the agrarian sector of Punjab economy. Suicides may occur on many accounts (economic, social, psychological, etc.) but are disturbing when the reported common cause of farmer suicides is the indebtedness-driven economic distress (Mohanakumar and Sharma 2006). A perusal of farmers' suicide cases of the green revolution state of Punjab apparently indicated that along with economic distress in rural agrarian economy, crop damage/failure, low farm incomes and acute burden debt have emerged as the most important causes of suicides especially among small and marginal farmers (Bhangoo 2006; Iyer and Arora 2010). Furthermore, there were other causes of suicides among farmers, but the scale of debt, purpose and use of loans and high share of informal sources in loans emerged as the most important ones. However, the rising debt burden was found out to be the leading cause of farmer suicides (Gill 2010).

New capitalist policies and agrarian distress have created the spirit of unbridled individualism and helplessness among the farmers, especially small and marginal, and agricultural labourers. This social development/phenomenon has resulted in breakdown of the traditional social and cultural values like social integration, belong-ingness and joint family system. The manifestation of all this was the failure of social institutions and set-up for timely moral and physical support to the farmers and agricultural labourers on the brink. This corroborates with the views of Durkheim, who has examined this phenomenon and stressed the role of social and family rela-tions and the system (Durkheim 1952). This demands necessary and urgent remedial measures as well as analysis and evaluation of causes and factors precipitating farm-ers' and agricultural labourers' suicides in the state. In Punjab, the emergence of agrarian distress and suicide phenomenon has become a subject of debate, analysis and evaluation among the concerned. The recently conducted census-based reports of Punjab government on farmers' and agricultural labourers' suicides showed that more than 7,000 farmers and agricultural labourers committed suicides in the state due to agrarian distress and indebtedness. Being a matter of concern having serious and severe political, social and economic ramifications, the state government and its agencies have funded some studies (IDC 1998, 2006; Shergill 1998, 2010; NSSO 2005; PSFC 2006, 2007; Sidhu *et al.* 2011) to gauge the gravity of the situation, and also some scholars on their own (AFDR 2000; Iyer and Manick 2000; Bhangoo 2005, 2006; Chahal 2005; Gill 2005; Gill and Singh 2006; Satish 2006) have studied the phenomenon empirically and analytically, and captured and analysed it at the micro- and macro-levels relying on primary as well as secondary sources. Review of the studies allows us to identify three approaches to study and analyse this problem; first, representational and journalistic (Movement Against State Repression 2001; Sridhar 2004) studies that have drawn the attention of the government/policymak-ers to the distressing plight of the farmers, but these studies remained at the level of impressionistic observations. Second, research studies based on field surveys, primary and secondary information which have analysed and evaluated the issue in depth to understand the root causes of the problem (IDC 1998, 2006; AFDR 2000; Iyer and Manick 2000; Chahal 2005; Bhangoo 2006; Satish 2006; Sidhu *et al.* 2011), have been carried out in different parts of the state. Third, analytical studies (Bhangoo 2005; Gill 2005; Gill and Singh 2006; Jodhka 2006; Satish 2006) examined the deter-minants of the problem on the basis of existing literature and secondary information.

The studies have identified the state's cotton belt comprising Sangrur, Bath-inda, Mansa, Ferozpur and old Faridkot districts with high farmer suicide proneness during 1991–2005 (IDC 1998, 2006; Chahal 2005; Bhangoo 2006; Sidhu *et al.* 2011). Studies also reveal the moderate and low farmer suicide proneness of the central plain and sub-mountainous districts of the state, respectively. It has also been reported that non-remunerative prices of crops, successive crop failures, non-implementation of crop diversification programme due to uncertain yield, prices and marketing of alternatives, high and increasing costs of cultivation and high and exorbitant interest rates charged by money lenders and banks have landed the farming community of Punjab, especially the small and marginal farmers, in a debt trap. Punjab's grave situation of farmers' indebtedness (Shergill 1998, 2010; NSSO 2005; PSFC 2007) and the resultant farmer suicides have been hitting the headlines continuously. Suicides among farmers are disheartening and awful due to indebtedness especially in a prosperous state like Punjab, which has seen strong peasant movements and notwithstanding the fact that political leadership of the state predominantly comes from farming communities, especially Jat-Sikhs, who committed maximum suicides (IDC 1998, 2006; AFDR 2000; Iyer and Manick 2000; Chahal 2005; Bhangoo 2006).

Conclusions and research gaps

Discussion and analysis based on review of studies of agrarian distress and rural suicides brought out that the issue is deep-rooted and complex and demands detailed and deeper investigation. Evidently, the collapse of public investment in agriculture along with erosion of public institutions catering to farmers and farming sector aggravated the problem. Further, changing agrarian political economy demonstrates that agriculture is facing a severe crisis along with heavy and unbearable burden of debt against farmers and agricultural labourers, especially small and marginal, towards the informal sources of credit, and it manifests into increasing the incidence of suicides among farmers and agricultural labourers. The review of literature has also revealed and thrown light on magnitude of indebtedness and its causes, suicides and finally remedial measures. Solutions suggested to the agrarian distress include access and equity in irrigation, access to institutional credit especially to the small and marginal farmers, delinking of input–output–credit markets, strengthening of research and extensions services in agriculture, provision of inputs at affordable prices and diversification of economy especially rural. Due to divergent estimates and conclusions, a precise and concrete idea and solution regarding the crisis remains lacking. Further, most of the studies on the subject have ignored and neglected agricultural labourers, who are the important section of rural Punjab and indispensable to agriculture. Some studies have shown that agricultural labourers were also under great distress due to the prolonged and prevailing agrarian crisis, and many of them have committed suicides in the recent past. At the same time, some gaps remain and the studies have been found to be incoherent. Given the overall economic environment and agrarian distress, some farmers with similar characteristics to deceased farmers are still surviving. However, the review of studies mentioned earlier suggests that comparative studies of deceased and surviving farmers and agricultural labourers are almost absent in economic literature, especially related to Punjab. Therefore, in this study an attempt has been made to overcome the shortcomings and strives to fill the gaps.

3

ECONOMIC DEVELOPMENT AND RURAL DISTRESS IN PUNJAB

The process of modern economic development has been started in Punjab with the ushering in of green revolution in the mid-1960s.[1] The green revolution raised factor productivity multiple times. Consequently, the income levels across households dramatically increased along with strong interaction with the market. The impact of rising agriculture productivity on income distribution among rural households at the most was proportional to the ownership of productive assets such as land. A noteworthy impact of green revolution on rural households was dramatic reduction of poverty in Punjab (Bhalla and Chadha 1983). Punjab economy after the green revolution, among the major Indian states, has emerged as the most prosperous state in terms of per capita income. The green revolution–based prosperity reflected in initiating economic development process in other sectors of the economy due to forward and backward linkages (Bhalla 1995). The agriculture-led development model of Punjab was presented as the role model of capitalist economic development not only to other Indian states but also to other developing economies.

Agricultural development has been considered as a prerequisite for subsequent modern capitalist economic development. The transition, as has been observed by Kuznets (1966), from agriculture to industrialization and at a mature stage of economic development to service sector, though, underlines substantial institutional changes that pave the way for modern economic growth to take firm roots. Obviously, this transition involves transfer of surpluses, both of savings and workforce from agriculture to industrial sector of the economy. It is usually observed that the industrial sector realizes increasing returns to scale, and expansion of the industrial sector makes best use of surpluses both of the savings generated by the agriculture sector and the workforce. The industrial sector provides employment to workforce released from the agricultural sector at a higher level of wages and returns on investment, which generates desired self-sustained dynamics in the economy.[2] This is historically observed patterns of economic development of both advanced countries of the western world and newly industrializing countries of East Asia.

When we examine the economic development experience of Punjab economy since the ushering in of the green revolution, the agricultural development has fulfilled the prerequisite of economic transformation. It has generated desired level of savings[3] and made workforce surplus but failed to transform the state's economy from agriculture to industrialization. Dismal economic performance of Punjab economy, during the past two decades of economic reforms period, compared with other states of India has generated a widespread economic distress in the state.[4] During this period, the farm debt in Punjab has more than doubled in real terms. The annual interest liability is almost equal to one-third of total revenue surpluses generated by the agricultural sector of Punjab (Shergill 2011). The large proportion of this indebtedness of the farm sector (37 per cent) is due to non-institutional sources, which is exploitative in nature. The small-sized farmers' access to institutional sources is quite low compared with large-sized farms, and their indebtedness is two and a half times higher than that of the large-sized farms (Singh, Kingra and Sangeeta 2011). Due to the withdrawal of state in making investment both in agricultural sector and in social sectors, it increased burden on rural households. The policy of freezing minimum support prices (MSP) recommended by the Abhijit Sen committee report reduced income of the farmers. Distress sale of paddy, during the 1997–2001, has added fuel to fire. The rising household expenditure due to cut in social sector as well as agricultural sector infrastructure investment has impinged heavily on the already-fragile economy of the small-sized farmers. This 'double squeeze strategy' under the liberalization, privatization and globalization regime increased rural distress without providing any escape route, which forced small-sized farmers and farm labourers to resort to committing suicides. In this context, an attempt has been made in this chapter to examine the changes in the structure of Punjab economy to identify the internal and external factors responsible for rural distress. The chapter is organized into four sections. Apart from the introductory section, the second section outlines the growth and structural dynamics of Punjab economy. In the third section, the changing structure of the agrarian economy and the process of depeasantization in Punjab agriculture is analysed. The rural economy of Punjab and distress among the farm sector has been analysed in the fourth section. The major conclusions emerging from this chapter are presented in the final section.

Growth and structural transformation of Punjab economy

Among the traditional measures of level of economic development per capita income remained the most handy and commonly used indicator of economic prosperity. The per capita income estimates of major states of the Indian Union are presented in Table 3.1 and Figure 3.1. The analysis of Table 3.1 and Figure 3.1

TABLE 3.1 Per capita income across major Indian states, 2011–12

State	2011–12 per capita income in rupees	Rank	Growth rate 2010–11 to 2011–12 percentages (at 2004–05 prices)	Rank
Andhra Pradesh	71,480	8	5.75	10
Bihar	23,435	15	15.44	1
Gujarat	75,115★	5	8.65★	4
Haryana	108,859	1	6.18	8
Himachal Pradesh	74,899	6	5.76	9
Karnataka	68,374	9	6.69	7
Kerala	83,725	4	7.13	5
Madhya Pradesh	38,669	13	10.48	2
Maharashtra	101,314	2	8.73	3
Odisha	46,150	12	4.64	12
Punjab	74,606	7	4.24	13
Rajasthan	47,506	11	3.72	15
Tamil Nadu	84,496	3	6.72	6
Uttar Pradesh	30,052	14	4.17	14
West Bengal	54,830	10	5.67	11
All India	60,603	–	5.16	–

Source: Government of India (2013).

Note: ★ Figures for the previous year.

reveals that Punjab on the basis of 2011–12 per capita income is ranked seventh. First three ranks go to Haryana, Maharashtra and Tamil Nadu, respectively. The per capita income of Punjab for 2011–12 was of the order of Rs 74,606. The gap in per capita income between first rank state (Haryana) and Punjab is Rs 34,253. During the past two decades, Punjab economy has drifted from first rank to seventh, and the gap between fast-growing states and Punjab has widened continuously. Two fast-growing states, that is Gujarat and Himachal Pradesh, have recently also crossed the level of per capita income of Punjab. As per the per capita income growth rate ranks, Punjab has reached to the bottom-ranking states. It is surprising to note that Punjab's per capita income has grown at 4.24 per cent during 2010–11 and 2011–12, and accordingly growth rate rank was 13th. This evidence clearly brings out the fact that the status of Punjab economy in the national reckoning has eroded and is going down at a fast pace. The falling behind of Punjab compared with other states has happened due to the achieving of slow rate of economic growth of Punjab economy, especially in post-reform period.

The plan-wise state domestic product (SDP) growth rates from the eighth Five-Year Plan to the 11th Five-Year Plan and target growth rates of the 12th Five-Year

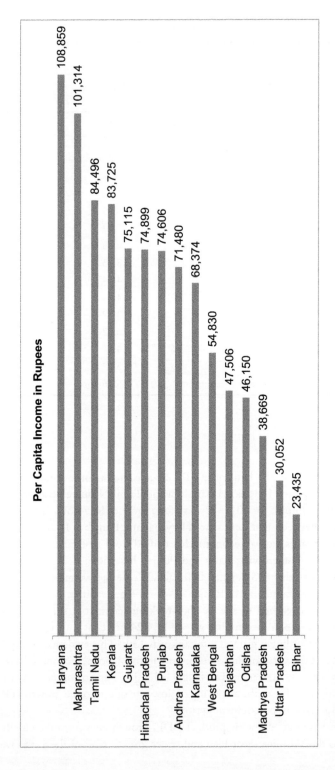

FIGURE 3.1 Rank–wise per capita income across major Indian states, 2011–12

Plan across Indian states are presented in Table 3.2. Punjab economy, during the eighth Five-Year Plan period recorded growth rate of SDP of the order of 4.7 per cent per annum against the national average growth rate of 6.5 per cent per annum. Among the 15 states, the SDP growth rate rank of Punjab economy was 13th. The growth performance further deteriorated marginally during the ninth Five-Year Plan (1997–2002) period, and the rate of economic growth was 4.4 per cent in the state of Punjab. However, there were general slow economic progresses during the ninth Five-Year Plan, and all-India average growth rate also slowed down to 5.5 per cent per annum. The growth rates, during 1997–2002, across the board decelerated except Bihar, Karnataka, Odisha and West Bengal, where the growth rates have actually increased.

Punjab economy has grown at a rate of 4.5 per cent per annum during the tenth Five-Year Plan (2002–07) against its own targeted rate of economic growth, that is 6.4 per cent per annum. It is important to note here that Indian economy, during the same period, entered into high growth trajectory. Indian economy has grown at the rate of 7.7 per cent per annum during the tenth Five-Year Plan period. The acceleration of Indian economic growth has further occurred during the 11th Five-Year Plan period. Indian economy recorded 7.9 per cent growth rate, which can be considered as the 'golden period' growth rate of the national economy. However, Punjab has recorded a growth rate much below the national average, that is 6.87 per cent per annum. Although Punjab economy registered acceleration in the growth rate during the 11th Five-Year Plan period, the rank of the growth rate among 15 states was 14th. Punjab economy consistently recorded relatively low growth rates as well as its rank remained second from below. The historical experience of the record of low economic growth of Punjab economy shows the growth target fixed in the 12th Five-Year Plan period is just 6.4 per cent, whereas the Planning Commission has set the target rate of growth of Indian economy at 8.2 per cent per annum for the same period. When Punjab economy is ranked in terms of target growth rate, its rank turns out be 15th, that is the bottom of all the 15 major states of India (Table 3.2).

The comparative analysis of Punjab state with all-India average in post-reform period shows that Punjab not only performed below the national average but has lagged far behind the progressive states of India such as Haryana, Maharashtra, Gujarat, Kerala, Tamil Nadu and Himachal Pradesh. The cause of worry is that it is expected to continue to perform much below the all-India average and also below the progressive states in the foreseeable future.

To disentangle the slow pace of growth of per capita income and SDP during the post-reform period, the sectoral net state domestic product growth rates have been estimated and presented in Table 3.3. A perusal of Table 3.3 reveals that the performance of Punjab is deteriorating when we compare with its own past performance and achievements. There is a strong evidence of deceleration in economic growth of Punjab's economy in terms of NSDP growth rates recorded during 1993–94 to 1999–2000. However, the growth rate has accelerated to 6 per cent during 2001–02 to 2011–12. The agricultural sector occupies prime place in the economy of

TABLE 3.2 Growth rates in state domestic product across states and over time (%)

S. No.	State/union territory	Eighth plan (1992–97)	Ninth plan (1997–02)	Tenth plan (2002–07)	Eleventh plan (2007–12)	Twelfth plan (2012–17) target growth rate
1.	Andhra Pradesh	5.4 (10)	4.6 (8)	6.7 (8)	8.33 (6)	8.4 (4)
2.	Bihar	2.2 (14)	4.0 (11)	4.7 (12)	12.11 (1)	9.1 (1)
3.	Gujarat	12.4 (1)	4.0 (11)	10.6 (1)	9.59 (2)	8.4 (4)
4.	Haryana	5.2 (11)	4.1 (10)	7.6 (4)	9.10 (4)	8.1 (8)
5.	Karnataka	6.2 (9)	7.2 (1)	7.0 (7)	8.04 (9)	7.6 (11)
6.	Kerala	6.5 (5)	5.7 (5)	7.2 (6)	8.04 (9)	8.2 (6)
7.	Madhya Pradesh	6.3 (7)	4.0 (11)	4.3 (15)	8.93 (5)	8.8 (3)
8.	Maharashtra	8.9 (2)	4.7 (7)	7.9 (3)	9.48 (3)	8.9 (2)
9.	Odisha	2.1 (15)	5.1 (6)	9.1 (2)	8.23 (8)	8.2 (6)
10.	Punjab	4.5 (13)	4.4 (9)	4.5 (14)	6.87 (14)	6.4 (15)
11.	Rajasthan	7.5 (3)	3.5 (15)	5.0 (11)	7.68 (11)	7.4 (14)
12.	Tamil Nadu	7.0 (4)	6.3 (3)	6.6 (9)	8.32 (7)	7.9 (9)
13.	Uttar Pradesh	4.9 (12)	4.0 (11)	4.6 (13)	6.90 (13)	7.6 (11)
14.	West Bengal	6.3 (7)	6.9 (2)	6.1 (10)	7.32 (12)	7.6 (11)
15.	Himachal Pradesh	6.5 (5)	5.9 (4)	7.3 (5)	5.50 (15)	7.9 (9)
	All India	6.5	5.5	7.7	7.9	8.2

Source: Planning Commission (2013).

Note: Figures in parenthesis are ranks.

TABLE 3.3 Sectoral growth rates of net state domestic product (average annual), 1993–94 to 2011–12 (at 2004–05 prices) (%)

Sector/year	1993–94 to 2011–12	1993–94 to 2000–01	2001–02 to 2011–12
Agriculture	1.9	2.4	1.6
Manufacturing	7.2	5.3	8.4
Electricity	5.6	1.9	8.0
Construction	10.0	8.9	10.7
Trade	4.5	5.4	3.9
Transport	13.2	13.3	13.1
Banking	13.9	13.7	14.0
Real estate	2.1	1.2	2.7
Public administration	7.6	7.2	7.8
Other services	4.7	3.1	5.8
NSDP	5.4	4.4	6.0
Per capita income	3.5	2.5	4.2

Source: Authors' estimates based on data available in CSO (2012).

Punjab. The relative share of the agricultural sector in the NSDP product was 31.25 per cent in 2010–11. It has declined from 44 per cent in 1990–91 to 39 per cent in 1999–2000 and further to 31.25 per cent in 2010–11 (Government of Punjab 2012). This clearly brings out the fact that the agricultural sector of the state of Punjab still constitutes the major contributing sector in the health of the state economy. The growth of the agricultural sector as indicated from the post-reform period not only remained quite slow (1.9 per cent) but decelerated in the second sub-period, that is 2001–02 to 2011–12. During the 1990s, the agricultural sector of the state had grown at a rate of 2.4 per cent, and it was 1.6 per cent during 2001–02 to 2011–12. However, the agricultural sector has grown at a rate of 5.15 per cent per annum during the 1980s (Singh and Singh 2002). The foregoing discussion brings out the fact that the deceleration of rate of growth of the agricultural sector has contributed substantially to the slowdown in the growth of per capita income of the economy of Punjab.

The industrial sector has been regarded as the most dynamic sector of an economy and provides desired economic transformation from low wage–low productivity economic activities to high wage–high productivity economic activities. However, in the case of Punjab, the industrial sector of Punjab economy in terms of its relative contribution to the NSDP remained quite small. The manufacturing sector of Punjab contributed 15.1 per cent of NSDP in 1990–91 and remained almost stagnant at 15.4 per cent in 2010–11. The relative share of the registered manufacturing sector in NSDP was 8.8 per cent in 1990–91, which has declined to 8.5 per cent in 2010–11. The manufacturing sector as a whole has recorded 7.2 per cent per annum growth rate in the post-reform period. The manufacturing sector growth rate during 1993–94 to 2000–01 was 5.3 per cent per annum much below the overall average. During 2001–02 to 2011–12, the manufacturing growth rate accelerated and recorded 8.4 per cent growth rate. The sectors, which have recorded deceleration of economic growth during the 2000s compared with the 1990s, are agriculture, trade and transport. Two sectors, electricity and other services, have shown faster rate of growth during 2001–02 to 2011–12, but other sectors such as construction, banking, real estate and public administration have recorded marginal acceleration in the growth rates in the second sub-period. The agricultural sector has remained the single-largest sector of the state economy, and slow growth in this sector impinges the overall growth performance of Punjab economy.

The agriculture sector of Punjab economy directly absorbs more than 35.6 per cent of the total workforce in 2011. The cultivators constitute 19.55 per cent of the total workforce of Punjab state, and agricultural workers were of the order of 16.05 per cent (Government of India 2011). It is significant to note that the agricultural sector generates more than 21.84 per cent of the gross SDP (Government of Punjab 2012) but employs 35.6 per cent of the workforce. This empirical evidence brings out clearly that the structure of Punjab economy is not only imbalanced but highly agricultural sector dependent both for income generation and for employment. Therefore, the growth performance of this sector heavily impinges on the well-being of the population living in the rural areas of Punjab. The performance of the agricultural sector also affects the growth prospects of the other sectors of Punjab economy directly and indirectly due to the interconnections between sectors. The manufacturing sector generated 20.12 per cent of the gross SDP in 2011–12 but employed only 10.24 per cent of the workforce out of the total workforce of the state in 2011 (Table 3.4). The analysis of Table 3.4 reveals that the absolute

TABLE 3.4 Changing structure of workforce across industrial categories in Punjab

Year	Cultivators	Agricultural workers	Industrial workers	Other workers	Total workers
2011	1,934,511 (19.55)	1,588,455 (16.05)	1,013,553 (10.24)	5,360,843 (54.16)	9,897,362 (100.00)
2001	2,099,330 (22.96)	1,498,976 (16.40)	769,047 (8.41)	4,774,407 (52.23)	9,141,760 (100.00)
1991	1,917,210 (31.44)	1,502,123 (24.63)	749,136 (12.28)	1,929,905 (31.65)	6,098,374 (100.00)
1981	1,767,286 (35.86)	1,092,225 (22.16)	665,442 (13.50)	1,402,806 (28.47)	4,927,759 (100.00)
1971	1,665,153 (42.56)	786,705 (20.11)	442,070 (11.30)	1,018,664 (26.03)	3,912,592 (100.00)

Source: Government of India (2011), and Government of Punjab, Statistical Abstract, Various Issues.

Note: Figures in parenthesis are percentages.

number of cultivators has increased from 1,665,153 in 1971 to 1,934,511 in 2011. But the relative share of cultivators declined from 42.56 per cent in 1971 to 19.55 per cent in 2011. It is important to note here that agricultural labourers in absolute number have increased from 786,705 in 1971 to 1,588,455 in 2011, which is more than two times' increase. However, the relative share of agricultural labour has marginally decreased during the past four decades, that is only four percentage points. Industrial workforce has more than doubled during the past four decades, but relative share marginally declined from 11.3 per cent in 1971 to 10.24 per cent in 2011. The relative share of this workforce should have increased so that the transformation process could have decreased the burden of growing population on the agricultural sector of Punjab economy.

Changing structure of agrarian economy and the process of depeasantization

The agrarian economy of Punjab has undergone substantial changes since the advent of the green revolution. These changes in the agrarian economy of Punjab can be traced with the help of distribution of land across farm size categories and over time. The availability of non-farm employment opportunities for the rural workforce and changes therein is the other important feature that helps us in understanding the transformation of the agrarian economy. There is a growing tendency of the small- and marginal-sized farmers becoming non-viable, and consequently, it leads to the process of depeasantization. The analysis of the three aspects – changing structure of agrarian economy, non-farm employment opportunities and depeasantization of the small cultivators – is helpful in enhancing our understanding about the functioning of the agrarian economy.

The analysis of Table 3.5 shows that the number of small and marginal holdings increased from 1980–81 to 1990–91. This is precisely because of the division in the joint family towards nuclear family and hence the emergence of large number of small-sized holders. This was also resulting from the experience of the scale-neutral agricultural technology witnessed by the farmers in the 1970s. This technology has increased productivity and returns irrespective of size of the farm. However, the mechanization process has started taking place at a massive scale in Punjab, especially mechanization of harvesting. This has reduced the scale neutrality of technology, and small and marginal farmers started turning non-viable, which is indicative of the fact that there was a drop in the number of small and marginal holdings, as observed from the table in the year 1995–96 and also 2010–11. There is a growing tendency of increase in the area under semi-medium and medium-size farms. It is basically due to the fact that economies of scale can be reaped only in these sizes of farms. The declining number of small and marginal farmers clearly brings out the fact that the long-held belief of depeasantization which was not occurring at the early stage of green revolution has been visible during the 1990s and more vigorously during the first decade of the 21st century.

TABLE 3.5 Distribution of farm size–wise operational landholdings, area operated and average size in Punjab

Years	Category	Marginal (below 1 ha)	Small (1–2 ha)	Semi-medium (2–4 ha)	Medium (4–10 ha)	Large (10 ha and above)	All holdings
1980–81	Number of landholdings (000)	197 (19.22)	199 (19.41)	287 (28.00)	269 (26.25)	73 (7.12)	1,025 (100)
	Area operated (000 ha)	126 (3.02)	291 (6.98)	841 (20.16)	1,672 (40.09)	1,241 (29.75)	4,171 (100)
	Average size of holding (ha)	0.64	1.46	2.93	6.22	17.00	4.07
1990–91	Number of holding (000)	296 (26.50)	204 (18.26)	289 (25.87)	261 (23.37)	67 (6.00)	1,117 (100)
	Area operated (000 ha)	164 (4.07)	328 (8.13)	841 (20.86)	1,622 (40.23)	1,077 (26.71)	4,032 (100)
	Average size of holding (ha)	0.55	1.61	2.91	6.21	16.07	3.61
1995–96	Number of holdings (000)	204 (18.66)	183 (16.74)	320 (29.28)	306 (28.00)	80 (7.32)	1,093 (100)
	Area operated (000 ha)	122 (2.94)	240 (5.79)	833 (20.08)	1,754 (42.30)	1,198 (28.89)	4,147 (100)
	Average size of holding (ha)	0.60	1.31	2.60	5.73	14.98	3.79
2010–11*	Number of holdings (000)	164 (15.59)	195 (18.54)	325 (30.89)	298 (28.33)	70 (6.65)	1,052 (100)
	Area operated (000 ha)	101 (2.55)	269 (6.78)	855 (21.55)	1,713 (43.18)	1,029 (25.94)	3,967 (100)
	Average size of holding (ha)	0.62	1.38	2.63	5.75	14.70	3.77

Source: www.planingcommission.nic.in/plans/stateplan/sdr_punjab/sdrpun_ch4.pdf.

Notes: 1. * 2010–11 data from Agricultural Census 2010–11.

2. Figures in parenthesis are percentages.

Non-farm rural sector

The rural non-farm employment has not only been supporting the livelihoods of rural people, especially the poor, but also generating additional employment opportunities and reducing the income gaps in rural areas (Pavithra and Vatta 2013). The declining labour absorption in agriculture, stagnated real wages of agricultural labourers, reduced man-days of farm work and high growth rate of labour force have resulted in a quantum transfer of rural workforce from farm to non-farm employment (Ghuman 2005; PAU 2009; Singh and Sangeet 2014). Therefore, it is important to look into the extent of rural non-farm-sector employment and share of earnings from non-farm employment in Punjab. The information of these two important indicators of rural non-farm-sector employment has been presented in Tables 3.6 and 3.7.

Analysis of distribution of rural non-farm workers shows that rural household industry, others industries, construction, trade and commerce, transport, storage and communication and other activities like repair shops have been major occupations of rural non-farm workers over the period of time. Further, construction, transport, storage and communications have emerged as leading activities of rural non-farm workers over the period of time.

Analysis of distribution of income of rural households of Punjab from different sources suggests that farmers of all categories were drawing major part of their income from agriculture; however, landless households of the state earned only 14.84 per cent of their income mainly as agricultural wages and 64.00 per cent from non-farm employment. It is also evident from the analysis that as farm size increases the share of agriculture income also increases and vice versa. Further, among the non-farm activities, manufacturing, construction, wholesale and retail trade, hotels and restaurants, transport, storage and communication, finance, insurance and real

TABLE 3.6 Percentage distribution of rural non-farm workers in Punjab

Sector / Year	1971	1981	1991	2001	2009–10
Mining and quarrying	0.0	0.12	0.0	0.05	0.22
Household industry	16.72	9.99	4.51	7.64	
Other than household industry	15.90	22.32	21.28	20.84	22.57
Construction	7.46	6.78	7.21	11.87	13.05
Trade and commerce	15.42	17.39	15.87	15.29	8.63
Transport, storage and communications	6.33	10.11	10.00	8.50	12.61
Other services	38.15	33.30	41.11	35.86	42.92
Total	100	100	100	100	100

Source: Singh (2011).

TABLE 3.7 Percentage distribution of income from all sources of rural households in Punjab

Category source		Landless	Marginal	Small	Medium	Large
Agriculture		14.84	36.2	84.9	84.2	84.1
Non-farm		64.0	26.7	7.0	8.5	–
Transfer		8.91	29.2	6.9	7.3	13.8
Others		8.9	7.9	1.2	–	2.1
Total		100	100	100	100	100
Non-farm	*A.*	*18.1*	*19.2*	*65.6*	*69.6*	–
sub-categories	*B.*	*19.3*	–	–	*4.3*	–
	C.	*12.1*	–	–	–	–
	D.	*13.2*	*23.1*	–	*21.7*	–
	E.	*9.8*	*57.7*	*26.2*	–	–
	F.	*27.5*	–	*8.2*	*4.4*	–
Non-farm total		100	100	100	100	–

Source: Compiled from Pavithra and Vatta (2013).

Notes
A – manufacturing,
B – construction,
C – wholesale and retail trade, hotels and restaurants,
D – transport, storage and communication,
E – finance, insurance and real estate,
F – community, social and personal services (CSP services).

estate and community, social and personal services (CSP services) have been the main sources of income of non-farm workers of Punjab.

Depeasantization: the process

The workforce from the farming sector moved away to non-farm sectors because of two factors: first, due to developmental factors such as growth and development of agriculture sector, secondary sector and tertiary sectors; and second, due to distress factors like increasing and high indebtedness, falling farm incomes, increasing cultivation costs and successive crop damage/failure. The latter phenomenon also known as the process of depeasantization has started taking place in Punjab agriculture after the adoption of new economic policies and became more prone during the first decade of the 21st century. The information related to some important issues and causes of depeasantization in Punjab agriculture has been depicted in Table 3.8.

Analysis of causes, issues and process of depeasantization in Punjab agriculture reveals that after 1991 many farmers left farming and engaged in other activities (Singh, Singh and Kingra 2009). During this period, around 26 per cent of marginal and small, 11 per cent of medium and 5 per cent of large farmers left

TABLE 3.8 Percentage distribution of causes and issues of depeasantization in Punjab

Variables	Farm size category	Marginal < 1 ha	Small 1–2 ha	Medium 2–4 ha	Large > 4 ha
Left farming		10.8	15.0	11.3	4.9
Reasons for leaving farming	Low income	71.4	59.9	58.2	45.7
	Division of land	43.3	25.5	29.1	21.7
	Debt repayment	35.5	29.7	31.3	21.7
New activity	Labour	28.1	20.8	12.7	–
	Milkmen	10.1	8.8	10.4	6.6
	Distress rentiers	2.3	13.5	16.4	37.0
	Others	59.5	56.9	60.5	56.4
Level of satisfaction from new activity	Full	21.7	24.5	33.6	69.6
	Less	16.1	22.4	16.4	4.3
	Dissatisfied	30.4	17.7	17.2	4.3
Land status after	Sale	45.2	29.2	31.3	8.7
	Partial sale	4.6	14.6	17.9	21.7
	No land sale	48.4	56.3	50.8	69.6

Source: Compiled from Singh, Singh and Kingra (2009).

agriculture and joined other occupations. Low income from agriculture, division of agricultural landholdings and accumulation of debt and its non-repayment have been identified as major causes for leaving agriculture among all the farm categories. Agricultural labour, non-farm labour, milkmen and distress rentiers were the leading activities pursued by farmers who left farming. Many of the small, marginal and medium farmers were dissatisfied with their new work, and many of them sold the whole land in the process. However, in the case of large farmers, they pursued other activities such as business and became entrepreneurs and were satisfied with the new occupation and did not sell the whole plot of land. It can been concluded that small, marginal and medium farmers left farming because of push factors and large farmers due to pull factors responsible for the depeasantization process.

Agrarian distress in the rural economy of Punjab

Agrarian distress has deepened during the period of economic reforms. It is widely recognized that agrarian distress has two dimensions, that is institutional and structural. Agricultural sector has been facing increasing marginalization and shrinking institutional support system. In fact, it is an underlying feature of the economic reforms programme to shift institutional emphasis from the state to the market (Reddy and Mishra 2009a). This shift has dramatic consequences for the small and marginal farmers who were intimately connected to commercial farming. The small and marginal farmers together constitute the poor peasantry of Punjab (Gill 2014). They could not face the onslaught of the market forces. Since their holdings turned non-viable due to weakening of the institutional support during the economic reform period, but without any alternative decent occupation to fall back upon, they have no alternative except to face the process of elimination. The crisis-prone situation of the small and marginal farmers has initiated the process of distress-driven depeasantization in Punjab.[5]

Punjab agriculture since the green revolution had undergone substantial structural changes.[6] The evolution of the structure of agricultural production and productivity was determined by two yardsticks. One, the most remunerative crops were preferred over less remunerative crops. Two, the cropping system which was using mechanical and biological innovations more efficiently over the less efficient ones was adopted. The changing cropping pattern is the testimony of this. There were more than 21 crops sown in Punjab in 1960–61. The crops sown in Punjab were just nine in 1990–91. A substantial change has occurred in the structure of the cropping system of Punjab from a more diversified to highly skewed in favour of few crops, and it continues to be so even today. There happened to be a dramatic rise in the area under wheat and paddy crops, which is now popularly known as wheat–paddy rotation. These two crops have turned out to be more profitable compared with other available alternative crops (Sidhu and Singh 2011; Shergill 2013).

Although it is a well-established empirical fact that the current cropping pattern is the most profitable and it has also attained a high degree of specialization, yet the yield saturation of these crops heavily impinges on the economy of the farmers. It is significant to note here that the yield attained by two crops, that is wheat and rice, is very high compared with all-India average and other states (Sidhu 2014). The average yield of wheat was 5,097 kg per hectare in 2011–12 and 3,741 kg per hectare in 2011–12 for rice crop. But there is an increasing tendency of declining the secular trend of yield in recent years. The yield of wheat crop has been increased at 2.06 per cent per annum between 1990 and 2000, but it decelerated during 2000–09 by –0.28 per cent. This was the period of productivity collapse for the wheat crop in Punjab (Nair and Singh 2014). It is pertinent to point out here that due to favourable weather conditions for wheat crop in the past two years reversal of productivity growth has occurred (Sidhu 2014). But this may be treated as an aberration due to the fact that science and technological-based productivity growth has shown long-term tendency of decreasing the productivity growth.

Economic reforms that have exposed the farmers to market transaction with dismantling control on industry-manufactured products and increasing privatization of services, which are being used as an input in agriculture production, raised the input cost of production of agricultural operations. The cost of production of 1 quintal (100 kg) of wheat crop during 1991–92 to 2011–12 has increased from Rs 190.79 to Rs 880.26.[7] Similarly, in the case of rice crop, during the same period, the cost of rice crop had gone up from Rs 206.77 to Rs 836.46. In the case of both the crops, the cost of cultivation has increased more than four times. When the data regarding cost of cultivation, MSP and margins is presented for both crops in Figures 3.2 and 3.3, the analysis

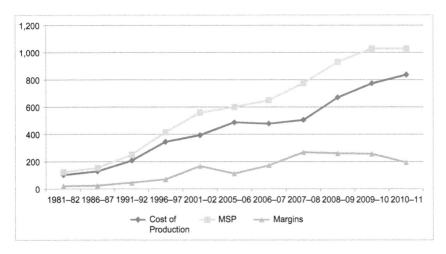

FIGURE 3.2 Trends of cost of production, MSP and margins of paddy crop, 1981–82 to 2010–11

Source: Authors.

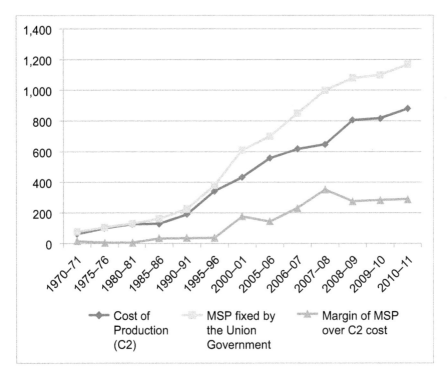

FIGURE 3.3 Trends of cost of production, MSP and margins of wheat crop, 1970–71 to 2010–11

Source: Authors.

of graphs clearly brings out an important point that the net margins from the two dominant crops grown in Punjab, that is wheat and paddy, have been decelerating. The stagnation/falling tendency of productivity growth along with falling profit margins of the dominant crops, that is wheat and rice, surely decreased the availability of income in the hands of the farming households. Both the factors, institutional and structural, together impacted severely the household economy of the agriculturists. This is a clear sign of the emergence of agrarian distress during the economic reforms period.

Punjab agriculture and farmers have been considered most progressive in adopting the contemporary mechanical and biological innovations. Consequently, the use of human labour in wheat and paddy production has dramatically declined from 428.07 and 818.37 man-hours per hectare in 1985 to 183.71 and 410.41 man-hours per hectare in 2006–07, respectively. This decline comes out to be 57.08 per cent for wheat and 50 per cent for paddy. During 1985 to 2006–07, there was overall decline of use of labour in farm operations to the extent of 23 per cent (Devi, Singh and Kumar 2011). The other noteworthy fact that needs to be noticed here is that there has been a dramatic fall of instability in the crop yield due to application of available innovations. Wheat and paddy crops turned out to be having lowest variability and instability so far as yield outcomes are concerned (Sidhu, Vatta and Kaur 2011). Except peak season, that is harvesting and sowing periods, most of the farm labour turn out to be surplus. The mechanical and biological innovations have even made small and marginal farm households own workforce surplus. In fact, the farm households turn out to be manager farmers.

The agricultural transformation has turned towards high degree of capital intensity. It is well known that there are an increasing number of tractors, tube wells and pump sets, harvester combines and other agricultural implements (Singh and Bhogal 2014). However, what is less known is the relative rise of prices of the agricultural machinery such as a tractor. A tractor cost equivalent to 28.8 tons of wheat in 1970. The same tractor was purchased by farmers by selling 60.7 tons of wheat in 2005 (Singh 2009). Similar is the case of tube wells, whose cost has gone up. Furthermore, the additional cost of deepening the tube wells has been incurred due to falling ground water table. This has increased cost of cultivation multiple times. Therefore, this has resulted in declining income of farmers, particularly marginal- and small-sized farmers. Small- and marginal-sized farms are increasingly becoming non-viable (Sekhon, Kaur, Sidhu and Mahal 2011).

The accumulated indebtedness is rising at a fast rate. The estimated per household debt among marginal farmers was Rs 118,820 in 2008–09. However, this was Rs 187,325 among the small farmers. It is significant to note that farm household indebtedness rises with the rise in the farm size, but per hectare indebtedness falls as the size of farm increases. This relationship clearly brings out the fact that the economies of scale are intimately connected to the size of the farm. When we analyse the source of indebtedness among the farm households, the large proportion of the farm debt belongs to the non-institution sources (Singh, Kingra and Sangeeta 2011). The non-institutional source of financing not only is exploitative in terms of charging high rates of interest but is also well known for charging differential interest rates. Higher rates of interest are charged from small-sized farmers compared with large-sized farmers. There is a growing incidence of interlinking the financing with input, consumption goods and output markets. This increasing practice of growing incidence of interlinked agrarian markets has been responsible for the rising level of indebtedness on the one hand and reducing otherwise legitimate surpluses of the farmers on the other hand (Gill 2006). These kinds of informal lending practices are counter-intuitive in a modern capitalist economy. But they are thriving and flourishing due to high transaction cost in formal financial institutions and tedious procedures adopted to grant credit by formal financial institutions.

The external or exogenous factors such as public support in terms of providing social overhead capital and terms of trade usually determine the sustainability of the farm sector. In the case of social overhead capital, the popularly used indicator is gross fixed capital formation (GFCF). The proportion of agriculture GFCF to gross state domestic product (GSDP) has declined from 21.74 per cent in 1980–81 to 11.91 per cent in 2000–01, but it took a nosedive to 7.85 per cent in 2010–11. The private capital formation has been steadily accelerated,[8] but the decline of GFCF in Punjab agriculture was mainly due to decline in public sources of capital formation. This change in the structure of capital formation in Punjab agriculture heavily impinged upon agricultural households across the categories, but its intensity in the case of small- and marginal farm-sized households was higher than that of medium and large farm households (Singh 2009). It is well known that during the liberalization period, Punjab government has dramatically reduced expenditure on social sectors such as health and education. This has further burdened rural households to bear rising expenditure on health and education, which affected the fragile economy of the small and marginal farm households severely compared with the large farm households. As stated in the 12th Five-Year Plan, the farm sector has suffered due to adverse terms of trade for the agricultural sector during the past two decades, which is the period of liberalization. This is the standard strategy of transferring surpluses from agriculture to other sectors of the economy. However, the data on workforce engaged in the agricultural sector amply shows that the workforce in absolute numbers has increased at a fast rate. This process is contrary to the transfer of surpluses from the agricultural sector but workforce stays back. This implies growing burden on the agricultural sector without generating any gainful employment opportunities. This phenomenon is known as jobless growth. All these factors combined together bring home the fact that the agricultural sector is operating under such circumstances and consequently cannot escape from entering into agrarian crisis/distress. The growing economic distress across rural households in general and small and marginal farmers and agricultural labourers in particular forced them to commit suicides.[9]

Apart from the grave economic crisis faced by agriculture, Punjab economy is also undergoing environmental disaster. The steady rise in the grain production in Punjab is highly dependent on the assured irrigation arrangements. Ninety-eight per cent of the gross cropped area in Punjab is irrigated. Over the period of time, irrigation is being increasingly done by tube wells/pump sets, which is mainly lifting water from the aquifer. Since the number of tube wells has gone up from 2.80 lakhs in 1980–81 to 11.42 lakhs in 2010–11 (Government of Punjab 2012), the ground water table of the aquifer is falling at a rapid rate. The large number of developmental blocks ('block' means an administrative unit) (more than 75 per cent) in Punjab has been declared as dark, meaning overexploited (Singh and Aggarwal 2010). This is due to the consequence of the policy of extracting more ground water to produce more grains. As the water table recedes, the cost of extraction of water has been increasing. This increases the cost of extracting ground water due to installing costly submersible pumps, which can lift water from the deep aquifer. Thus, it increases the capital cost of installing more powerful tube wells that also consume more electric power. The rising cost of extracting water from the deep aquifer has in fact generated monopoly on public resource such as ground water by the large-sized farmers. Small and marginal farmers, who cannot afford the heavy cost of tube wells, are forced to buy water for irrigating their farms from the big farmers. There is a growing imbalance across various geographic areas of Punjab and social classes so far as the uses of ground water are concerned. On the one side there has been an extreme depletion of ground water, and on the other side, there is rise of water table leading to water logging in certain areas of Punjab (Kulkarni and Shah 2013). The increasing ground water pollution due to increasing and indiscriminate pesticide and chemical fertilizer uses has been the root cause of increasing the incidence of many deadly diseases like cancer. The model of agricultural development as a by-product has amazingly generated severe environmental disaster. During the paddy growing season, Punjab state suffers from high humidity and high degree of temperature. This kind of atmosphere is ideal for pests to multiply. The pest attack on crops such as cotton leads to increasing use of pesticides. The rising pesticide consumption is due to crops grown with high doses of water, which were alien to the local environment. In fact, the changing climate conditions result in reduction of area under other crops such as cotton. The occasional failure of cotton crop due to pest attacks leads to fall in income and increase in the cost of cultivation.

The burning of wheat and paddy biomass waste (stubble) causes air pollution while adding to toxic gases, especially burning of biomass waste of paddy. It also burns the micro-nutrients of the top soil, flora and fauna and several other species. The foregoing analysis shows that the economic crisis and environmental degradation are intimately connected. All factors combined together lead us to conclude that the rising number of farmers' and agricultural labourers' suicides in Punjab is the outcome of the deep-rooted multidimensional crisis of the model of economic growth.

Conclusions

The economic development experience of Punjab economy during the phases of liberalization, globalization and privatization remained dismal. Slow growth of Punjab economy during the past two decades not only reduced the status of the state in national reckoning from first to seventh number but also generated widespread distress. Rural suicides are the manifestation of this economic distress prevailing in the state's economy. Despite the early agriculture revolution and substantial economic surpluses, structural transformation in Punjab economy failed to occur. The slow process of structural change is distress driven, which is playing the role of push factors. But pull factors which are required to play a dominant role are nearly absent, and consequently, a very limited upward mobility of the workforce is taking place.

Agricultural workforce is increasing in absolute numbers, but slow relative decline compared with fast relative decline of income shares has generated structural imbalance in Punjab economy. The rural workforce has been trapped in the low-income agricultural sector of the economy. However, the agrarian economy of Punjab has been undergoing dramatic change from more diversified to less diversified. Wheat–paddy rotation has emerged as the dominant cropping patterns in Punjab. Biological and mechanical innovations have been harnessed by the farmers of Punjab, and intensity of use of these innovations is almost comparable to advanced countries' agriculture. This has raised the cost of cultivation multiple times on the one hand and dramatically decreased use of human labour on the other hand. The adverse terms of trade and falling social sector expenditure have far-reaching consequences for the rural economy of Punjab.

A high degree of indebtedness among the various categories of farmers and agricultural labourers is the consequence of deep-rooted agrarian distress in Punjab economy. Apart from structural problems faced by Punjab economy, the recent phase of liberalization has generated the environment, which impinged heavily on the already-fragile household economy of small and marginal farmers and agricultural labourers in Punjab. Agrarian credit markets interlinked with other markets have been eating away the surpluses generated in the agricultural sector of the state's economy. Due to lack of alternative remunerative occupations and reduction of manpower use in agriculture, the rural workforce has been increasingly becoming seasonal/disguisedly employed. Rising indebtedness and falling agriculture-based income across the categories of small and marginal farmers and agriculture labourers have no other alternative except to commit suicide.

The agriculture-based model of economic development has generated environmental disaster. The ground water depletion is taking place at an alarming rate. High-degree temperature with high level of humidity allows pests to grow at a phenomenal rate. Consequently, high doses of pesticides are required to save crops from increasing pest attacks. Increasing pesticide use has contaminated ground water. In fact, the food chain has been contaminated with high residues of chemicals, which are carcinogenic in nature and cause diseases. The burning of biomass leads to increase in toxicity of the gases in the air. There is a positive relationship between agrarian distress and environmental degradation in Punjab. The growing and continuing suicides of farmers and agricultural labourers in Punjab cannot be arrested until dramatic changes in economic policy are made that will provide stimulus to the structural transformation in Punjab economy. This transformation also includes the changes in the organization of agriculture from individual to collective for harnessing economies of scale of operation both in production and in marketing. The rural workers need to be provided necessary wherewithal along with comprehensive retirement plan and pensioner benefits on the pattern of Taiwanese's rural workforce.

Notes

1 The arrival of green revolution was the outcome of technological breakthrough in the form of new seeds of high-yielding varieties of wheat and rice. The green revolution technological breakthrough flourished in Punjab due to fulfilment of preconditions in the form of agrarian reforms, institutional changes and development of irrigation network. The preconditions of suitable institutional arrangements were followed by extensive and intensive use of modern farm inputs such as research, extension, input supply, credit, marketing and price support system (Chand 2009).

2 An important underlying aspect of economic transformation, which involves technological innovations supported by institutional arrangements, is the matching social norms and ideological change facilitating modernization in terms of both organizations of production and the culture. If there is any constraint obstructing this dramatic change, the state comes forward to develop suitable rules of the game and regulatory mechanism (Kuznets 1966). This process of structural change has been described by Chang (2003: 41) as 'government-engineered transformation'.

3 Since the mid-1960s and up to the early 1980s, the green revolution has generated surpluses which were mobilized by the banking system. Due to several regulations on industrial investment, the large proportion of these surpluses could not be invested in Punjab. Therefore, these surpluses have been siphoned off by the universal nature of operation of the banking system of India. This is supported by the empirical evidence of very low credit-deposit ratio witnessed for Punjab (Singh 2002). However, this ratio remained below the minimum prescribed by the Reserve Bank of India – a monetary authority of the country.

4 An important factor that has contributed to the increasing agrarian distress in the economic reform era was the dysfunction of the fiscal policy of the state. During this period, the state expenditure on rural and agriculture capital formation suffered. The burden of reduction of public agriculture capital formation resulted in the heavy burden on the households. This has given to increase not only the cost of production but also social expenditure such as health and education. This singular constraint generated diseconomies in the rural sector of the economy due to interdependencies and the consequence was widespread rural distress.

5 In a recent study, it was estimated that during the economic reforms period, that is from 1991 to 2012–13, 14.40 per cent of the total number of farmers of Punjab left farming (Singh and Bhoghal 2014). Out of the total number of farmers who left agriculture, the proportion of the small and marginal farmers is alarming, that is 18.26 and 26.50 per cent, respectively. Among the identified reasons, lack of profitability was the predominant factor that forced the farmers to leave agriculture as an occupation for livelihood. High debt burden has forced more than 9 per cent of the farmers to sell their most prized possession, that is land. It is important to note that of those who left farming a large proportion of marginal farmers (47 per cent) and small farmers (22 per cent) took up labour as an occupation. This clearly brings home the fact that distressed-driven depeasantization process has entailed downward mobility. This social transformation process is quite difficult, painful and dehumanizing in nature and has severe economic, social and political consequences.

6 There is a growing tendency of concentration of operational landholdings in Punjab. The semi-medium category of operational holdings has gained currency. But all other categories of landholdings in terms of proportion of area operated have decreased except small and marginal farms. The proportion of area operated and number of households has increased from 1971–72 to 2002–03 as per the NSSO estimates during different rounds (Nair and Singh 2014). This shows the structural change that has occurred over a long period of time. The growing tendency of small and marginal operational holdings in Punjab and a large proportion from them turning economically non-viable. This structural feature of Punjab agriculture is counter-intuitive and is a cause of worry.

7 The cost of cultivation taken is C2, which includes all actual expenses in cash and kind incurred in cultivation, rent paid for leased-in land and imputed value of family labour, interest in value of owned capital assets (excluding land) and rental value of land (net of land revenue).

8 An important feature of the economic reform period is the falling growth rate of public investment in Indian agriculture, but there was a marginal rise in the growth rate of private investment from 2.67 per cent during 1981–90 to 3.71 per cent per annum during 1991–2003 (Chand 2009). However, in the case of Punjab, there is growing evidence of substantial rise in private investment with regard to tractors, tube wells/pump sets, harvester combines and other agricultural implements (Singh and Bhogal 2014).

9 It is strange that a very strong and steady community of farmers had witnessed dramatic rise in suicides. Keeping in view the increasing incidence of suicides by farmers and agricultural labourers, the government of Punjab ordered census survey. This census survey was conducted by Punjab's three universities on behalf of Punjab government so that the extent of suicides can be ascertained and suitable policy for compensation can be formulated. This survey covered the period of suicides between 2000 and 2010. The total number of persons, which include farmers and agricultural labourers, was 6,926 who committed suicides during the period of survey. The debt-stressed suicides among them were 4,686 persons. The farmers who committed suicides due to debt stress were 2,943 persons, and 1,743 were the agricultural labourers who committed suicides because of unbearable debt burden (Dhaliwal 2014).

4

FARMER AND AGRICULTURE LABOURER SUICIDES IN PUNJAB

Analysis of the census survey

Introduction

Agrarian distress is widespread. Its intensity is increasing over time. The prevailing agrarian crisis is the result of liberalized public policy adopted by the Indian government and the free play of market forces. The individual impact from the increasing intensity of agrarian crisis has been farmer and agricultural labourer suicides. Recently, the various farmer organizations have formed a national coordination committee and are struggling to register their protest to put agrarian distress on the agenda of political parties. With the increasing involvement of the distressed rural community in political mobilization for collective action, several measures have come to the domain of public policy to provide immediate relief and long-term measures to solve the crisis. The Union government of India in the interim budget 2019–20 announced the Pradhan Mantri Kisan Samman Nidhi (PM-KISAN) income support scheme of Rs 6000 per annum in three equal instalments to be deposited in the accounts of small and marginal farmers. The minimum income guarantee scheme by the state governments of Odisha, named Krushak Assistance for Livelihood and Income Augmentation (KALIA), and Telengana, named Agriculture Investment Support Scheme (Rythu Bandhu), was also enacted and implemented. A large number of other states in India have enacted debt waiver schemes for farmers. In the 17th Lok Sabha election (2019), the Indian National Congress proposed in its manifesto a wider measure to cover poor families by supplementing the income of poor families currently earning income less than Rs 72,000 per annum. The proposed scheme is expected to cover poor families, both landed and non-landed, and is named Nyuntam Aay Yojana (NYAY).

The affirmative public policy actions were attempted by the government of Punjab as early as in the budget of 2002. It was then proposed to compensate the family of the farmer who had died by suicide. The amount of compensation was two lakh rupees to the victim's family. However, this scheme was implemented in 2016, also because of the intervention of the Punjab and Haryana High Court. Recently, the government of Punjab authorized the deputy commissioner of the district to grant compensation to the suicide victims' families, from 1 April 2013 onwards, after verification that the farmer's suicide was caused by indebtedness. Earlier, during the implementation of this scheme of compensation to left-behind family members, the government of Punjab entrusted the task of counting the number of farmer suicides to three universities: Punjab Agriculture University, Ludhiana; Punjabi University, Patiala; and Guru Nanak Dev University, Amritsar. A census survey was conducted by the research teams of three universities, and reports were submitted to the government of Punjab in 2017. The reference period for census survey was 2000 to 2013. This chapter is based on this unique data set for Punjab. Importantly, the government of Punjab also started a debt waiver scheme for the small and marginal farmers. These two schemes are operational in Punjab, but farmers and agriculture labourers continue to die by suicide. From March 2017 to January 2019, 900 farmers died by suicide due to agrarian distress (Chaba, 2019). It seems that despite some affirmative action by the government of Punjab, the agrarian distress continues to intensify in the state of Punjab, which is leading to the rise in farm suicides – that is, suicides by farmers and agricultural labourers. In this chapter, an attempt is made to understand the extent and causes of suicides in Punjab on the basis of a census survey conducted in Punjab. The analysis of this comprehensive data allows us to gauge the intensity of the agrarian crisis over space and time and also enables us to suggest remedial measures that can help to mitigate agrarian distress in the foreseeable future. The present chapter is divided into five sections. Section two presents the agriculture transformation that generates the agrarian crisis. It also examines the trends of farmer suicides across Indian states. In section three, the analysis of farmers and agriculture labourer suicides occurring across the state of Punjab is presented. This section presents a district-level analysis of agriculture suicides and causes of suicides. The final section presents the major conclusions that emerged from the empirical analysis.

Agrarian crisis in India: farm suicides

The historical roots of the agrarian crisis can be identified as early as in the mid-1980s, when several scholars expressed their concern about stagnating productivity levels and recommended diversifying cropping patterns as a remedy to the problems in the agricultural sector (Johl, 1986; Singh, 2016). The agrarian crisis is attributed partly to the public policies pursued by the government and also to other factors: first, stagnation of yield, especially of wheat and decline in rice and cotton and successive crop failures due to natural and human made factors (spurious pesticides, seeds and fertilizers) along with the failure and non-implementation of the crop diversification programme due to uncertain yields, low prices and poorly marketing alternative crops. The crisis in the Punjab agricultural sector has been supplemented by the increased operational and fixed costs of cultivation and the consequently declining income from agriculture. Around 30 per cent of the operational holdings of the state are in small and marginal farms, and their economic viability and sustainability are dubious due to the squeezing profitability of major crops and increasing production costs. Small and marginal farmers are most affected by the crisis, and their survival is under threat. These farmers are victims of over-capitalization and high mechanization, but use of farm machinery and capital assets is very low. The transfer of agricultural land for non-agricultural purposes and unfavourable terms of trade has only worsened the agrarian crisis. Thus, the impact of such conditions translated more into hardship for small and marginal farmers.

The policies pursued by the state under the new world economic order emerged after the formation of the World Trade Organization that have added to the woes of farmers, because it prematurely pushed them to compete with farmers of developed nations enjoying high subsidies without a level-playing field. The policies of liberalization, privatization and globalization (LPG) have mainly promoted and incentivized private investment. The reduction of public investment in agriculture decreased capital formation, and thus, institutional support dried up for small and marginal farmers. This critical public input deficiency wreaked havoc on the farmers. State politics turned against the interests of the farmers as strong political position of farmers emerging during green revolution weakened and fragmented in 1980s, and they are now on the margins during liberalization due to the shift in the political affiliations and the disjuncture between the interests of farmers and politicians. Punjab politicians who once advocated the cause of agriculture development and farmer interests developed interests in industry and business and were no more interested in agriculture, because agriculture no longer remained the main source of their income. As a result, small and marginal farmers suffered, and the marginalization of agriculture further deepened the crisis and clearly resulted in farm suicides across the county, especially in agriculturally developed areas. Information regarding farm suicides in India, in Indian states and in comparative rates of suicides among main cultivators, all cultivators and the general population is presented in Tables 4.2, 4.3 and 4.4 and in Chart 4.1.

In India, especially in the advanced agriculture areas, the symptoms of agrarian crisis had started appearing soon after the implementations of LPG polices during early 1990s, which were further augmented by the World Trade Organization policies. As a result of these policies, reports of farm suicides started pouring in across the country during the mid-1990s. Table 4.1 shows that farm suicides in India have increased from 10,720 in 1995 to a peak of 18,241 in 2004; they thereafter started declining marginally to 11,370 in 2016. Further, information regarding this suggests that farm suicides in rural India have been continuing unabatedly. According

TABLE 4.1 Farm suicides in India

Year	Number	Year	Number
1995	10,720	2006	17,060
1996	13,729	2007	16,632
1997	13,622	2008	16,796
1998	16,015	2009	17,368
1999	16,082	2010	15,964
2000	16,603	2011	14,027
2001	16,415	2012	13,754
2002	17,971	2013	11,772
2003	17,164	2014	12,360
2004	18,241	2015	12,602
2005	17,131	2016	11,370

Source: Compiled by the authors, from NCRB, Accidental Deaths and Suicides in India, various issues

to National Crimes Record Bureau (NCRB), from 1995 to 2016, the total number of farmers and agricultural labourers who had died by suicide due to the agrarian crisis was 333,398.

Table 4.2 presents the comparative state-level picture of farmer suicides and percentage change during 2015 and 2016, which suggests that farm suicides declined by 9.5 per cent in 2016 compared to 2015. But the analysis shows that Punjab has recorded its highest percentage increase, namely 118.0 per cent, in farmer suicides, followed by Haryana at 54.32 per cent, Gujarat at 35.5 per cent, Karnataka at 32.50 per cent and Madhya Pradesh at 2.4 per cent in 2016 as compared to 2015. However, during the same period, Telangana registered a decline of 54.0 per cent, followed by Chhattisgarh at 28.5 per cent, Maharashtra at 15 per cent and Andhra Pradesh at 12.2 per cent. From, this analysis, it can be safely concluded that major agricultural states of India are facing severe agrarian distress and the problem of farm suicides.

Many individuals and governments and government agencies have been questioning and doubting the occurrence of farmers and agriculture labourer suicides due to agrarian distress in the country and branding farm suicides as normal suicides of the population. But the comparative per one lakh rates of suicides among the general population and all cultivators and main cultivators during 2001 and 2011 clearly answer the doubts regarding the farmer and agriculture labour suicides. Analysis shows that the per one lakh rates of suicides for male main cultivators were the highest, at 17.7 per cent in 2001 and 18.3 in 2011, when compared to all male cultivators and the general male population during the same period (see Table 4.3 and Chart 4.1). Similarly, the per

TABLE 4.2 Farm suicides: state-level comparison, 2015 and 2016

State	2015 Number	2016 Number	Percentage change
Punjab	124	271	118.0
Haryana	162	250	54.32
Karnataka	1569	20,79	32.50
Gujarat	301	408	35.5
Madhya Pradesh	1290	1321	2.4
Telangana	1400	645	−54.0
Maharashtra	4291	3661	−15.0
Andhra Pradesh	916	804	−12.2
Chhattisgarh	954	682	−28.5
All India total★	12,602	11,370	−9.8

Source: Compiled by the authors, from Mukherjee (2018)

Note: ★Total might not match, because only states prone to farm suicide were included

TABLE 4.3 Comparative rates of suicides among main cultivators, all cultivators and the general population in India, 2001 and 2011 (per lakh/100,000)

Category	2001			2011		
	Male	Female	Persons	Male	Female	Persons
All cultivators	16.2	6.2	12.9	16.1	6.4	13.2
Main cultivators	17.7	10.1	15.8	18.3	10.1	16.3
General population	12.5	8.5	10.6	14.3	8.2	11.3

Source: Compiled by the authors, from Nagaraj et al. (2014), NCRB and Census 2001–11

one lakh rates of suicides among female main cultivators and main cultivators were higher than those of women and others in the general population during the same period. Therefore, according to the analysis, the main cultivators and all cultivators of India were clearly under agrarian distress, due to which they resorted suicide.

Figure 4.1 presents the comparative picture of the per lakh rates of suicides of general population, all cultivators and main cultivators during 2001 and 2011. The rate of suicides increased among cultivators and all cultivators when compared to the general population, from 2001 to 2011, which suggests that the farming community has been facing hardships and that these hardships have led to farm suicides.

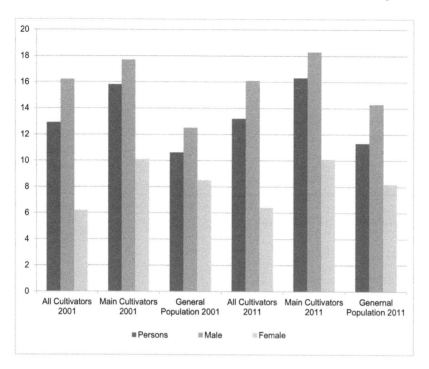

FIGURE 4.1 Comparative per lakh rates of suicides among all cultivators, main cultivators and the general population in India, 2001 and 2011

Source: Based on Table 4.4

Punjab agrarian crisis: farm suicides

In India between 2001 and 2011, Maharashtra, Karnataka, Andhra Pradesh, Chhattisgarh and Madhya Pradesh accounted for approximately two-thirds of the farm suicides against around 55 per cent to 57 per cent of the total general suicides (Nagaraj et al., 2014). These traditionally farm-suicide-hotbed states experienced a fall in farm suicides in 2016 as compared to 2015 (Table 4.2). However, comparatively, the agriculturally advanced states of Punjab, Haryana, Gujarat and Karnataka, having large irrigation facilities and high agricultural production yield levels, witnessed a surge in farm suicides during the same period (Mukherjee, 2018). However, there are variations in terms of the number and rate of farm suicides across the states, so it would be important to identify the states emerging on the farm suicide map of the country and the farm suicide problem (see Table 4.2). In this light, when we look at this phenomenon during 2015 and 2016, the farm suicide rates in Punjab have registered a high percentage change in the country (see Table 4.2). An attempt has been made to study the farm suicides in Punjab during 2000 to 2013, and the information regarding this is presented in Table 4.4 and Figures 4.2, 4.2a and 4.2b.

TABLE 4.4 The extent of farmer and agricultural labourer suicides in Punjab, 2000–13

Category	Causes		
	Debt	Non-debt	Total
Farmers	3681 (*57.63%*) (94.75%)	204 (*36.69%*) (5.25%)	3885 (*55.96%*) (100%)
Agricultural labourers	2706 (*42.37%*) (88.78%)	342 (*63.31%*) (11.22%)	3048 (*44.04%*) (100%)
Total	6387 (*100%*) (91.99%)	556 (*100%*) (8.01%)	6943 (*100%*) (100%)

Source: Compiled by the authors, from government of Punjab, Survey Reports of Punjabi University, Patiala; Punjab Agriculture University, Ludhiana; and Guru Nanak Dev University, Amritsar, 2017

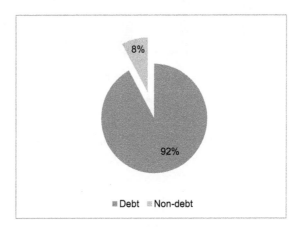

FIGURE 4.2a Causes of farm suicides in Punjab

Source: Based on Table 4.4

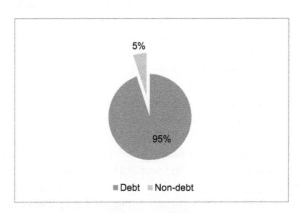

FIGURE 4.2b Causes of farmer suicides in Punjab

Source: Based on Table 4.4

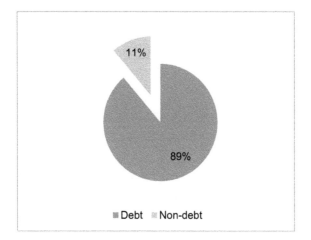

FIGURE 4.2c Causes of agriculture labourer suicides in Punjab

Source: Based on Table 4.4

In Punjab, as can be seen through the Table 4.4, the total number of farmers and agriculture labourers who died by suicide from 2000 to 2013 was 6943. Of those, 55.96 per cent were farmers, and 44.04 per cent were agricultural labourers. Analysis suggests that 6387, or 91.99 per cent, of farm suicides were due to debt, and only 556, 8.01 per cent, were due to non-debt reasons. In the case of farmers, a high percentage – that is, 94.75 per cent – died by suicide due to debt and only 5.25 per cent due to non-debt causes. Similarly, 88.78 per cent of the agricultural labourers died by suicide due to debt and 11.22 per cent due to other reasons. Analysis of Table 4.4 further revealed that 6387 farm suicides were reported due to debt, and out of these, 57.63 per cent were farmers and 42.37 per cent were farm labourers. Due to non-debt reasons, 556 farm suicides were reported: a majority, of 63.31 per cent, were farm labourers, and 36.69 per cent were farmers. All indicators revealing the extent of farm suicides in Punjab shows that farmers and agricultural labourers of the state are facing severe crisis, and they are dying by suicide due to the agrarian crisis.

Farm suicides in Punjab: district-level distribution

For a deeper analysis and understanding of the prevailing farm suicides – that is, farmer and agriculture labourer suicides – in the state of Punjab, it is better to investigate into the issue at the micro level: a district-level comparative analysis of farm suicides in Punjab. The district-level information and data regarding farm suicides has been depicted in Table 4.5; Figures 4.3, 4.3a and 4.3b; and Figure 4.4.

The analysis of Table 4.5 suggests that between 2000 and 2013, the state can be divided, on the basis of rural suicides, into two geographical regions. First, the districts that reported a high intensity of agrarian distress were witnessing a higher

TABLE 4.5 District-level numbers and comparisons of farm suicides in Punjab, 2000–13

| District | Causes of Farm Suicides | | | | | | Share in Rural Population 2011 |
| | Debt | | Non-debt | | Total | | |
	Number	%	Number	%	Number	%	%
Highly affected districts							
Bathinda	1163	18.21	110	19.78	1273	18.33	5.13
Barnala	738	11.56	20	3.60	758	10.92	2.33
Faridkot	65	1.02	8	1.44	73	1.05	2.31
Fazilka	27	0.42	16	2.88	43	0.62	4.38
Ferozpur	32	0.50	11	1.98	43	0.62	4.14
Ludhiana	309	4.84	79	14.21	388	5.59	8.24
Mansa	1359	21.28	74	13.31	1433	20.64	3.49
Moga	563	8.81	75	13.49	638	9.19	4.43
Mukatsar	384	6.01	43	7.73	427	6.15	3.75
Patiala	176	2.76	13	2.34	189	2.72	6.53
Sangrur	1456	22.80	78	14.03	1534	22.09	6.57
Subtotal (A)	6272	98.21	527	94.78	6799	97.92	51.30
Slightly affected districts							
Amritsar	8	0.13	10	1.80	18	0.26	6.67
Fatehgarh Sahib	14	0.22	1	0.18	15	0.22	2.39
Gurdaspur	31	0.49	2	0.36	33	0.48	7.27
Hosiharpur	7	0.11	2	0.36	9	0.13	7.22
Jalander	12	0.19	2	0.36	14	0.20	5.95
Kapurthala	4	0.06	1	0.18	5	0.07	3.07
Mohali	13	0.20	5	0.90	18	0.26	2.59
Rupnagar	6	0.09	–	–	6	0.09	2.92
SBS Nagar	8	0.13	2	0.36	10	0.14	2.81
Pathankot	–	–	–	–	–	–	2.18
Tarn Taran	12	0.19	4	0.72	16	0.23	5.64
Subtotal (B)	115	1.81	29	5.22	144	2.08	48.70
Total (A) + (B)	6387	100	556	100	6943	100.00	100.00

Source: Compiled by the authors, from Government of Punjab, Survey Reports of Punjabi University, Patiala; Punjab Agriculture University, Ludhiana; and Guru Nanak Dev University, Amritsar, 2017, and Economic and Statistical Organization (ESO), Punjab

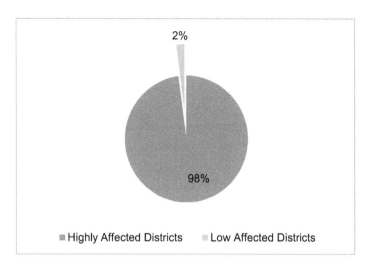

FIGURE 4.3 District-level comparison of farm suicides in Punjab

Source: Based on Table 4.5

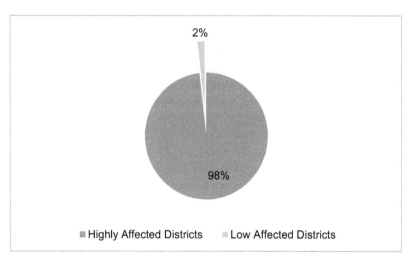

FIGURE 4.3a District-level comparison of farmer suicides in Punjab, 2000–13

Source: Based on Table 4.5

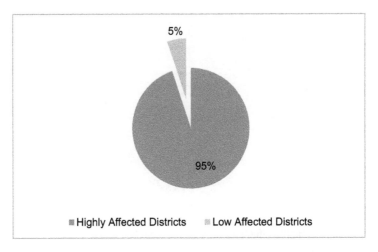

FIGURE 4.3b District-level comparison of agriculture labourer suicides in Punjab, 2000–13
Source: Based on Table 4.5

number of rural suicides and, second, the districts that were recording low-intensity agrarian distress accounted for a low number of suicides. In the first category, there were 11 districts – Bathinda, Barnala, Faridkot, Fazilka, Ferozepur, Ludhiana, Mansa, Moga, Mukatsar, Patiala and Sangrur of the Malwa belt – that have reported large numbers of farm suicides. Almost 50 per cent of the rural population of the state resides in these districts, but during the period of census survey, 97.92 per cent of farm suicides were reported from this belt only. In Punjab, the total number of farm suicides due to debt was 6387, and 98.21 per cent of the debt-related suicides were from the Malwa region alone. Similarly, 556 farm suicides were caused by other reasons in the state, and 94.79 per cent of these were also from these highly distressed districts. Out of total 6799 farm suicides in this area, 92.25 per cent were due to debt, and 7.75 per cent due to other reasons. Therefore, Punjab's Malwa region is clearly highly distressed and prone to farm suicides, and the main reason for this seems to be its high dependence on agriculture for the small and marginal farmers and agriculture labour.

The analysis of agrarian distress and farm suicides clearly shows that the districts that fall in the Shiwalik foothills belt – that is, SAS Nagar, Rupnagar, Fateh Garh Sahib, SBS Nagar, Hoshiarpur, Pathankot and Gurdaspur, the districts of Amritsar and Tarn Taran that lie in the Majha region and the districts of Jalandhar and Kaporthala (which belong to the Doaba region) – were not as distressed as the districts in the Malwa region of Punjab. Almost 50 per cent of rural population of the state is residing in these districts. However, the share of farm suicides in these districts was only 2.08 per cent. The debt-related farm suicides accounted for only 1.81 per cent, and 5.22 per cent of farm suicides were due to other reasons. Yet no farm suicides were reported in the Pathankot district, which has 2.18 per cent of the population of the state living in the countryside. In two districts of Punjab – Kapurthala and Rupnagar – there were only five and cases of farm suicides, respectively, but the population living in the countryside was 3.07 per cent and 2.92 per cent, respectively. The main reason for the low farm suicides in these districts has been reportedly partly because farmers and agriculture labour engaged in non-farm and allied activities. Thus, they earn a significant share of income from these activities. Therefore, a district-level comparative analysis of farm suicides, especially due to debt as the major reason, clearly depicts that the agrarian sector of the Malwa region/cotton belt of Punjab seems to be extremely distressed (see Figure 4.4).

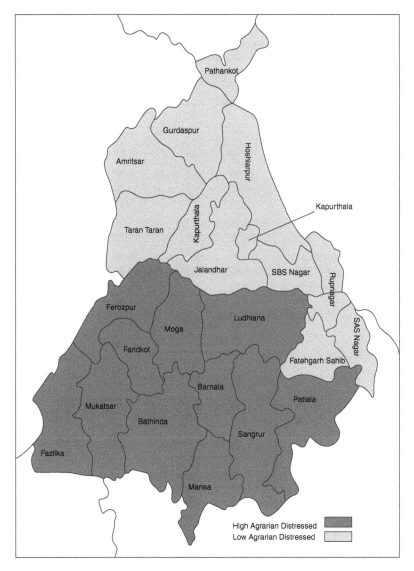

FIGURE 4.4 District-level comparative picture of agrarian distress in Punjab, 2000–13

Source: By authors

Farmer suicides in Punjab: district-level distribution

Analysis of farmer suicides (Table 4.6) during 2000–13 suggests that, in total, 3885 farmers in Punjab have died by suicide; out of these, 3786, or 97.45 per cent, were in the Malwa belt, comprising of districts of Bathinda, Barnala, Faridkot, Fazilka, Ferozpur, Mansa, Moga, Mukatsar, Ludhiana, Patiala and Sangrur. The highest percentage of farmer suicides (22.29 per cent) has been reported in Sangrur, followed by Mansa at 20.93 per cent, Bathinda at 17.07 per cent and Barnala at 11.53 per cent (Table 4.6). The overriding cause for farmer suicides in Punjab was debt: 3885

TABLE 4.6 District-level numbers and comparisons of farmer suicides in Punjab, 2000–13

District	Causes of Farmer Suicides					
	Debt		Non-debt		Total	
	Number	%	Number	%	Number	%
Highly affected districts						
Bathinda	629	17.09	34	16.67	663	17.07
Barnala	440	11.95	8	3.92	448	11.53
Faridkot	32	0.87	5	2.45	37	0.95
Fazilka	20	0.54	7	3.43	27	0.69
Ferozpur	28	0.76	4	1.96	32	0.82
Ludhiana	201	5.46	31	15.20	232	5.97
Mansa	784	21.30	29	14.22	813	20.93
Moga	364	9.89	23	11.27	387	9.96
Mukatsar	175	4.75	13	6.37	188	4.84
Patiala	87	2.36	6	2.94	93	2.39
Sangrur	833	22.63	33	16.18	866	22.29
Subtotal (A)	3593	97.60	193	94.61	3786	97.45
Slightly affected districts						
Amritsar	6	0.16	5	2.45	11	0.28
Fatehgarh Sahib	9	0.24	–	–	9	0.23
Gurdaspur	28	0.76	2	0.98	30	0.77
Hosiharpur	5	0.14	–	–	5	0.13
Jalander	11	0.30	1	0.49	12	0.31
Kapurthala	4	0.11	–	–	4	0.10
Mohali	8	0.22	–	–	8	0.21
Rupnagar	–	–	–	–	–	–
SBS Nagar	6	0.16	2	0.98	8	0.21
Pathankot	–	–	–	–	–	–
Tarn Taran	11	0.30	1	0.49	12	0.31
Subtotal (B)	88	2.40	11	5.39	99	2.55
Total (A) + (B)	3681	100.00	204	100.00	3885	100.00

Source: Compiled by the authors, from Government of Punjab, Survey Reports of Punjabi University, Patiala; Punjab Agriculture University, Ludhiana; and Guru Nanak Dev University, Amritsar, 2017

farmer suicides, or 94.75 per cent, were due to debt. Furthermore, in the Malwa belt alone, 3681 farmer suicides, or 97.60 per cent, were due to debt, and here 94.61 per cent of the farmer suicides were due to non-debt reasons.

During the period under discussion, not a single farmer has died by suicide due to debt or non-debt in the Pathankot and Rupnagar districts, which are in the foot-hill zone of the state. Similarly, the other districts of the Shiwalik foothills belt and the districts of Majha and Doaba have reported only 99 farmer suicides, or 2.55 per cent of the whole state; out of these, 88 farmers, or 2.40 per cent of the farmers of Punjab, have died by suicide due to debt, and 11 farmers, or 5.39 per cent of the farmers of the state, died by suicide due to other reasons during the same period. Again, the main reason for the lesser number of farmer suicides in these districts has been occupational diversification and earning income from non-farm and allied activities.

Farmer suicides in Punjab: farm-size distribution

To understand the agrarian crisis, it is important and essential to analyse the suicides of the farmers in Punjab by farm size. Therefore, an attempt is made to look into the farm-size distribution of farmer suicides in the state during 2000–2013. The data and information of the same is depicted in Table 4.7, Figures 4.5a, 4.5b and 4.5c.

An analysis of farmer suicides according to farm-size distribution suggests that out of 3885 farmer suicides in Punjab, 43.84 per cent were marginal farmers, followed by 30.12 per cent small, 17.99 per cent semi-medium, 7.03 per cent medium and only 1.03 per cent large. Further, 94.75 per cent of all farmers died by suicide

TABLE 4.7 Farm-size distribution of farmer suicide cases due to debt and other reasons, in Punjab, 2000–13

Farmer category (acres)	Debt	Non-debt	Total
Marginal (up to 2.5)	1585 (93.07%) (43.06%)	118 (6.93%) (57.84%)	1703 (100.00%) (43.84%)
Small (2.5–5.0)	1122 (95.90%) (30.48%)	48 (4.10%) (23.53%)	1170 (100.00%) (30.12%)
Semi-medium (5.0–10.0)	677 (95.85%) (18.39%)	22 (4.15%) (10.78%)	699 (100.00%) (17.99%)
Medium (10.0–25)	263 (96.34%) (7.14%)	10 (3.66%) (4.90%)	273 (100.00%) (7.03%)
Large (more than 25)	34 (85.00%) (0.92%)	6 (15.00%) (2.94%)	40 (100.00%) (1.03%)
Total	3681 (94.75%) (100.00%)	204 (5.25%) (100.00%)	3885 (100.00%) (100.00%)

Source: Compiled by the authors, from Government of Punjab, Survey Reports of Punjabi University, Patiala; Punjab Agriculture University, Ludhiana; and Guru Nanak Dev University, Amritsar, 2017

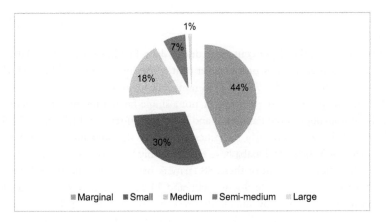

FIGURE 4.5 Farmer suicides, according to farm size, in Punjab

Source: Based on Table 4.7

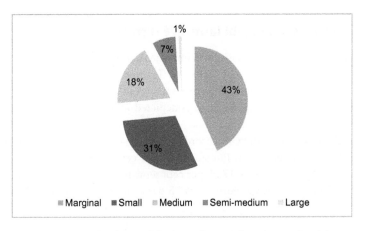

FIGURE 4.5a Farmer suicides due to debt, according to farm size, in Punjab

Source: Based on Table 4.7

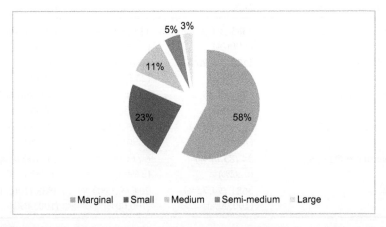

FIGURE 4.5b Farmer suicides for non-debt reasons, according to farm size, in Punjab

Source: Based on Table 4.7

due to debt as the main reason: out of the total 3681 farmers, 43.06 per cent were marginal farmers, 30.48 per cent small, 18.39 per cent semi-medium, 7.14 per cent medium and only 0.92 per cent large. A large majority of deceased farmers who died by suicide due to non-debt causes, specifically 81.37 per cent, also belonged to marginal and small farmer categories. From the above analysis, it seems that there is some relationship between non-debt causes and the production levels of the farmers. The analysis clearly revealed that a large majority, specifically 70 per cent, of the deceased farmers belonged to marginal and small farmer categories. Therefore, it can be safely concluded that in Punjab marginal and small farmers have been facing the severe and cruel agrarian distress. Thus, it is pertinent to add here that the small and marginal section of the farming community needs the supportive remedial measures.

For a deeper and regional analysis of farmer suicides due to debt and non-debt, it is necessary to study the farmer suicides through district-level distribution according to farm size in the state. Again, for this purpose, the districts of Punjab are divided into two parts. First, the districts highly affected by agrarian distress and, second, the districts less affected by farmer suicides. The information related to debt and non-debt causes of farmer suicides is presented in Table 4.8 and Table 4.9.

TABLE 4.8 District-level and farm-size distribution of farmer suicides due to debt in Punjab, 2000–13

Category (acres) District	Marginal (up to 2.5)	Small (2.5–5.0)	Semi-medium (5.0–10.0)	Medium (10.0–25)	Large (more than 25)	Total
Highly affected districts						
Bathinda	263 (16.59)	196 (17.47)	118 (17.43)	48 (18.25)	4 (11.76)	629 (17.09)
Barnala	191 (12.05)	129 (11.50)	83 (12.26)	37 (14.07)	–	440 (11.95)
Faridkot	13 (0.82)	6 (0.53)	7 (1.03)	4 (1.52)	2 (5.88)	32 (0.87)
Fazilka	10 (0.63)	5 (0.45)	1 (0.15)	4 (1.52)	–	20 (0.54)
Ferozpur	13 (0.82)	10 (0.90)	3 (0.44)	2 (0.76)	–	28 (0.76)
Ludhiana	91 (5.74)	56 (4.99)	38 (5.61)	15 (5.70)	1 (2.94)	201 (5.46)
Mansa	346 (21.83)	251 (22.37)	142 (20.97)	44 (16.73)	1 (2.94)	784 (21.30)
Moga	192 (12.11)	106 (9.45)	42 (6.20)	21 (7.98)	3 (8.82)	364 (9.89)
Mukatsar	52 (3.28)	52 (4.62)	33 (4.87)	21 (7.98)	17	175 (4.75)
Patiala	38 (2.40)	29 (2.58)	15 (2.22)	3 (1.14)	2 (5.88)	87 (2.36)

(Continued)

TABLE 4.8 (Continued)

Category (acres) District	Marginal (up to 2.5)	Small (2.5–5.0)	Semi-medium (5.0–10.0)	Medium (10.0–25)	Large (more than 25)	Total
Sangrur	331	258	182	61	1	833
	(20.88)	(22.99)	(26.88)	(23.18)	(2.94)	(22.63)
Subtotal (A)	1540	1098	664	260	31	3593
	(97.16)	(97.86)	(98.08)	(98.86)	(91.18)	(97.61)
Slightly affected districts						
Amritsar	4	2	–	–	–	6
	(0.25)	(0.18)				(0.16)
Fatehgarh Sahib	–	3	2	2	2	9
		(0.27)	(0.30)	(0.76)	(5.88)	(0.24)
Gurdaspur	17	7	4	–	–	28
	(1.07)	(0.62)	(0.60)			(0.76)
Hosiharpur	2	1	2	–	–	5
	(0.13)	(0.09)	(0.30)			(0.14)
Jalander	7	3	1	-	-	11
	(0.44)	(0.27)	0.15)			(0.30)
Kapurthala	1	3	–	–	–	4
	(0.06)	(0.27)				(0.11)
Mohali	3	1	3	1	–	8
	(0.19)	(0.09)	(0.44)	(0.38)		(0.22)
Rupnagar	–	–	–	–	–	–
SBS Nagar	4	1	1	–	–	6
	(0.25)	(0.09)	(0.15)			(0.16)
Pathankot	–	–	–	–	–	–
Tarn Taran	7	3	–	–	1	11
	(0.44)	(0.27)			(2.94)	(0.30)
Subtotal (B)	45	24	13	3	3	88
	(2.84)	(2.14)	(1.92)	(1.14)	(8.82)	(2.39)
Total (A) + (B)	1585	1122	677	263	34	3681
	(100.00)	(100.00)	(100.00)	(100.00)	(100.00)	(100.00)

Source: Compiled by the authors, from Government of Punjab, Survey Reports of Punjabi University, Patiala; Punjab Agriculture University; Ludhiana and Guru Nanak Dev University, Amritsar, 2017

Note: Figures in parentheses are percentages

TABLE 4.9 District-level and farm-size distribution of farmer suicides due to reasons other than debt in Punjab, 2000–13

Category (acres) District	Marginal (up to 2.5)	Small (2.5–5.0)	Semi-medium (5.0–10.0)	Medium (10.0–25)	Large (more than 25)	Total
Highly affected districts						
Bathinda	20	10	2	2	–	34
	(16.95)	(20.83)	(9.09)	(20)		(16.67)
Barnala	4	1	2	1	–	8
	(3.39)	(2.08)	(9.09)	(10)		(3.92)

Category (acres) District	Marginal (up to 2.5)	Small (2.5–5.0)	Semi-medium (5.0–10.0)	Medium (10.0–25)	Large (more than 25)	Total
Faridkot	3 (2.54)	1 (2.08)	–	–	1 (16.67)	5 (2.45)
Fazilka	6 (5.08)	1 (2.08)	–	–	–	7 (3.43)
Ferozpur	3 (2.54)	1 (2.08)	–	–	–	4 (1.96)
Ludhiana	20 (16.95)	8 (16.67)	3 (13.64)	–	–	31 (15.20)
Mansa	12 (10.17)	10 (20.83)	2 (9.09)	4 (40)	1 (16.67)	29 (14.22)
Moga	15 (12.71)	3 (6.25)	5 (22.73)	–	–	23 (11.27)
Mukatsar	7 (5.93)	3 (6.25)	1 (4.55)	–	2 (33.33)	13 (6.37)
Patiala	6 (5.08)	–	–	–	–	6 (2.94)
Sangrur	15 (12.71)	6 (12.50)	7 (31.82)	3 (30)	2 (33.33)	33 (16.18)
Subtotal (A)	111 (94.07)	44 (91.67)	22 (100.00)	10 (100.00)	6 (100.00)	193 (94.61)
Slightly affected districts						
Amritsar	2 (1.69)	3 (6.25)	–	–	–	5 (2.45)
Fatehgarh Sahib	–	–	–	–	–	–
Gurdaspur	2 (1.69)	–	–	–	–	2 (0.98)
Hosiharpur	–	–	–	–	–	–
Jalander	1 (0.85)	–	–	–	–	1 (0.49)
Kapurthala	–	–	–	–	–	–
Mohali	–	–	–	–	–	–
Rupnagar	–	–	–	–	–	–
SBS Nagar	1 (0.85)	1 (2.08)	–	–	–	2 (0.98)
Pathankot	–	–	–	–	–	–
Tarn Taran	1 (0.85)	–	–	–	–	1 (0.49)
Subtotal (B)	7 (5.93)	4 (8.33)	–	–	–	11 (5.39)
Total (A) + (B)	118 (100.00)	48 (100.00)	22 (100.00)	10 (100.00)	6 (100.00)	204 (100.00)

Source: Compiled by the authors, from Government of Punjab, Survey Reports of Punjabi University, Patiala; Punjab Agriculture University; Ludhiana and Guru Nanak Dev University, Amritsar, 2017

Note: Figures in parentheses are percentages

The data show that out of 3885 farmers, 94.75 per cent had died by suicide due to debt as the main reason, whereas 5.25 per cent died due to other causes. As far as the districts that fall in the Malwa region of Punjab are concerned, 97.61 per cent of the farmers of all categories had died by suicide. But it was only 2.39 per cent in other districts. This clearly reveals that the Malwa region of Punjab faced the worst crisis in the agrarian economy. As far as the farm-size distribution of farmer suicides was concerned, 97.16 per cent of the marginal farmers, 97.86 per cent of the small farmers, 98.08 per cent of the medium farmers, 98.86 per cent of the semi-medium farmers and 91.18 per cent of the large farmers died by suicide in the high incidence of agrarian distress–prone districts of the state, and only around 2 per cent to 3 per cent of the suicides were reported from other districts during 2000–13. Among the highly distressed districts, in the case of marginal farmers that died by suicide, was Mansa: it is ranked first with a 21.83 per cent share of the state, followed by Sangrur with 20.88 per cent, Bathinda with 16.59 per cent, Moga with 12.11 per cent and Barnala with 12.05 per cent. In the case of small and semi-medium farmers, the Sangrur district was highest with a 22.99 per cent and a 26.88 per cent share respectively, followed by Mansa, Bathinda, Barnala and Moga in the ranking order. Another, similar situation has been prevailing with regard to farmer suicides due to debt in the case of medium and large farm-size categories of the farmers.

An analysis of the suicides of various categories of farmers in the less agrarian distressed areas due to debt suggests that not even a single case of suicide has been reported from the Pathankot and Rupnagar districts. Further, the other districts of this region have also reported few cases of farmer suicides due to debt as the main reason. Therefore, it emerged from this analysis that farmer suicides due to debt have dominated in the highly agrarian distressed districts of the state. Importantly, the small and marginal farmers were prone to suicides mainly because of the fact that their main occupation is agriculture, though a few are also engaged in non-farm activities.

The farmer suicides were also due to reasons other than debt. An attempt has been made in this chapter to analyse the district-level variations of farmer suicides due to non-debt reasons during 2000–13. The information and data regarding this are depicted in Table 4.9. The analysis of the Table 4.9 reveals that a large major-ity, specifically 81.37 per cent, of victim farmers in this category were small and marginal farmers and nearly 93 per cent of these farmers belonged to the highly agrarian distressed districts of the state. Three districts, specifically Bathinda, San-grur and Ludhiana, represent the highest numbers of suicides in the non-debt category. Among these districts, the small and marginal farmers mainly died by suicide even in the category of non-debt reasons. Among the districts where farm-ers died by suicide for non-debt-related reasons, Amritsar was on the top. From the foregoing analysis, it can be concluded that the real reasons behind the suicides of these farmers may be related to the economy of the farmers since the predomi-nant number of victim farmers belong to the districts highly affected by agrarian distress.

Farm labour suicides in Punjab: district-level distribution

It is important to understand the state of the situation of the other half of the work-force engaged in agriculture: the agriculture labourers. The agriculture labour is an equal partner in the development of agriculture. During the years of prosperity, they gain less, and when distress occurs, they are the most affected. The agrarian distress in Punjab has severely affected the agriculture labour of the state. In this section, an attempt is made to look into the impact this distress.

The information regarding for agriculture labourer suicides in Punjab is presented in Table 4.10. The analysis of Table 4.10, displaying agriculture labour suicides in Punjab, shows that 3048 farm labourers died by suicide in the state between 2000 and 2013. Out of 3048 labourer suicides, a large majority, specifically 88.78 per cent, was caused by debt. The remaining 11.22 per cent died by suicide due to reasons other than debt. The trend of farm labour suicides found to be somewhat similar to that of farmer suicides: the leading cause in both the cases has been debt. It can be safely inferred that agriculture labour is also a victim of agrarian distress, which is widespread in Punjab.

The district-level analysis of agriculture labour suicides gives us insights into the spread and extent of the incidence. It is important to examine the farm labour suicides at the district level in order to better understand the prevailing distress among the farm labour in different regions of the state. The district-level distribution of farm labour suicides in Punjab during 2000–13 is depicted in Table 4.11.

In the case of farm labour suicides, the districts of Punjab have been divided into two parts. First, the districts highly affected by agrarian distress, the extent of it and its causes are described. Second, the number and the proportion of agriculture labour that died by suicide in slightly affected districts are described. On the whole, 98.52 per cent of farm labourers died by suicide in the districts highly affected by agrarian distress of the state, and only 1.48 per cent of agriculture labourer suicides were reported from districts in Punjab that were slightly affected by distress. When we look at the agriculture labourer suicides, it is clear from the analysis of the data that the suicides were mainly caused by debt. The proportion of agriculture labourers who died by suicide due to indebtedness was 88.78 per cent. The proportion is quite small when we look at the non–debt reasons for dying by suicide by agriculture labourers, which is only 11.22 per cent.

TABLE 4.10 Agriculture labour suicides in Punjab, 2000–13

Causes	Number	Percentage
Debt	2706	88.78
Non-debt	342	11.22
Total	3048	100.00

Source: Compiled by the authors, from Government of Punjab, Survey Reports of Punjabi University, Patiala; Punjab Agriculture University; Ludhiana and Guru Nanak Dev University, Amritsar, 2017

TABLE 4.11 District-level numbers of agricultural labourer suicides in Punjab, 2000–13

District	Causes of Agricultural Labourer Suicides					
	Debt		Non-debt		Total	
	Number	%	Number	%	Number	%
Highly affected districts						
Bathinda	534	19.73	76	22.22	610	20.01
Barnala	298	11.01	12	3.51	310	10.17
Faridkot	33	1.22	3	0.88	36	1.18
Fazilka	7	0.26	9	2.63	16	0.52
Ferozpur	4	0.15	7	2.05	11	0.36
Ludhiana	108	3.99	48	14.04	156	5.12
Mansa	575	21.25	45	13.16	620	20.34
Moga	199	7.35	42	12.28	241	7.91
Mukatsar	209	7.72	30	8.77	239	7.84
Patiala	89	3.29	7	2.05	96	3.15
Sangrur	623	23.02	45	13.16	668	21.92
Subtotal (A)	2679	99.00	324	94.74	3003	98.52
Slightly affected districts						
Amritsar	2	0.07	5	1.46	7	0.23
Fatehgarh Sahib	5	0.18	1	0.29	6	0.20
Gurdaspur	3	0.11	–	–	3	0.10
Hosiharpur	2	0.07	2	0.58	4	0.13
Jalander	1	0.04	1	0.29	2	0.07
Kapurthala	–	–	1	0.29	1	0.03
Mohali	5	0.18	5	1.46	10	0.33
Rupnagar	6	0.22	–	–	6	0.20
SBS Nagar	2	0.07	–	–	2	0.07
Pathankot	–	–	–	–	–	–
Tarn Taran	1	0.04	3	0.88	4	0.13
Subtotal (B)	27	1.00	18	5.26	45	1.48
Total (A) + (B)	2706	100.00	342	100.00	3048	100.00

Source: Compiled by the authors, from Government of Punjab, Survey Reports of Punjabi University, Patiala; Punjab Agriculture University; Ludhiana and Guru Nanak Dev University, Amritsar, 2017

Furthermore, the analysis of the table shows that 99.00 per cent deceased agriculture labour has been reported from the districts highly affected by agrarian distress in Punjab and only 1.00 per cent of farm labour suicides were reported from slightly affected districts. Among the highly affected districts, the Sangrur district was ranked first, at 23.02 per cent of labour suicides in the state, followed by Mansa at 21.25 per cent, Bathinda at 19.73 per cent, Barnala at 11.01 per cent and Moga and Sri Mukatsar Sahib at over 7 per cent. Importantly, during the period of study, not even a single agriculture labourer suicide was reported from the Pathankot and Kapurthala districts.

Similarly, 94.74 per cent of the farm labour suicides that were due to non-debt reasons occurred in the districts highly affected by agrarian distress, and 5.26 per cent of farm labour suicides were reported from slightly affected districts. Again, no farm labourer suicides have been reported from Gurdaspur, Rupnagar, SBS Nagar or Pathankot in this category. From this analysis, it can be concluded that in Punjab, the farm labour has also been facing the onslaught of agrarian distress, especially in the Malwa region of the state, which needs to be addressed by introducing concrete policy initiatives.

Conclusions

The Punjab economy has been showing structural changes, and the green revolution resulted in rapid growth of state's net state domestic product. Punjab agriculture has made remarkable progress and is unparalleled in the history of world agriculture. Punjab state, with only 1.5 per cent of the geographical area of the country (besides feeding its growing population), has been contributing 35 per cent to 40 per cent of the rice and 45 per cent to 70 per cent of the wheat to the central pool. But the gains of the green revolution cannot be sustained, because presently, the agrarian sector of the state is suffering an unprecedented crisis.

The agrarian crisis is the result of policies pursued by the government and many other factors; first, stagnation of yield, especially for wheat, and a decline in rice and cotton and successive crop failures due to natural and human made factors (spurious pesticides, seeds and fertilizers), along with failures in and not implementing the crop diversification programme due to uncertain yields, low prices and poorly marketing alternative crops. The crisis in Punjab's agriculture has also been compounded by the increased operational and fixed costs of cultivation and the consequential declining income from agriculture. World Trade Organization policies added to the woes of farmers by prematurely pushing them to compete with farmers in developed nations who receive high subsidies. New economic agendas focused on industry and other sectors have resulted in stagnation in the public investment in agriculture, and it has consequently marginalized he agrarian sector and also wreaked havoc on the farmers and agriculture labourers. State politics turned against the interests of the workforce in the rural sector of the economy due to strong political positions of *certain* farmers who have emerged during the green revolution. It was weakened and fragmented in the 1980s and now on the margins during the liberalization period due to the shift in political affiliations and a disjuncture between the interests of farmers and those of politicians.

A comparative state-level picture of farm suicides shows that the Indian agricultural sector is facing severe agrarian distress and resulting farm suicides. Further, the comparative per one lakh rate of suicides among the general population, all cultivators and main cultivators (respectively) shows that all cultivators and the workforce working as main cultivators in India were under agrarian distress, due to which they resorted to dying by suicide. Recently, agriculturally advanced states, specifically Punjab, Haryana, Gujarat and Karnataka, which have large irrigation facilities and high agricultural production and yield levels, witnessed a surge in farm suicides. For the purpose of the analysis herein, Punjab has been divided into two parts: first, the highly agrarian distressed districts, mainly Malwa, and, second, the less agrarian distressed districts of the Shiwalik foothills, Doaba and Majha. All indicators of the extent of farm suicides in Punjab reveal that farmers and agricultural labourers of the state are facing a severe crisis and continue to die by suicide due to indebtedness. Punjab's Malwa region in specific is highly distressed by the agrarian crisis. It is especially prone to farm suicides, and the overriding reason for a large majority of the farm suicides was debt. In Punjab, marginal and small farmers have been facing the severe agrarian distress, and this section of the farming community needs supportive, remedial measures.

Further, the deceased farmers who have died by suicide due to reasons other than debt were small and marginal farmers and belonged to agrarian distressed districts, and a small number of them belonged to less distressed districts. Some of the farmers in the medium farm and large farm categories also died by suicide. Again, the reasons behind the suicides of these farmers may be related to the economic crisis that farmers are facing, because these farmers also reside in the distressed areas of the state. The trends in agriculture labourer suicides were found to be somewhat similar to those for the farmer suicides, the leading cause of which in both was debt. Thus, it can be concluded that the agriculture sector in Punjab is in the grip of a deep agrarian crisis.

5

RURAL HOUSEHOLDS

Socioeconomic characteristics

The study of socioeconomic characteristics of the sampled villages, rural households and respondents, that is deceased farmers and agricultural labourers and control group farmers and agricultural labourers, is crucial and important to gauge the gravity of the rural and agrarian distress in Punjab. Indian society traditionally has been characterized by the dominance of cultural factors like extended family systems/joint family system, dependence on the family and the fact that some time family loyalty overrides individual concerns. Social norms predominantly determine the socioeconomic behaviour of the rural households. These cultural and social factors may help elucidate some of the patterns of suicide among farmers and agricultural labourers. In this chapter, an attempt has been made to analyse various important personal, social, cultural, religious and economic variables of the village and rural households.

Almost all the studies and investigations have established that the Malwa region of Punjab is under unprecedented agrarian rural distress as more than 80 per cent of the rural suicides committed by farmers and agricultural labourers have been reported from this region alone during 1990–2010 (IDC 1998, 2006; AFDR 2000; Iyer and Manick 2000). Recent census surveys conducted by the universities of the state on behalf of the Punjab government also confirmed the same scenario in this region of the state. Since the earlier studies purely concentrated on the victim farmers and agricultural labourers, they could not take into consideration the control groups' characteristics. Therefore, the comparative analysis of victim and control group of farmers and agricultural labourers is attempted while taking into consideration the three highly distressed districts of the state: Bathinda, Mansa and Sangrur. The rest of the chapter is organized into five sections. The geographical characteristics of the study area are described in the first section. In the second section, the field survey coverage across districts is analysed. The social characteristics of the sampled households across the victim farmers and agricultural labourers and the control group are analysed in the third section. The resource base and sources of irrigation of the sampled households are examined in the fourth section. In the final section, the concluding observations are presented.

Description of the study area

Punjab lies on the north-west border of India and is surrounded by Haryana, Himachal Pradesh, Jammu and Kashmir, Rajasthan and West Punjab of Pakistan. The location of Punjab in India has been shown in Figure 5.1. Administratively, Punjab

FIGURE 5.1 Location of study area within India and Punjab

Source: Courtesy of the authors.

has been divided into 20 districts and four divisions, culturally into Majha, Malwa and Doaba and geographically Shiwalik Hills range, central plains and southern plains. This study has been confined to Bathinda, Mansa and Sangrur districts of Punjab. These three districts constitute a major part of Malwa region and the cotton belt of the state, and are considered as the epicentre of agrarian distress and prone to farmers' and agricultural labourers' suicides. These districts are also a part of southern plains and share boundaries with Haryana. The main feature of the study area has been its contiguity, that is all the three districts are contiguous. Almost the area and area-related profile, agriculture and cropping pattern, village community and culture, climate, topography and many other features of the three selected districts have been indistinguishable.

Bathinda district: profile, climate and topography

Bathinda district is situated in the southern part of Punjab in the heart of Malwa region and is situated between 29° 33′ and 30° 36′ north latitude and 74° 38′ and 75° 46′ east longitude. The district is surrounded by Sirsa and Fatehabad districts of Haryana in the south, Sangrur and Mansa districts in the east, Moga in the north-east and Faridkot and Muktsar districts in the north-west. It consists of 285 villages, out of which 281 are inhabited and four are uninhabited; eight towns; and one census town. According to the Surveyor General of India, the district covers an area of 336,725 hectares and is sixth in terms of area in the state. Subdivision-wise area of Bathinda district is shown in Table 5.1.

Bathinda lies on the southern-western part close to the Thar Desert of Rajasthan far away from the Shiwalik range and major rivers of the state. As a result of this, climatically, the district has very hot summers and scorching heat. It has a scanty rainy season and dry but harsh winter. The average annual rainfall was 307.5 mm during 2006–10, which is much below the state average (437.6 mm) and temperature ranges 47°C in summer and 0°C in winter. Subdivision-wise area of Bathinda is much larger than other subdivisions of Rampura Phul and Talwandi Sabo.

TABLE 5.1 Subdivisions and area of Bathinda district

Name of the subdivision	Area in hectares
Bathinda	151,845
Rampura Phul	87,516
Talwandi Sabo	97,364
Total	336,725

Source: http://bathinda.nic.in/html/district_at_a_glance.html; accessed on 29 July 2012.

Sangrur district: profile, climate and topography

Sangrur is one of the four districts in Patiala division. It is one of the southern districts of the state and lies between 29° 4' and 30° 42' north latitude and 75° 18' and 76° 13' east longitude. It is bounded by Ludhiana district in the north, Barnala district in the west, Patiala district in the east and Fatehabad district (state of Haryana) in the south. It consists of 585 villages, out of which 581 are inhabited and four are uninhabited; and 13 towns. According to the Deputy Economic and Statistical Advisor, Sangrur, the area of Sangrur is 361,452 hectares. In terms of area, the district has ranked 13th in the state. Subdivision-wise area of Sangrur district is shown in Table 5.2. There are substantial differences in terms of the size across the various subdivisions. The analysis of Table 5.2 reveals that Sunam subdivision is the largest in terms of area and Dhuri is the smallest subdivision. However, other subdivisions are having marginal differences in terms of size (areas in hectares).

The climate of the district is on the whole dry and is characterized by a short monsoon, a hot summer and a bracing cold winter. The year may be divided into four seasons. The cold season from November to March is followed by the hot season lasting up to the end of June. The period from July to mid-September constitutes the rainy season, of south-west monsoon, the second half of September and October may be termed the post-monsoon or transition period. The average annual rainfall was 369.7 mm during 2006–10.

Mansa district: profile, climate and topography

Mansa district is situated in the southern part of Punjab in the heart of Malwa region and is situated between 29° 32' and 30° 12' north latitude and 75° 10' and 75° 46' east longitude. The district is surrounded by Sirsa and Fatehabad of Haryana state in the south, and Sangrur and Bathinda in the east. It consists of 242 villages and 5 towns. This district is the newly created one of Punjab by reorienting parts of adjoining Bathinda district in 1992; it covers an area of 2,192.25 square kilometres and is divided into five development blocks and three subdivisions. According to

TABLE 5.2 Subdivision-wise area of Sangrur District

Subdivision	Area in hectares
Sangrur	78,079
Malerkotla	69,536
Sunam	93,617
Moonak	60,286
Dhuri	59,934
Total	361,452

Source: Deputy Economic and Statistical Advisor, Sangrur, Punjab.

TABLE 5.3 Subdivisions and area of Mansa district

Name of the subdivision	Area in hectares
Mansa	76,628
Budhladha	72,735
Sardulgarh	69,862
Total	219,225

Source: http://mansa.nic.in/html/area.html; accessed on 2 August 2012.

the Surveyor General of India, the district covers an area of 219,225 hectares and is 4.3 per cent of area of the State. Subdivision-wise area of Mansa district is shown in Table 5.3. Subdivision-wise distribution of area of Mansa district suggests that all three subdivisions have marginal differences in size as far as the geographical coverage of the area is concerned.

The climate of the district is typical semi-arid type, with distinct wet and dry seasons. The normal average annual rainfall of the district is 121.8 mm during 2006–10 and temperature ranges 47°C in summer and 0°C in winter. The climate of Mansa district is classified as subtropical steppe, semi-arid and hot, which is mainly dry except in rainy months and characterized by intensely hot summers and cold winters. All the three districts have on an average low rainfall compared to the overall average rainfall of the state. There are wide variations across the three districts regarding area under irrigation. In the Bathinda district, the main source of irrigation is government canal irrigation system, but Sangrur district mainly depends on tube well irrigation system. There is balance between tube well and government canal irrigation so far as the irrigated area of Mansa district is concerned.

Socioeconomic characteristics of the sampled villages

For a fruitful and meaningful understanding of the problem in hand, an attempt has been made to include all the developmental blocks of the three districts. Furthermore, an attempt has also been made to provide more representation in the sample to highly distressed villages (see Appendix II), blocks and districts. This is done with a view to capture the intensity of agrarian distress. District-wise and block-wise details of the sample of farmers on the brink/control group, deceased farmers, control group agricultural labourers on the brink and deceased agricultural labourers drawn are presented in Table 5.4.

In all 1,020 farmers, 510 deceased farmers and 510 farmers on the brink/control group, and 372 agricultural labourers, 186 deceased and 186 agricultural labourers on the brink/control group, have been included in this study. The chosen sample design gives more representation to highly agrarian distressed district of Sangrur and followed by Bathinda and Mansa of Punjab in the sample. In case of Sangrur, Lehra Gaga, Sunam and Andana blocks have been more affected and distressed;

TABLE 5.4 District-wise classification and distribution of the sample

Category	Farmers			Labourers		
District	Deceased	Control group	Total	Deceased	Control group	Total
Sangrur	199	199	398	69	69	138
Bathinda	172	172	344	60	60	120
Mansa	139	139	278	57	57	114
Total	510	510	1,020	186	186	372

Source: Field survey.

therefore, more respondents have been approached in these blocks as compared to other blocks of the district. Similarly on the same ground from Bathinda district, Rampura, Bathinda and Maur blocks have been given more representation as compared to other blocks. Budhladha, Jhunir and Mansa developmental blocks of Mansa district have more distress and hence been given more representation in the sample as compared to other blocks (see Table 1.1).

Socioeconomic profile

The concept of economic development has been considered and treated as a growth of gross national product, growth of per capita gross national product and other similar economic indicators. It is widely recognized now that the apparent failure of this narrow economic approach to development (McGranahan 1971; UNDP 2012) leads to a rapid upsurge of interest to investigate social factors. Human resources development approach to development argued that the social factors are part and parcel of the process of development and should not be ignored (UNDP 2012). The informal rules based on social setting govern and shape the economic behaviour of the economic agents of production. Therefore, socioeconomic variables must be viewed, analysed and considered as interdependent aspects of social and overall development. In the following sections, an attempt is made to analyse major personal, social and economic variables of the respondents.

Age-wise distribution

Age is one of the important personal factors that influence and determine the other variable of economic progress and choices of the individuals. The study of suicide victims can be helpful in understanding which of the age group is more prone to suicides. Suicide is an act, which socially is non-acceptable and legally is treated as a crime. Therefore, there is a social stigma attached to a family whose member commits suicide. This adds to the sufferings of the living members of the family with grave social and economic consequences. On the one hand, the person who commits suicide is the most important member of the family and most of the time the sole bread earner of the family and, on the other hand, leaves behind a heap of debt burden without any repayable capacity of the surviving family members. In this section, an attempt is made to capture these variables of the farmers and agricultural labourers by classifying the respondents into various age groups. The information and data collected from the field survey regarding age-wise distribution of respondents is presented in Table 5.5 and Figure 5.2.

When we look at the age-wise distribution of the deceased group of farmers and agricultural labourers, it is evident from the analysis of Table 5.5 that a large number of victim farmers and agricultural labourers were below the age of 35 years. In the two districts, that is Sangrur and Mansa, more than 50 per cent of the deceased farmers belonged to the age group of below 35 years. This group has committed maximum suicides as compared to middle-aged and elder farmers and

TABLE 5.5 Age-wise distribution of number of deceased and control group farmers and labourers (age in years)

District	Farmers		Labourers	
	Deceased	Control group	Deceased	Control group
Sangrur				
Below 35	100 (53.3)	39 (19.6)	38 (55.1)	10 (14.5)
36–55	77 (38.7)	107 (53.8)	24 (34.8)	35 (50.7)
Above 56	16 (8.0)	53 (26.6)	7 (10.1)	24 (34.8)
Total	199 (100)	199 (100)	69 (100)	69 (100)
Bathinda				
Below 35	69 (40.1)	30 (17.4)	36 (60.0)	9 (15.0)
36–55	81 (47.1)	81 (47.1)	21 (28.3)	29 (48.3)
Above 56	22 (12.8)	61 (35.5)	7 (11.7)	22 (36.7)
Total	172 (100)	172 (100)	60 (100)	60 (100)
Mansa				
Below 35	73 (52.5)	21 (15.1)	33 (57.9)	18 (31.6)
36–55	51 (36.7)	75 (54.0)	20 (35.1)	29 (50.9)
Above 56	15 (10.8)	43 (30.9)	4 (7.0)	10 (17.5)
Total	139 (100)	139 (100)	57 (100)	57 (100)
Overall				
Below 35	248 (48.6)	90 (17.6)	107 (57.5)	37 (19.9)
36–55	209 (41.0)	263 (51.6)	61 (32.8)	93 (50.0)
Above 56	53 (10.4)	157 (30.8)	18 (9.7)	56 (30.1)
Total	510 (100)	510 (100)	186 (100)	186 (100)

Source: Field survey.

Note: Figures in parenthesis are percentages.

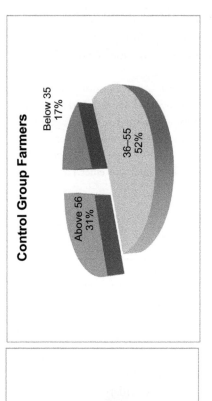

Deceased Farmers

Above 56
10%

36–55
41%

Below 35
49%

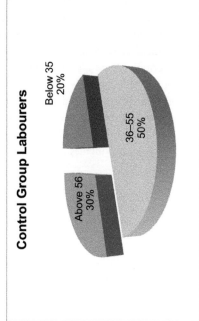

Control Group Farmers

Below 35
17%

Above 56
31%

36–55
52%

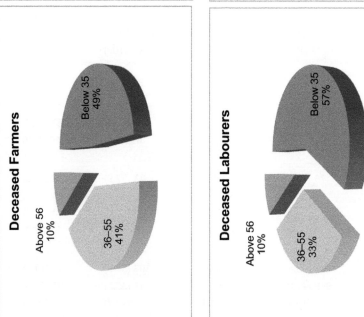

Deceased Labourers

Above 56
10%

36–55
33%

Below 35
57%

Control Group Labourers

Below 35
20%

Above 56
30%

36–55
50%

FIGURE 5.2 Age–wise distribution of farmers and agricultural labourers

predominantly labourers across the districts under consideration. It is significant to note that on the whole 57.5 per cent of the victim agricultural labourers belonged to the age group of below 35 years. However, for the victim farmers, this percentage is 48.6. This means that the younger-age group farmers and agricultural labourers are suffering from the syndrome of non-fulfilment of a brighter future. They do also leave behind tales of suffering for the other members of the family. An important fact that emerged from the analysis of Table 5.5 is that more than 90 per cent of the farmers and agricultural labourers who committed suicides belonged to the age group of below 55 years. This implies that the victim farmers and agricultural labourers had long experience and skill base for doing agriculture operations efficiently. There were perceptible differences across districts among the victim farmers and agriculture labourers. In Bathinda, the lowest percentage of victim farmers and the highest percentage of victim agricultural labourers belonged to below the age group of 35 years.

So far as the control group of farmers and agricultural labourers was concerned, the large number was falling between the age group of 36 and 55 years. The overall analyses of the control group of farmers and agricultural labourers show no marked differences when we compare their age group. But one can notice marginal differences across three districts under examination regarding age distribution of the control group of farmers and agricultural labourers.

From the foregoing analysis, it can be safely concluded that agrarian distress has been affecting the young farmers and young agricultural labourers in Punjab. Earlier studies also found that 60 per cent (IDC 1998), 89 per cent (Iyer and Manick 2000), 86 per cent (AFDR 2000), 76 per cent (Chahal 2005), 82 per cent (IDC 2006) and 74 per cent (Bhangoo 2006) of the cases fall in the young and middle-age categories. This amply demonstrates the emerging stress and hardships faced by young and middle-aged farmers. It seems that agrarian crisis is hitting hard the household economy of the younger farmers and agricultural labourers. Their capability to tolerate and resist the agrarian crisis seems to be diminishing at a fast pace.

Sex-wise distribution

Since the green revolution, agricultural operations had remained the domain of the male members of the households. It is significant to note that female participation in the workforce has remained quite low in Punjab. Therefore, there is a prevailing myth that the agrarian distress affects only the male members of the family. To empirically verify whether this myth is true, we have included in the field survey the category of the deceased farmers and agricultural labourers as males and females. Therefore, the analysis of sex-wise distribution of the deceased and control group farmers and agricultural labourers is significant to gauge the intensity of distress among males and females. In this light, an attempt is made to examine the sex-wise distribution of the respondents, which is another important social profile factor. The information regarding sex-wise distribution of the respondents is presented in Table 5.6.

TABLE 5.6 Sex-wise distribution of farmers and agricultural labourers

District	Sex	Farmers		Labourers	
		Deceased	Control group	Deceased	Control group
Sangrur	Male	196 (98.49)	193 (96.98)	60 (86.96)	67 (97.10)
	Female	3 (1.51)	6 (3.02)	9 (13.04)	2 (2.99)
	Total	199 (100)	199 (100)	69 (100)	69 (100)
Bathinda	Male	156 (90.69)	171 (99.41)	56 (93.33)	57 (95.00)
	Female	16 (9.30)	1 (0.58)	4 (6.67)	3 (5.00)
	Total	172 (100)	172 (100)	60 (100)	60 (100)
Mansa	Male	134 (96.40)	136 (97.84)	54 (94.34)	55 (96.49)
	Female	5 (3.60)	3 (2.16)	3 (5.26)	2 (3.51)
	Total	139 (100)	139 (100)	57 (100)	57 (100)
All over	Male	486 (95.29)	500 (98.03)	170 (91.39)	179 (96.24)
	Female	24 (4.70)	10 (1.96)	16 (8.60)	7 (3.76)
	Grand total	510 (100)	510 (100)	186 (100)	186 (100)

Source: Field survey.

Note: Figures in parenthesis are percentages.

It is a well-known fact that operations of agriculture in Punjab is the domain of male members of the households. It implies that the prevailing agrarian distress should have impacted only the male members of the households. But the analysis of the data collected from the field survey and presented in Table 5.6 shows that the distress was so cruel that it also engulfed the women members of the rural households. Sex-wise distribution of households' analysis further showed that women of the households also committed suicides due to economic distress. The highest number of female members of the farm households who committed suicides was reported from Bathinda district, that is nine females, which was 9.30 per cent of the total number of suicides. However, the female farmers in the Mansa district, who committed suicides, were just 3.6 per cent. The lowest incidence of female farmers' suicides was reported in Sangrur district, which was 1.51 per cent. The fact is that females also committed suicides due to a high degree of agrarian distress. However, the female agricultural labourers who have committed suicides were much higher than the female farmers. The highest incidence of suicides of female farm labourers was in Sangrur (13.04 per cent), followed by Bathinda (6.67 per cent) and Mansa (5.2 per cent). A similar trend and evidence has been brought out by the earlier studies (Iyer and Manick 2000) as well. Thus, an important conclusion that emerges from the analysis of the distribution of the deceased male and female farmers and agricultural labourers is that distress-driven suicides are predominantly committed by men. But the distress has not spared the females, and the proportion of suicides and female participation in the workforce is in consonance.

Caste-wise analysis

Indian caste system is deep rooted and segregates the society occupationally and hierarchically. As a consequence of this, the position of an individual in the society is determined by his or her birth in a particular caste, and not by selection/choice or by his or her accomplishments. Historically, the caste in Indian society is based on a hierarchical system, and each caste has a preset occupation to be followed by its members. Furthermore, each caste has its own customs, traditions, practices and rituals, and members of the castes are bounded by these. Therefore, it is important to analyse the respondents by their caste category.

The analysis of Table 5.7 and Figure 5.3 shows that a large majority of the deceased and control group farmers belong to Jat Sikh caste – a general and superior caste of Punjab. Thus, the farmers are among the upper strata of the caste

TABLE 5.7 Caste-wise distribution of farmers and agricultural labourers

District	Caste	Farmers		Labourers	
		Deceased	Control group	Deceased	Control group
Sangrur	Jat Sikh	188 (94.5)	184 (92.5)	9 (13.0)	6 (8.7)
	OBCs	2 (1.0)	–	1 (1.5)	3 (4.3)
	SCs	9 (4.5)	6 (3.0)	56 (81.2)	55 (79.1)
	Brahmins	–	9 (4.5)	3 (4.3)	5 (7.3)
	Total	199 (100)	199 (100)	69 (100)	69 (100)
Bathinda	Jat Sikh	162 (94.2)	160 (93.0)	1 (1.7)	–
	OBCs	5 (2.9)	5 (2.9)	1 (1.7)	–
	SCs	4 (2.3)	4 (2.3)	54 (90.0)	60 (100)
	Brahmin	1 (0.6)	3 (1.7)	4 (6.7)	–
	Total	172 (100)	172 (100)	60 (100)	60 (100)
Mansa	Jat Sikh	131 (94.3)	126 (90.6)	1 (1.7)	1 (1.7)
	OBCs	2 (1.4)	1 (0.7)	2 (3.6)	1 (1.7)
	SCs	1 (0.7)	11 (7.9)	54 (94.7)	53 (93.1)
	Brahmin	5 (3.6)	1 (0.7)	–	2 (3.5)
	Total	139 (100)	139 (100)	57 (100)	57 (100)
Overall	Jat Sikh	481 (94.3)	47 (92.2)	11 (5.9)	7 (3.8)
	OBCs	9 (1.8)	6 (1.2)	4 (2.1)	4 (2.1)
	SCs	14 (2.7)	21 (4.1)	164 (88.2)	168 (63.5)
	Brahmin	6 (1.2)	13 (2.5)	7 (3.8)	7 (30.6)
	Total	510 (100)	510 (100)	186 (100)	186 (100)

Source: Field survey.

Note: Figures in parenthesis are percentages; SCs: scheduled castes; OBCs: other backward castes.

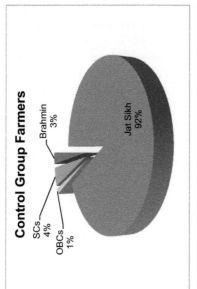

Control Group Farmers

Brahmin 3%
SCs 4%
OBCs 1%
Jat Sikh 92%

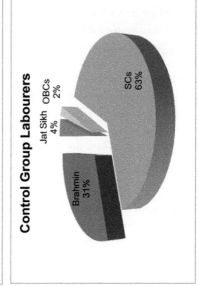

Control Group Labourers

Jat Sikh 4%
OBCs 2%
SCs 63%
Brahmin 31%

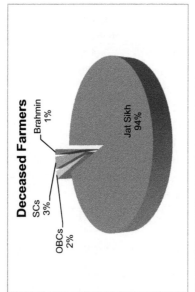

Deceased Farmers

Brahmin 1%
SCs 3%
OBCs 2%
Jat Sikh 94%

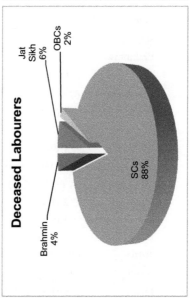

Deceased Labourers

Jat Sikh 6%
OBCs 2%
SCs 88%
Brahmin 4%

FIGURE 5.3 Caste–wise distribution of farmers and agricultural labourers

hierarchy in Punjab. High incidence of suicides among them indicates that they did not seem to compromise over social values and loss of social status (Chahal 2005) and also that economic factors are not sparing Jat Sikh farmers irrespective of their caste hierarchy (Iyer and Manick 2000).

In case of deceased and control group of farmers, a very large majority of the respondents belonged to Jat Sikh caste, as can be noticed from the overall empirical evidence from the field survey. This is true due to the fact that Jat Sikh caste has been dominating the agrarian scene of the state. A similar situation and trend has been noticed across the three districts, that is Bathinda, Sangrur and Mansa. It is important to note here that the two castes dominate the rural society of Punjab, that is Jat Sikhs as farmers and scheduled castes (SCs) as agricultural labourers. But the overall and across the districts empirical evidence shows that the higher castes such as Jat Sikhs and Brahmins also engaged in agriculture as agricultural labourers. However, the proportion of these households as agricultural labourers is quite small.

Although the high incidence of suicides was prevalent among the high-caste Jat Sikhs, yet other minority castes engaged in agriculture could not save themselves from this menace of suicides. The foregoing analysis amply brings out the fact that the spread of agrarian distress was so wide and far that it could not spare the high- and low-caste farmers who had been engaged in this occupation. Furthermore, the analysis of the caste-wise distribution of the deceased and control group of agricultural labourers indicated that SCs were the most dominant caste followed by others at Punjab level as well as in Bathinda, Sangrur and Mansa districts. Again, it is pertinent to mention here that SCs of Punjab, especially in rural areas, engaged in farm work as labourers in different forms since time immemorial. Therefore, the analysis of social category of agricultural labourers suggests that lower castes and downtrodden people of rural Punjab constitute this class. It is pertinent to add here that non-landed households engaged in farm labour even if they belonged to the higher caste could not manage to escape from committing suicides. This allows us to conclude that agrarian distress was so deep rooted and its spread was so wide that it took the toll of labourers across the castes categories.

Religion

Religion is an important source of informal institutional arrangement through which society functions. The norms, beliefs, customs, traditions, culture and ideology are the fundamental sources that determine and shape human interaction and human beings forms expectations of how others will behave. These institutions are also acting as constraints on the formal rules and regulations that govern the society. The continuity and enforcement of informal rules and regulations affect economic outcomes. The relationship between institutions and economic performance is complex but simultaneous (North 2003). The role of religion-based institutions is quite predominant in the rural society of India in general and Punjabi society in particular.

Religion may be among one of the most important defensive factor against suicides, both at the individual and at the societal levels, and this effect may be mediated by the degree to which a given religion sanctions suicide. This argument is consistent with ecological studies that have observed suicide rates to be high in societies where religious beliefs are not actively promoted by the state, and to be low in countries where they are (Vijayakumar *et al.* 2012). In this study efforts have been made to analyse the religion of the deceased and control group of farmers and agricultural labourers to ascertain the extent of suicides across religious groups. The field survey-based evidence regarding religious categories is depicted in Table 5.8 and Figure 5.4.

Analysis of the deceased farmers and agricultural labourers suggests that a large majority, over 97 per cent, of them belonged to the Sikh religion followed by the Hindu religion and Muslim religion, respectively. It is quite natural that in Punjab Jat Sikhs dominate agriculture, and scheduled castes, especially Majabhi, Balmiki and Ramdasia Sikhs, dominate the rural areas in the landless agricultural labour class. High incidence of suicides among Sikh farmers and agricultural labourers has been astonishing and is against the Sikh tenets. Reincarnation, karma is part of Sikhism, and meditation is part of the practice, just as seva, which is a selfless service to the humanity. The values of Sikhism are very humbling. Sikhs are supposed to make a decent, honest living by working, which is really a virtue for them. Sikhs also

TABLE 5.8 Religion-wise distribution of farmers and labourers

Districts	Religion	Farmers		Labourers	
		Deceased	Control group	Deceased	Control group
Sangrur	Sikh	194 (97.5)	190 (95.5)	64 (92.8)	60 (86.9)
	Hindu	5 (2.5)	9 (4.5)	5 (7.2)	6 (8.7)
	Muslim	–	–	–	3 (4.3)
	Total	199 (100)	199 (100)	69 (100)	69 (100)
Bathinda	Sikh	171 (99.4)	169 (98.3)	52 (86.7)	57 (95.0)
	Hindu	1 (0.6)	3 (1.7)	4 (6.7)	2 (3.3)
	Muslim	–	–	4 (6.7)	1 (1.6)
	Total	172 (100)	172 (100)	60 (100)	60 (100)
Mansa	Sikh	133 (95.6)	138 (99.2)	54 (94.7)	55 (96.4)
	Hindu	6 (4.3)	1 (0.7)	3 (5.3)	2 (3.5)
	Muslim	–	–	–	–
	Total	139 (100)	139 (100)	57 (100)	57 (100)
Overall	Sikh	498 (97.6)	497 (97.5)	170 (91.6)	172 (92.5)
	Hindu	12 (2.4)	13 (2.5)	12 (6.4)	10 (5.4)
	Muslim	–	–	4 (2.1)	4 (2.1)
	Total	510 (100)	510 (100)	186 (100)	186 (100)

Source: Field survey.

Note: Figures in parenthesis are percentages.

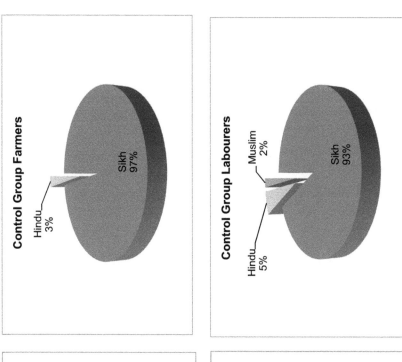

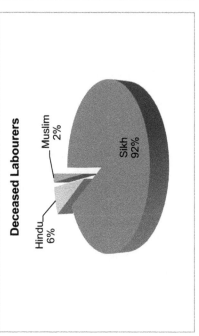

FIGURE 5.4 Religion–wise distribution of farmers and agriculture labourers

Source: Authors.

maintain the idea of Chardi kala, which means to keep your spirits high even when confronted by something unusual like death. Hence, it emerged from the earlier analysis that agrarian distress was so cruel that it undermined the religious values. This provides evidence for upholding the new institutional economics, which states that rules of the market economy are dominating informal institutions. Therefore, the economic factors overshadowed tradition and economic distress for a prolonged period of time and has forced the otherwise sturdy community of farmers and agricultural labourers to commit suicides despite the presence of the norms backed by religion to remain in high spirits.

Education

Education has been widely recognized as an important determinant of economic growth and development. The higher the educational attainments, the higher is the general level of living. In fact, it is the enabling factor of social capability that determines the participation of economic agents of production in economic activities and also of returns. It is a widely believed and empirically tested fact that education among farmers and agricultural labourers positively influences the level of agricultural productivity and agricultural sector growth (Schultz 1988). It is also suggested that education among farmers and farm workers results in cost-cutting and yield-raising techniques and expansion and promotion of agricultural institutions such as cooperatives, marketing and banking. Education also improves wages and conditions of employment of agricultural labourers (Chaudhri 1979). In this light, an attempt is made in this section to analyse the literacy and level of education across farmers and the agricultural workforce. The distribution of educational levels and proportions based on the field survey are presented in Table 5.9.

The level of education and literacy among the rural population is very low. This is evident from the analysis of Table 5.9. More than 55 per cent of the farmers – deceased and control group – and more than 78 per cent of the deceased landless workers were illiterate. However, more than 81 per cent of the control group landless workers were illiterate. Lack of education among deceased farmers and agricultural labourers and control group farmers and agricultural labourers was clearly evident as the large proportion has no schooling at all.

For agricultural production and marketing activities, it has been noticed in various studies that middle-level education gives higher returns in terms of agricultural productivity (Schultz 1988). It is significant to note that the level of education to deal with complex agricultural output and credit markets is matriculation. However, in this category, the proportion of deceased farmers was nearly 12 per cent. It is little higher in the control group, that is 16.27 per cent. This proportion among landless workers is very low (4 to 6 per cent). The survey results regarding the low level of education also corroborate with the overall trend of illiteracy and education of these three districts. Therefore, comparative analysis reveals that agricultural labourers were more illiterate than farmers in all the districts and at the overall level. A similar trend was pointed out by earlier studies (IDC 1998, 2006; AFDR 2000; Iyer and

TABLE 5.9 Education level-wise distribution of farmers and labourers across districts

	Farmers		Labourers	
	Deceased	*Control group*	*Deceased*	*Control group*
Sangrur				
Illiterate	108 (54.27)	108 (54.27)	52 (75.36)	55 (79.71)
Primary	27 (13.57)	13 (6.53)	9 (13.04)	3 (4.35)
Middle	24 (12.06)	26 (13.07)	4 (5.80)	4 (5.80)
Matriculation	28 (14.07)	39 (19.60)	4 (5.80)	5 (7.24)
10+2	10 (5.03)	9 (4.52)	–	1 (1.45)
Above 10+2	2 (1.00)	4 (2.01)	–	1 (1.45)
Total	199 (100)	199 (100)	69 (100)	69 (100)
Bathinda				
Illiterate	89 (51.74)	99 (57.56)	45 (75.00)	49 (81.67)
Primary	28 (16.28)	18 (0.10)	4 (6.67)	3 (5.00)
Middle	23 (13.37)	20 (11.63)	7 (11.67)	5 (8.33)
Matriculation	22 (12.79)	30 (17.44)	3 (5.00)	3 (5.00)
10+2	8 (4.65)	4 (2.32)	1 (1.67)	–
Above 10+2	2 (1.16)	1 (0.58)	–	–
Total	172 (100)	172 (100)	60 (100)	60 (100)
Mansa				
Illiterate	90 (64.75)	76 (54.68)	49 (85.96)	47 (82.46)
Primary	12 (8.63)	24 (17.27)	3 (5.26)	5 (8.77)
Middle	24 (17.27)	16 (11.51)	3 (5.26)	1 (1.75)
Matriculation	11 (7.91)	14 (10.07)	1 (1.75)	4 (7.02)
10+2	2 (1.44)	6 (4.32)	1 (1.75)	–
Above 10+2	–	3 (2.16)	–	–
Total	139 (100)	139 (100)	57 (100)	57 (100)
Overall				
Illiterate	287 (56.27)	283 (55.49)	146 (78.49)	151 (81.18)
Primary	67 (13.14)	55 (10.78)	16 (8.60)	11 (5.91)
Middle	71 (13.92)	62 (12.16)	14 (7.53)	10 (5.38)
Matriculation	61 (11.96)	83 (16.27)	8 (4.30)	12 (6.45)
10+2	20 (3.92)	19 (3.73)	2 (1.08)	1 (0.54)
Above 10+2	4 (0.78)	8 (1.57)	–	1 (0.54)
Total	510 (100)	510 (100)	186 (100)	186 (100)

Source: Field survey.

Note: Figures in parenthesis are percentages.

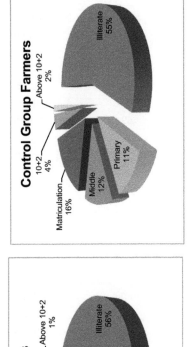

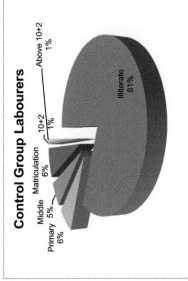

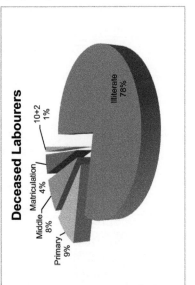

FIGURE 5.5 Education level-wise distribution of farmers and agricultural labourers

Source: Authors.

Manick 2000; Chahal 2005; Bhangoo 2006). This not only limits the occupational choices of the farmers but results in failure of farmers to grasp the nitty-gritty of modern agriculture and also increases their dependency on non-viable traditional agriculture and on costly non-institutional sources of credit (PSFC 2007).

Marital status

Marriage is a social institution and foundation for generating social capital. Social capital and agricultural development are positively correlated. Recent studies showed that there are higher returns from economic activities if the household has a higher level of social capital (Kumar 2014). Rural households are largely engaged in agricultural activities and agriculture requires transmission of externalities. To internalize the externalities, social capital plays an important role.

Traditionally, in agriculture, the main agricultural operations have been performed by the male members of the households and supported by the women members of the family. Moreover, life partners come to the rescue of each other in the case of any exigencies. Therefore, it seems useful to look at the marital status of the respondents to investigate the impact of this variable on agriculture. The information of marital status of farmers and agricultural labourers is presented in Table 5.10.

TABLE 5.10 Distribution of farmers and agriculture labourers across deceased and control group

District	Marital status	Farmers		Labourers	
		Deceased	Control group	Deceased	Control group
Sangrur	Married	141 (70.85)	184 (92.46)	58 (84.06)	65 (94.20)
	Unmarried	58 (29.15)	15 (7.54)	11 (15.94)	4 (5.79)
	Total	199 (100)	199 (100)	69 (100)	69 (100)
Bathinda	Married	135 (78.49)	170 (98.83)	44 (73.33)	60 (100)
	Unmarried	37 (21.51)	2 (1.16)	16 (26.67)	–
	Total	172 (100)	172 (100)	60 (100)	60 (100)
Mansa	Married	101 (72.66)	126 (90.65)	42 (73.68)	52 (91.23)
	Unmarried	38 (27.38)	13 (9.35)	15 (26.31)	5 (8.77)
	Total	139 (100)	139 (100)	57 (100)	57 (100)
Overall	Married	377 (73.92)	480 (94.12)	144 (77.42)	177 (95.16)
	Unmarried	133 (26.08)	30 (5.88)	42 (22.58)	9 (4.84)
	Total	510 (100)	510 (100)	186 (100)	186 (100)

Source: Field survey.

Note: Figures in parenthesis are percentages.

A total of 73.92 per cent farmers and 77.42 per cent agricultural labourers, who had committed suicides, were married. The analysis of marital status further shows that the percentage of married persons was higher among the control group of farmers and agricultural labourers as compared to the deceased group of farmers and agricultural labourers of Sangrur, Bathinda, and Mansa districts and also at the overall levels. The unmarried deceased farmers and landless labourers were the highest in Sangrur district followed by Mansa and Bathinda districts. They seem to lack social capital. This may be due to failure and absence of support from spouses in the time of crisis. In general, the capitalist mode of production has reduced social support system without providing alternative institutional support system. This kind of evidence was supported and also verified by earlier studies conducted to ascertain the factor behind rural suicides in the Malwa region of Punjab (AFDR 2000; Bhangoo 2006). It is pertinent to add here that the control group of farmers and agricultural labourers in terms of proportion of marital status (94.12 per cent and 95.16 per cent, respectively) clearly brings out the fact that social capital was higher than the deceased group of farmers and agricultural labourers. This may be one of the most important factors that allowed similarly placed group of farmers and agricultural labourers to survive.

Size of landholding

Land is the most prized possession of rural households. It is the only source of livelihood and social security. The scale of production in agriculture is usually determined by the size of the farm. Therefore, it is pertinent to point out that the difference between owned landholdings and operational landholdings is precisely the reason that operational holdings indicate the scale of production. The ownership of the land does not mean that it is being operated. Farmers lease in and lease out land. Thus, the operational landholding unit is distinct from the ownership landholding unit, because of the fact that it is the operational landholding, which is a fundamental unit of agricultural operations and economic decisions. Ownership of landholdings includes all land owned or held in owner-like possession by the households. The operational landholding is the extent of land managed, whether the land be owned, leased or otherwise possessed, as a techno-economic unit of production in which some agricultural production had been carried out in the reference period. Operational landholdings are thus a better measure of access to land for production purposes than ownership of the landholdings. Therefore, we have employed the concept of operational landholdings in this study.

One of the significant problems faced by the agricultural sector of the state and of India is the fragmentation of landholdings. Fragmentation of ownership landholdings in India is a major challenge and problem facing Indian and Punjab agriculture; due to this, the majority of the farmers are increasingly becoming small and marginal farmers. As per the agricultural census, the proportion of small and marginal farmers in India was 83.3 per cent in 2005–06 and this proportion for Punjab was 31.6 per cent. This leads us to the conclusion that the majority of landholdings in India are too small to be economically viable to promote modern agricultural development. These do not generate enough income to buy modern agricultural implements and farm inputs and make heavy investments in agriculture. Small and marginal size of the landholdings accompanied with fragmentation landholdings also prevents the use of new farm machines which are very essential for modern agricultural growth. Information and data regarding operational landholdings, in the select districts of the Malwa region of Punjab, of deceased and control group of farmers is presented in Table 5.11 and Figure 5.6.

Analysis of size-wise distribution of operational landholdings reveals that more than 81 per cent of the deceased farmers belonged to the category of small and marginal farmers. This finding provides ample evidence to the argument that the agrarian distress is more severe in the small-sized group of farmers due to non-viability of the farms. Further, in Sangrur, Bathinda and Mansa districts and at the overall level, more than 90 per cent of the farmers of both the groups (deceased and control group) belonged to small, marginal and medium categories. The farm size-wise analysis of the deceased and control group of farmers brings out the fact that in Sangrur and Mansa districts 97 per cent, in Bathinda 94 per cent and overall 96 per cent suicides have been committed by small-sized (marginal, small and semi-medium) category of the farmers. An important fact that emerged from the analysis is that the farmers engaged in agricultural operations of the non–viable farm sizes are prone to distress and hence suicides.

Average landholding size-wise

Size of the landholding is an important determinant of agricultural development. The size of average landholdings in Indian and Punjab agriculture has been declining over the period of time, which is a constraint as well as a challenge for agricultural development. The average holding size in Punjab had improved to nearly 3.80 hectares, though it still remained considerably below the level attained in 1980–81. However, except marginal and small farms, all other categories of farmers have considerably increased the scale of owned landholdings. Thus, there is an increasing tendency of concentration and centralization of landholdings. The earlier study on Punjab reveals that the Gini coefficient (a measure concentration) of land is dangerously high (Singh 2008). The average size of landholdings of deceased and control group of farmers across three districts and blocks of the districts is presented in Table 5.12 to ascertain the average ownership of the landholding in the study area.

The analysis of average size of landholdings of deceased and control group farmers across districts and blocks suggests that there existed perceptible differences. It is pertinent to notice here that except Sangrur district, the average ownership of landholding is large with the control group of farmers compared with the deceased

TABLE 5.11 Operational landholding size-wise distribution of farmers

District	Sangrur		Bathinda		Mansa		Overall	
Category (ha)	Deceased	Control group	Deceased	Control group	Deceased	Control group	Deceased	Control group
Marginal (<1)	116 (58.29)	102 (51.25)	92 (53.49)	53 (30.81)	50 (35.97)	53 (38.10)	258 (50.59)	208 (40.80)
Small (1–2)	54 (27.14)	59 (29.65)	44 (25.58)	62 (36.00)	58 (41.72)	36 (25.90)	156 (30.59)	157 (30.80)
Semi-medium (2–4)	23 (11.56)	29 (14.50)	26 (15.12)	36 (20.93)	27 (19.42)	34 (24.50)	76 (14.90)	99 (19.40)
Medium (4–10)	6 (3.02)	8 (4.00)	10 (5.81)	20 (10.00)	4 (2.88)	16 (11.50)	20 (3.92)	44 (8.60)
Large (>10)	–	1 (0.50)	–	1 (0.60)	–	–	–	2 (0.60)
Total	199 (100)	199 (100)	172 (100)	172 (100)	139 (100)	139 (100)	510 (100)	510 (100)

Source: Field survey.

Note: Figures in parenthesis are percentages.

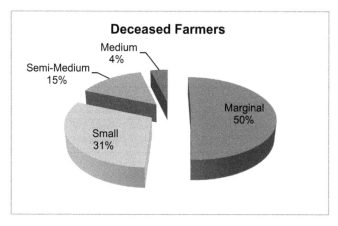

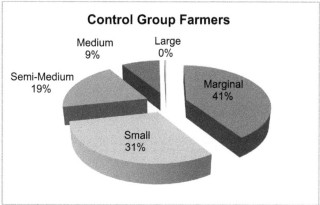

FIGURE 5.6 Operational landholding size-wise distribution of farmers

Source: Authors.

group of farmers. The overall average landholding with the deceased group of farmers was 2.61 acres, whereas the average landholding with the control group of farmers was 3.49 acres. The block-wise comparison of average landholding across the deceased group of farmers and control group of farmers show that a large majority of the blocks having higher average owned landholdings compared with the control group of farmers.

Furthermore, the average landholding size in this study has also been almost similar to those prevailing in Punjab. Block-wise analysis of average size of landholding also suggests the somewhat similar trend. Therefore, a strong trend that emerges from the analysis is that similar problems were being confronted by the sampled farmers across the three districts under consideration.

TABLE 5.12 District-wise and block-wise average size of landholding of deceased and control group farmers

Category	Deceased			Control group		
District and block	Number of farmers	Land in acres	Average land in acres	Number of farmers	Land in acres	Average in land acres
Bathinda						
Sangat	15	45.4	3.02	15	47.4	3.16
Bathinda	29	109.5	3.77	29	156.0	5.37
Nathana	14	51.4	3.67	14	41.6	2.97
Bhagta Bhai Ka	14	28.9	2.06	14	48.0	3.43
Phul	18	74	4.11	18	86.2	4.79
Talwandi Sabo	17	46.3	2.72	17	53.3	3.13
Maur	25	75.2	3.00	25	82.2	3.28
Rampura	40	138.3	3.46	40	125.4	3.13
Average	172	568.9	3.31	172	640.1	3.72
Sangrur						
Sunam	38	109	2.87	38	130.0	3.42
Malerkotla I	18	71	3.94	18	69.0	3.83
Malerkotla II	14	34.5	2.46	14	38.0	2.71
Sherpur	17	51	3.00	17	27.5	1.62
Dhuri	12	25	2.08	12	28.5	2.38
Bhawanigarh	21	49.5	2.36	21	3.5	0.17
Andana	23	64.5	2.80	23	44.0	1.91
Lehragaga	46	103.2	2.24	46	98.5	2.14
Sangrur	10	27.5	2.75	10	39.0	3.90
Average	199	535.2	2.69	199	478.0	2.42
Mansa						
Bhikhi	14	42	3.00	14	109.0	7.78
Mansa	24	56.2	2.34	24	77.0	3.20
Sardulgarh	21	97	4.62	21	121.0	5.76
Jhunir	29	144.4	4.98	29	131.0	4.52
Budhladha	51	225.5	4.42	51	223.6	4.38
Average	139	565.1	4.06	139	661.6	4.76
Overall	510	1,330	2.61	510	1,779.7	3.49

Source: Field survey.

Irrigation: area and sources

Irrigation is the lifeline of modern agriculture. Assured irrigation allows farmers to use water for plants in right doses at the right time. The modern agriculture based on high-yielding seed varieties, chemical fertilizers and other inputs needs timely irrigation. The availability of water for irrigation substantially affects productivity of agriculture given the modern agricultural inputs.

An important source of success of the green revolution in Punjab was the availability of assured irrigation. The multiple cropping patterns lead to cropping intensity, and higher level of yields across the crops was mainly due to the right doses of irrigation. The state government with the help of the union government was able to develop canal irrigation networks. But it is the tube well–based irrigation in the early green revolution that supplemented canal irrigation. Nowadays, tube wells turn out to be the dominant source of irrigation for Punjab agriculture. This shift has put enormous pressure on ground water. Ground water depletion is the main cause of the growing dependence of irrigation on tube wells. Thus, the high degree of intensity of agricultural crops was possible by the growth and development of irrigation systems (Faurès, Hoogeveen and Bruinsma 2013). The non-availability of timely water for irrigation purpose spoils crops and bleak the source of income of rural households.

Therefore, it is a matter of paramount importance to look into the irrigation scenario of the deceased and control group of farmers. Block-wise and district-wise information of irrigated and un-irrigated land area and proportions across deceased and control group of farmers is presented in Table 5.13.

The analysis of the division of irrigated and un-irrigated area across the deceased as well as of control group of farmers in Sangrur, Bathinda and Mansa districts reveals substantial variations. The area under irrigation in the Bathinda district was the lowest and was also below the sample average. However, the Sangrur and Mansa districts were above the sample average. But, when we look at the block-wise analysis, there exists some differentials in the irrigation of agricultural land. The analysis further suggests that more farmer suicide–prone blocks have more un-irrigated area, especially in Bathinda and Mansa districts. It is pertinent to point out here that those differences across deceased and control group of farmers regarding irrigated area are somewhat similar. Furthermore, during the survey, it was revealed by the respondent farmers and confirmed by the field survey team that despite the provisions of canal irrigation, lack of irrigation in especially canal tail-end villages was one of the important causes for failure of crops and agrarian distress causing farmer suicides.

The analysis of Table 5.14 reveals an important fact that the area under tube well irrigation is much higher in districts of Mansa and Sangrur. But in the Bathinda district, the predominant source of irrigation is canal water. However, there are wide variations across the blocks so far as the sources of irrigation are concerned. In one of the blocks (Talwandi Sabo) falling in the district of Bathinda, 94.1 per cent of area was under canal irrigation and rest of the area (5.9 per cent) was under tube well irrigation. This is an exception because tube well irrigation has emerged as the most dominant form of irrigation in Punjab, and this has added substantial

TABLE 5.13 Details of irrigated and un-irrigated area of farmers (acres)

District	Block	Deceased			Control group		
		Irrigated	Un-irrigated	Total	Irrigated	Un-irrigated	Total
Bathinda	Sangat	31.8 (83.9)	6.1 (16.1)	37.9 (100)	47 (100)	–	47.4 (100)
	Bathinda	16.5 (80.5)	4 (19.5)	20.5 (100)	152 (97.4)	4 (2.6)	156 (100)
	Nathana	30.5 (100)	–	30.5 (100)	41.6 (100)	–	41.6 (100)
	Bhagta Bhai Ka	16 (100)	–	16 (100)	48 (100)	–	48 (100)
	Phul	24 (100)	–	24 (100)	86.2 (100)	–	86.2 (100)
	Talwandi Sabo	56.5 (98.2)	1 (1.8)	57.5 (100)	53.25 (100)	–	53.25 (100)
	Maur	25 (100)	–	25 (100)	74.2 (90.3)	8 (9.7)	82.2 (100)
	Rampura	12.5 (68.3)	5.8 (31.7)	18.3 (100)	122.4 (97.6)	3 (2.4)	125.4 (100)
	Total	212.8 (92.6)	16.9 (7.4)	229.7 (100)	625.1 (97.7)	15 (2.3)	640.1 (100)
Sangrur	Sunam	109 (100)	–	109 (100)	130 (100)	–	130 (100)
	Malerkotla I	71 (100)	–	71 (100)	69 (100)	–	69 (100)
	Malerkotla II	34.5 (100)	–	34.5 (100)	38 (100)	–	38 (100)
	Sherpur	51 (100)	–	51 (100)	27.5 (100)	–	27.5 (100)
	Dhuri	25 (100)	–	25 (100)	28.5 (100)	–	28.5 (100)
	Bhawanigarh	48.5 (98.0)	1 (2.0)	49.5 (100)	0.5 (14.3)	3 (85.7)	3.5 (100)
	Andana	64.5 (100)	–	64.5 (100)	42 (95.5)	2 (4.5)	44 (100)
	Lehragaga	101.2 (98.0)	2 (2.0)	103.2 (100)	98.5 (100)	–	98.5 (100)
	Sangrur	27.5 (100)	–	27.5 (100)	39 (100)	–	39 (100)
	Total	532.2 (99.4)	3 (0.6)	535.2 (100)	473 (98.9)	5 (1.1)	478 (100)
Mansa	Bhikhi	41.5 (98.5)	0.5 (0.5)	42 (100)	109 (100)	–	109 (100)
	Mansa	51.2 (91.1)	5 (6.9)	56.2 (100)	77 (100)	–	77 (100)
	Sardulgarh	97 (100)	–	97 (100)	121 (100)	–	121 (100)
	Jhunir	144.4 (100)	–	144.4 (100)	131 (100)	–	131 (100)
	Budhladha	224.5 (99.6)	1 (0.5)	225.5 (100)	221.6 (99.1)	2 (0.9)	223.6 (100)
	Total	558.6 (99.0)	6.5 (1.0)	565.1 (100)	659.6 (99.7)	2 (0.3)	661.6 (100)
Overall		1,303.6 (98.5)	26.4 (1.5)	1,330 (100)	1,757.7 (98.7)	22 (1.3)	1,779.7 (100)

Source: Field survey.

Note: Figures in parenthesis are percentages.

TABLE 5.14 Distribution of farmers according to sources of irrigation

District	Block	Deceased			Control group		
		Tube well	Canal	Total	Tube well	Canal	Total
Sangrur	Sunam	24 (63.2)	14 (36.8)	38 (100)	21 (55.3)	17 (44.7)	38 (100)
	Malerkotla I	12 (66.7)	6 (33.3)	18 (100)	14 (77.8)	4 (22.2)	18 (100)
	Malerkotla II	14 (100)	–	14 (100)	12 (85.7)	2 (14.3)	14 (100)
	Sherpur	17 (100)	–	17 (100)	15 (88.2)	2 (11.8)	17 (100)
	Dhuri	10 (83.3)	2 (16.7)	12 (100)	8 (66.7)	4 (33.3)	12 (100)
	Bhawanigarh	20 (95.2)	1 (4.8)	21 (100)	16 (76.2)	5 (23.8)	21 (100)
	Andana	18 (78.3)	5 (21.7)	23 (100)	11 (47.8)	12 (52.2)	23 (100)
	Leharagaga	33 (71.7)	13 (28.3)	46 (100)	34 (73.9)	12 (26.1)	46 (100)
	Sangrur	10 (100)	–	10 (100)	10 (100)	–	10 (100)
	Total	157 (78.9)	42 (21.1)	199 (100)	141 (70.9)	58 (29.1)	199 (100)
Bathinda	Bathinda	20 (69.0)	9 (31.0)	29 (100)	21 (72.4)	8 (27.6)	29 (100)
	Sangat	3 (20.0)	12 (80.0)	15 (100)	4 (26.7)	11 (73.3)	15 (100)
	Nathana	8 (57.1)	6 (42.9)	14 (100)	8 (57.1)	6 (42.9)	14 (100)
	Bhagta Bhai Ka	–	14 (100)	14 (100)	–	14 (100)	14 (100)
	Phool	5 (27.8)	13 (72.2)	18 (100)	4 (22.2)	14 (77.8)	18 (100)
	Talwandi Sabo	1 (5.9)	16 (94.1)	17 (100)	2 (11.8)	15 (88.2)	17 (100)
	Maur	9 (36.0)	16 (64.0)	25 (100)	8 (32.0)	17 (68.0)	25 (100)
	Rampura	28 (70.0)	12 (30.0)	40 (100)	34 (85.0)	6 (15.0)	40 (100)
	Total	74 (43.0)	98 (57.0)	172 (100)	80 (46.5)	92 (53.5)	172 (100)
Mansa	Mansa	8 (33.3)	16 (66.7)	24 (100)	13 (54.2)	11 (45.8)	24 (100)
	Bhikhi	4 (28.6)	10 (71.4)	14 (100)	7 (50.0)	7 (50.0)	14 (100)
	Sardulgarh	13 (61.9)	8 (38.1)	21 (100)	15 (71.4)	6 (28.6)	21 (100)
	Jhunir	12 (41.4)	17 (58.6)	29 (100)	12 (41.4)	17 (58.6)	29 (100)
	Budhladha	35 (68.6)	16 (31.4)	51 (100)	22 (43.1)	29 (56.9)	51 (100)
	Total	72 (51.8)	67 (48.2)	139 (100)	69 (49.6)	70 (50.4)	139 (100)
Overall		303 (59.4)	207 (40.6)	510 (100)	290 (56.0)	220 (44.0)	510 (100)

Source: Field survey.

Note: Figures in parenthesis are percentages.

burden on the limited quantity of ground water. In the absence of any ground water recharging system, the falling water table further increases the cost of lifting ground water through tube wells. On the one hand it adds to the cost of production, and on the other hand when tube wells go dry due to falling water table crop production also fails.

Conclusions

The above analysis and discussion regarding socioeconomic characteristics of the deceased and control group farmers and agricultural labourers suggests that all the developmental blocks of the three districts have received required representation in the sample. Furthermore, highly distressed villages of all the blocks of the three districts have also been given adequate representation in the sample. We can state that the sample drawn was a representative sample and findings based on this sample may be generalized. The analysis of age-wise distribution of the deceased group of farmers and agricultural labourers amply brings out the fact that a large majority was below 35 years of age, that is young group, and were found to be highly distressed as this group has committed maximum suicides as compared to middle-aged and elder farmers and labourers. This demonstrates that the burden of agrarian distress has been faced by the young and middle-aged group of farmers. It is noteworthy that the distress was so cruel that it also engulfed the women members of the households of farmers and agricultural labourers as some women members of the households also committed suicides due to economic distress.

High incidence of suicides among Jat Sikh farmers indicates that they did not seem to compromise over social values and loss of social status, and also those economic factors are not sparing Jat Sikh farmers irrespective of their caste hierarchy. Analysis of the deceased farmers and agricultural labourers suggests that a large majority of them belonged to Sikhism. Analysis of the high incidence of suicides among Sikh farmers and agricultural labourers shows that agrarian distress was so cruel that it has undermined the existing social norms and values. Lack of education among deceased farmers and agricultural labourers and control group farmers and agricultural labourers was clearly evident as none of the respondents was postgraduate/professionally qualified, and only few were graduates. This not only limits the occupational choices of the farmers but results in failure of farmers to grasp the nitty-gritty of modern agriculture and also increases their dependency on non-viable farms. These non-viable farms were being operated with the help of costly non-institutional sources of credit. Comparatively higher percentage of unmarried farmers and agricultural labourers among the deceased group may be due to near absence of social capital and public security system.

The analysis of average size of landholdings of deceased and control group farmers across districts and blocks leads us to conclude that there existed perceptible differences. Except Sangrur district, the average ownership of landholding is large with the control group of farmers compared with the deceased group of farmers. The overall average landholding with the deceased group of farmers was 2.61 acres, whereas the average landholding with the control group of farmers was 3.49 acres. The block-wise comparison of average landholding across the deceased group of farmers and control group of farmers shows that a large majority of the blocks having higher average owned landholdings compared with the control group of farmers. On an average, the small and marginal landholders due to non-viability of their farms were prone to suicides.

The analysis of sources of irrigation reveals that the predominant source of irrigation in the sample districts is tube wells. However, in Bathinda district, the major source of irrigation is canal water. The variation among the developmental blocks is very high, especially in Bathinda district. The tube well-based irrigation has put substantial pressure on ground water in the absence of ground water recharging system. The non-availability of canal water to the villages located at the tail end of the canals was also the root cause of suicides in the sample districts.

6

DETERMINANTS OF AGRARIAN DISTRESS IN PUNJAB

Magnitude and manifestation

The agrarian crisis of Punjab economy is multidimensional and has been deepening progressively. Marginalization of agriculture and slowdown of industrial growth has been attributed to the economic crisis of Punjab, especially agrarian crisis. Un-remunerative prices of farm products, low and stagnated yields, fall in net farm incomes, successive crop failure and high and increasing costs of cultivation have landed the small and marginal farmers in a debt trap and suicides (Bhangoo 2005; Punjab State Farmers' Commission 2006). Punjab farmers are driven to a debt trap not only because of imprudent borrowing from high-cost informal sources and for unproductive purposes but also because of the fall in net farm incomes. Punjab farmers have also borrowed heavily for farm machinery, for digging/ deepening and replacing old bore wells with submersible pumps and for cultivating input-intensive high-value crops (Singh, Kaur and Kingra 2008). Unproductive nature and use of loans, exorbitant interest rates and indebtedness towards informal sources are disturbing dimensions of indebtedness. Punjab agriculture seems to be no longer a viable and profitable/rewarding occupation. Earnings from crop cultivation are not enough to meet the annual cultivation expenditure in most of the states, including Punjab, since this leads to farmers' indebtedness (NSSO 2005). Indebtedness depends on availability of credit, cost of credit, ability to service it and cost of cultivation. Unproductive use of loans along with exorbitant interest rates and indebtedness towards moneylenders/commission agents are disturbing dimensions of indebtedness clearly identified by Shergill (1998, 2010) and NSSO (2005). The gravity of indebtedness is deepening in Punjab as it increased from Rs 5,700.91 crores in 1997 (Shergill 1998) to Rs 12,506.37 crores in 2002 (Satish 2006) to Rs 24,000 crores (Punjab State Farmers' Commission 2007) and further to Rs 35,000 crores in 2011.

National Sample Survey Organization reported that in 2003 (NSSO 2005) at all-India level 48.6 per cent farm households were reported to be indebted, led by

Andhra Pradesh (82 per cent) and followed by Tamil Nadu (74.5 per cent) and Punjab (65.4 per cent). Average outstanding loan per farm household at all-India level was Rs 12,585 and a highest of Rs 41,576 in the state of Punjab followed by Kerala, Haryana, Andhra Pradesh and Tamil Nadu. Another estimate put per farm household outstanding loan at Rs 45,193 and Rs 28,082 per farm household of small and marginal farmers of Punjab (Chahal 2005). All the indicators of farmers' indebtedness highlighted and pointed out the grave/crisis situation prevailing in the state, which corroborates the views of Darling (1925).

Keeping in mind the aforementioned state of affairs of Punjab agriculture, in this chapter, an attempt is made to examine the different dimensions of indebtedness, to trace the source-wise and purpose-wise distribution of debt among different categories of farmers, to estimate the extent and magnitude of indebtedness among various categories of farmers, to identify factors affecting farmers' indebtedness, to know the perceptions of farmers regarding indebtedness and to suggest suitable policy measures. The chapter is organized in the following eight sections.

Agrarian setting: sampled households

In this section, an attempt has been made to examine the existing agrarian structure and setting of the sampled farm households. For this purpose, the type of landholdings such as owned and leased has been worked out for the sampled farm households. The information in this regard has been presented in Table 6.1.

Analysis of nature of landholding type of deceased and control group of farmers of all the three districts and at overall level shows that major share in operational landholdings of small, marginal and semi-medium farmers has been leased in holdings. It is also evident that as the size of farmer category increases, that is from marginal to large, the leased-in area decreases across the districts and at overall level. Therefore, it can be concluded that marginal, small and semi-medium farmers in the state have been surviving in agriculture by leasing in land as tenants.

Income–expenditure gap

The gravity of the agrarian crisis can be judged from the rise in the household expenditure on the one side and from the decline in the surpluses generated from agriculture-related economic activities on the other. Due to declining farm incomes and escalating farm costs over the period of time, the economy of the farmers, especially of small and marginal, has turned into a mess and disarray. Undoubtedly, farmers in Punjab are driven to a debt trap not only because of imprudent heavy borrowing from high-cost informal sources and for non-productive purposes but also because of fall in net farm incomes far below expectations (Shergill 1998; Bhangoo 2005). This resulted in increasing and widening of income–expenditure gap among the farmers and further causing high incidence of indebtedness and outstanding loans.

TABLE 6.1 Distribution of landholdings on the basis of ownership/leased in

District	Category	Holding type	Marginal (<1 ha)	Small (1–2 ha)	Semi-medium (2–4 ha)	Medium (4–10 ha)	Large (>10 ha)	Total
Sangrur	Deceased	Owned	61.68 (25.81)	69.2 (32.32)	60.8 (28.40)	22.4 (10.46)	–	214.08 (100)
		Leased in	26.2 (64.85)	3.8 (9.41)	10.4 (25.74)	–	–	40.4 (100)
	Control group	Owned	65.77 (33.97)	71.12 (36.74)	38.07 (19.66)	8.51 (4.40)	10.13 (5.23)	193.6 (100)
		Leased in	48 (47.52)	41 (40.59)	7 (6.93)	5 (4.95)	–	101 (100)
Bathinda	Deceased	Owned	38.79 (16.84)	69.86 (30.32)	66.68 (28.94)	55.08 (23.91)	–	230.41 (100)
		Leased in	15.59 (29.38)	9.11 (17.17)	26.33 (49.62)	2.03 (3.83)	–	53.06 (100)
	Control group	Owned	35.86 (13.83)	81.41 (31.40)	77.15 (29.76)	54.68 (21.09)	10.13 (3.91)	259.23 (100)
		Leased	34.02 (48.84)	13.77 (19.77)	20.25 (29.07)	–	1.62 (2.33)	69.66 (100)
Mansa	Deceased	Owned	17.51 (7.65)	67.03 (29.2)	92.95 (40.60)	51.44 (22.47)	–	228.93 (100)
		Leased in	11.14 (45.08)	5.47 (22.14)	8.1 (32.78)	–	–	24.71 (100)
	Control group	Owned	20.25 (7.51)	49.94 (18.52)	108.74 (40.33)	90.72 (33.64)	–	269.65 (100)
		Leased in	4.54 (33.24)	3.65 (26.72)	3.24 (23.72)	2.23 (16.33)	–	13.66 (100)

						Overall
Deceased	Owned	117.98 (17.52)	206.09 (30.60)	220.43 (32.73)	128.92 (19.14)	—	673.42 (100)
	Leased in	52.93 (44.79)	18.38 (15.55)	44.83 (37.94)	2.03 (1.72)	—	118.17 (100)
Control group	Owned	121.88 (16.87)	202.47 (28.02)	223.96 (31)	153.91 (21.30)	20.26 (2.80)	722.48 (100)
	Leased in	86.56 (46.96)	58.42 (31.69)	30.49 (16.54)	7.23 (3.92)	1.62 (0.88)	184.32 (100)

Source: Field survey.

Note: Figures in parenthesis are percentages.

TABLE 6.2 Estimated average income–expenditure gap of farmers and agricultural labourers (rupees)

Category	Variable	District			
		Sangrur	Bathinda	Mansa	Overall
Deceased farmers (suicide year)	Income	84,318	54,308	79,235	72,811
	Expenditure	137,065	140,555	109,323	130,681
	I–E gap	−52,747	−86,247	−30,088	−57,870
Control group farmers (2010–11)	Income	77,996	57,700	103,750	78,170
	Expenditure	131,041	175,492	116,218	141,992
	I–E gap	−53,045	−117,792	−12,648	−63,822
Deceased labourers (suicide year)	Income	14,780	18,062	17,639	16,715
	Expenditure	65,345	53,829	47,973	56,306
	I–E gap	−50,565	−35,767	−30,334	−39,591
Control group labourers (2010–11)	Income	19,191	18,333	25,372	20,807
	Expenditure	67,355	64,135	44,332	59,261
	I–E gap	−48,164	−45,802	−18,960	−38,454

Source: Field survey.

Note: I–E gap = income–expenditure gap.

Therefore, it is important to look into this aspect, to grasp the ground realties of the issue. The information and data regarding this is shown in Table 6.2.

Analysis of Table 6.2 reveals that across the households – deceased farmers, control group farmers and agricultural labourers – deceased and control group clearly indicate that there occurred huge income–expenditure gap. There is a marked difference between the deceased and control group of farmers' income–expenditure gap. However, the income–expenditure gap of the deceased and control group of labourer households is quite similar but is very high compared with their absolute level of income. Comparatively, two most distressed and suicide-prone Sangrur and Bathinda districts have larger income–expenditure gaps as compared to Mansa district across the categories of farmers and agricultural labourers. This shows that due to huge income–expenditure gaps, the farmers and labourers have no alternative except to resort to borrowings in order to survive in social order. The borrowing, in the absence of repaying capacity, has cumulative effect in increasing debt across the households. As a result of heavy burden of debt, deceased farmers and agricultural labourers have committed suicides.

Incidence of indebtedness

The extent as well as growing degree of indebtedness among the farmers and agricultural labourers is determined by numerous socioeconomic factors such as size of holding, purpose of debt, use of debt, sources of debt, cropping pattern, credit policy of the state, agriculture policy and socioeconomic factors. Agriculture credit is not a problem till it is serviced properly through income generated from farm produce and would not turn into indebtedness (Satish 2006). In this study an attempt has been made to probe the total outstanding debt against farmers, average per farm household debt and average per acre debt in three districts and at overall level. The information and data regarding the farmer category-wise burden of indebtedness across deceased farmers and control group farmers has been presented in Table 6.3 and Figure 6.1.

Indebtedness: deceased farmers

The information regarding indebtedness at the overall level shows that deceased small, marginal and semi-medium farmers were heavily indebted as their share amounts to 95 per cent of the total debt against this category, that is 41 per cent marginal farmers, 34 per cent small farmers and 19 per cent semi-medium farmers. In this regard, almost a similar situation was prevailing in all the three districts. In Sangrur district, the deceased small, marginal and semi-medium farmers' share in indebtedness was around 98 per cent. In Bathinda district, it was 90 per cent, and in Mansa district, the share of indebtedness of this category of farmers was 95 per cent. Analysis of per farm household average debt shows that small and marginal farmers' households were heavily indebted in all the three districts and at overall level compared to medium and large farm households. Further, similarly per acre debt against small and marginal farmers was also on the higher side as compared to large farmers of the three districts and at overall level. It emerged from the discussion that, in fact, this is a very high degree of indebtedness, because all three important indicators of indebtedness were high in the case of deceased small and marginal farmers.

Indebtedness: control group farmers

The information regarding indebtedness at the overall level shows that control group farmers, that is small, marginal and semi-medium, were also very highly indebted, but comparatively slightly less indebted as compared to deceased category of farmers, as their share in indebtedness was around 90 per cent at the overall level. In this regard, almost a similar trend has prevailed in all the three districts as well. In Sangrur, control group small, marginal and semi-medium farmers' share in indebtedness has been around 93 per cent, in Bathinda it was 89 per cent and in Mansa the share of this category of farmers was 82 per cent. Analysis of per farm household average debt against control group of farmers shows that small and marginal farmers' households were heavily indebted in all the three districts and at overall level compared to medium and large farm households, but some slightly low as compared to deceased group. Similarly, per acre debt against control group small and marginal farmers was also on the higher side as compared to large farmers of the three districts and at overall level, again slightly low as compared to deceased group. It emerged from the discussion that, in fact, this

TABLE 6.3 Farm size-category-wise distribution of total outstanding debt, debt per farmer household and per acre debt among farmers (amount)

District	Category	Debt	Marginal (<1 ha)	Small (1–2 ha)	Semi-medium (2–4 ha)	Medium (4–10 ha)	Large (>10 ha)	Total
Sangrur	Deceased	Total debt	23,918,008 (61.21)	11,045,008 (28.27)	3,145,008 (8.05)	965,000 (2.47)	–	39,073,024 (100)
		Per farmer debt	206,190	204,537	136,739	160,833	–	196,348
		Per acre debt	272,167	151,301	44,171	43,080	–	153,541
	Control group	Total debt	11,316,242 (43.09)	10,156,200 (38.67)	3,879,753 (14.77)	410,892 (1.56)	500,000 (1.90)	26,263,087 (100)
		Per farmer debt	110,944	172,139	133,785	51,362	500,000	131,975
		Per acre debt	40,270	36,673	34,851	12,313	–	36,092
Bathinda	Deceased	Total debt	10,551,172 (30.69)	9,906,162 (28.81)	10,037,169 (29.19)	3,885,501 (11.30)	–	34,380,004 (100)
		Per farmer debt	114,687	225,140	386,045	388,550	–	199,884
		Per acre debt	78,553	50,786	43,690	27,545	–	49,102
	Control group	Total debt	11,968,616 (28.20)	12,335,491 (29.07)	6,173,491 (14.55)	6,816,865 (16.06)	5,140,865 (12.11)	42,435,328 (100)
		Per farmer debt	225,823	198,960	171,486	340,843	5,140,865	246,717
		Per acre debt	69,342	52,470	25,661	50,473	–	52,237

		Col 1	Col 2	Col 3	Col 4	Col 5	Col 6
Mansa	Deceased	Total debt	2,800,180	9,216,192	1,409,186	1,270,000	—	14,695,558
			(19.05)	(62.71)	(9.59)	(8.64)		(100)
		Per farmer debt	56,004	158,900	52,192	317,500	—	105,723
		Per acre debt	39,570	51,465	5,646	9,996	—	23,457
	Control group	Total debt	3,987,340	3,959,342	3,006,302	2,581,382	—	13,534,366
			(29.46)	(29.25)	(22.21)	(19.07)		(100)
		Per farmer debt	75,233	109,982	88,421	161,336	—	97,370
		Per acre debt	65,119	29,912	10,869	11,244	—	19,341
Overall	Deceased	Total debt	37,269,360	30,167,362	14,591,363	6,120,501	—	88,148,587
			(42.28)	(34.22)	(16.55)	(6.94)		(100)
		Per farmer debt	144,455	193,381	191,992	306,025	—	172,840
		Per acre debt	88,285	54,410	22,270	18,923	—	45,084
	Control group	Total debt	27,272,198	26,451,033	13,059,546	9,809,140	5,640,865	82,232,782
			(33.16)	(32.17)	(15.88)	(11.93)	(6.86)	(100)
		Per farmer debt	131,116	168,478	131,915	222,935	2,820,433	161,241
		Per acre debt	52,971	41,048	20,779	24,645	—	36,714

Source: Field survey.

Note: Figures in parenthesis are percentages.

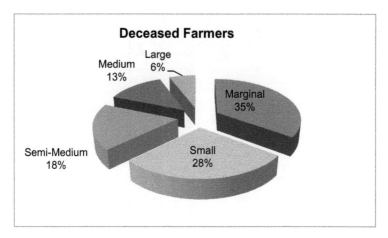

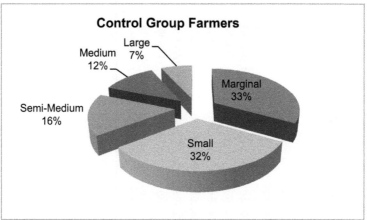

FIGURE 6.1 Farm size–category-wise distribution of indebtedness among farmers

Source: Authors.

is a very high degree of indebtedness, because all three important indicators of indebtedness were high in the case of control group small and marginal farmers.

Analysis evidently suggests that small and marginal farmers were heavily indebted as their share in the debt was 75 per cent in the case of both groups of farmers at the overall level. Almost same burden of debt has been observed in all the districts among deceased and control group farmers. Interestingly, across the districts and at overall level negligible burden of debt has been reported in the case of medium and large farmers' category of both the groups of deceased and control group farmers. This clearly shows that small and marginal farmers of both the groups in the state have been under great distress and committing suicides. Therefore, a greater degree of attention needs to be given when resolving the problems faced by the aforementioned category of farmers and labourers.

Outstanding loan

Average outstanding loan against farmers and agricultural labourers of both groups has been another important indicator of the indebtedness and rural distress. District-wise and block-wise information regarding average outstanding loan is shown in Table 6.4 and Figure 6.2.

At overall level average outstanding loan per deceased and control group of farmers' and labourers' households was found to be similar though there were

TABLE 6.4 Average amount of outstanding loan per deceased and control group farmers' and agricultural labourers' households (rupees)

District	Block	Average outstanding loan			
		Deceased farmers	Control group farmers	Deceased agricultural labourers	Control group agricultural labourers
Sangrur total		196,347	131,975	45,855	44,620
1	Sunam	238,684	21,289	34,167	29,750
2	Malerkotla I	121,667	323,611	22,500	39,375
3	Malerkotla II	387,143	87,857	41,000	26,750
4	Sherpur	179,412	35,294	67,500	41,500
5	Dhuri	164,583	204,167	17,500	36,667
6	Bhawanigarh	17,619	122,905	20,000	35,000
7	Andana	232,609	242,304	66,111	80,222
8	Leharagaga	219,783	84,783	70,313	54,062
9	Sangrur	153,800	329,500	26,667	22,922
Bathinda total		199,884	246,717	24,117	15,267
1	Bathinda	147,828	249,655	14,286	4,286
2	Sangat	121,867	67,733	33,667	12,750
3	Nathana	149,643	179,571	2,500	7,500
4	Bhagta Bhai Ka	205,000	74,857	12,750	9,500
5	Phool	350,889	80,278	3,667	20,000
6	Talwandi Sabo	222,882	186,176	21,667	23,917
7	Maur	187,760	1,113,000	60,000	37,500
8	Rampura	212,525	184,900	39,445	10,333
Mansa total		105,724	97,370	41,596	18,158
1	Mansa	12,857	160,000	46,889	27,222
2	Bhikhi	83,500	61,454	46,222	1,556
3	Sardulgarh	91,191	68,381	19,500	1,250
4	Jhunir	161,069	86,897	14,091	45,545
5	Budhladha	130,039	95,647	61,100	13,251
Overall		172,840	161,241	37,537	27,042

Source: Field survey.

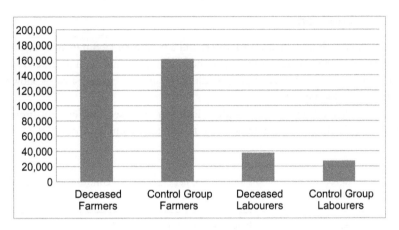

FIGURE 6.2 Average outstanding loan per deceased and control group farmers' and agricultural labourers' households

minor differences. The information regarding this clearly shows that farmers of both groups as well as labourers of both groups were heavily burdened under debt. Further, analysis suggests that amount of outstanding average loan against deceased farmers was Rs 172,840, Rs 179,306 for control group of farmers, Rs 37,537 for deceased labourers and Rs 27,042 in the case of control group of labourers at the overall level.

But variations have been reported as far as the district-wise and block-wise average outstanding loan against the farmers' and labourers' households of two groups is concerned. In the case of deceased farmers, comparatively amount of outstanding average loan against farmers of Sangrur (Rs 196,347) and Bathinda (Rs 199,884) districts was more as compared to Mansa (Rs 105,724) farmers of the same category. Block-wise analysis in this regard suggests that amount of outstanding average loan against deceased farmers of Malerkotla II (Rs 387,143), Sunam (Rs 238,684), Andana (Rs 232,609) and Leharagaga (Rs 219,783) blocks of Sangrur district; Phool (Rs 350,889), Talwandi Sabo (Rs 222,882), Rampura (Rs 212,525) and Bhagta Bhai Ka (Rs 205,000) blocks of Bathinda district; and Jhunir (Rs 161,069) and Budhladha (Rs 130,039) blocks of Mansa district was more as compared to other blocks of the three districts. Similarly, in the case of control group farmers, amount of outstanding average loan against farmers of Sangrur (Rs 131,975) and Bathinda (Rs 300,285) districts was more as compared to Mansa (Rs 97,370) farmers of the same category. Block-wise analysis in this regard suggests that amount of outstanding average loan against control group farmers of Sangrur (Rs 329,500), Malerkotla I (Rs 323,611) and Andana (Rs 242,304) blocks of Sangrur; Maur (Rs 1,113,000) and Bathinda (Rs 249,655) blocks of Bathinda; and Mansa (Rs 160,000) and Budhladha (Rs 95,647) blocks of Mansa district was more as compared to other blocks of the three districts.

As far as amount of outstanding average loan against deceased agricultural labourers was concerned, it was Rs 45,855 in Sangrur, Rs 41,596 in Mansa and Rs 24,117 in

Bathinda. Block-wise analysis of amount of outstanding average loan against deceased agricultural labourers shows that Leharagaga (Rs 70,313), Andana (Rs 66,111) and Sherpur (Rs 67,500) blocks of Sangrur; Maur (Rs 60,000), Rampura (Rs 39,445) and Sangat (Rs 33,667) blocks of Bathinda; and Budhladha (Rs 61,100), Mansa (Rs 46,889) and Bhikhi (Rs 46,222) of Mansa district were having more outstanding loans. Similarly, in the case of control group agricultural labourers, amount of outstanding average loan against labourers of Sangrur (Rs 44,620) and Mansa (Rs 18,158) districts was more as compared to Bathinda (Rs 15,267) labourers of the same category. Block-wise analysis of amount of outstanding average loan against control group agricultural labourers shows that Andana (Rs 80,222) and Leharagaga (Rs 54,062) blocks of Sangrur; Maur (Rs 37,500) and Talwandi Sabo (Rs 23,917) blocks of Bathinda; and Jhunir (Rs 45,545) and Mansa (Rs 27,222) blocks of Mansa district were having more outstanding loans.

Analysis of average outstanding loan per deceased and control group farmers and agricultural labourers' households reveals that at the overall level and at the district level farmers' and agricultural labourers' households were heavily indebted. But no significant differences have been observed in this regard between deceased and control group farmers as well as agricultural labourers across the districts and at overall level. However, differences across the blocks of the three districts have been noticed and reported, and it was also found that heavy burden of debt has been reported against deceased and control group farmers as well as agricultural labourers in more agrarian-distressed blocks. This also confirms the prevailing distress among farmers and agricultural labourers in the state, which demands urgent solution to the problem so that farmers and agricultural labourers on the brink can be saved.

Outstanding debt: sources

Source-wise outstanding debt towards institutional and non-institutional is indeed a matter of concern and one of the most disturbing dimensions of indebtedness among farmers (Government of India 2007) and agricultural labourers. In spite of all the efforts made for the spread of institutional finance by the state, it accounted for only two-fifths of agricultural labourers and about one-third of farmers of total outstanding debt. Generally and particularly in the present case, since the interest rates charged by the non-institutional sources are high and exorbitant, this might have imposed heavy burden of debt on the farmers and agricultural labourers. The information of source-wise outstanding debt against farmers and agricultural labourers is shown in Tables 6.5 to 6.8 and Figures 6.3 and 6.4.

Analysis of source-wise distribution of outstanding amount of debt against both the categories of farmers clearly shows that farmers of all the three districts and at overall level depend upon institutional sources, non-institutional sources and multiple sources for borrowing funds. It is interesting to note that in the case of both deceased and control group farmers, the share of co-operative debt is found to be meagre in the case of all the districts and at overall level. About 49 per cent of the deceased farmers and 58 per cent of the control group farmers depend upon multiple sources of finance for

TABLE 6.5 Percentage distribution of farmers according to outstanding debt across sources and districts

S. No.	Sources	Sangrur		Bathinda		Mansa		Overall	
		Deceased	Control group	Deceased	Control group	Deceased	Control group	Deceased	Control group
Institutional sources									
1	Commercial bank	18.0	38.6	22.4	31.7	26.0	28.5	21.8	32.2
2	Co-operative	1.7	8.9	2.9	11.0	9.2	3.8	4.1	7.7
3	Commercial bank and co-operative	3.5	5.0	2.4	5.5	5.3	1.3	3.5	3.7
4	Sub-total	23.3	52.5	27.6	48.3	40.5	33.5	29.4	43.6
Non-institutional sources									
1	Commission agent	25.0	34.7	18.1	18.6	13.0	43.7	19.1	32.4
2	Relative	1.7	2.0	1.9	1.4	–	3.8	1.4	2.5
3	Commission agent and relative	29.7	3.0	24.3	9.7	–	–	19.9	4.2
4	Sub-total	56.4	39.6	44.3	29.7	13.0	47.5	40.4	39.1
Multiple sources									
1	Commercial bank, co-operatives and others	20.3	7.9	28.1	22.1	46.6	19.0	30.2	17.3
	Grand total	100	100	100	100	100	100	100	100

Source: Field survey.

District	Sangrur		Bathinda		Mansa		Overall	
Source Category	Deceased farmers	Control group	Deceased farmers	Control group	Deceased farmers	Control group	Deceased farmers	Control group
Institutional sources								
Commercial bank	6,455,012 (16.5)	6,718,000 (25.6)	4,973,000 (14.5)	2,825,002 (6.7)	1,160,000 (7.9)	3,372,684 (24.9)	12,588,012 (14.3)	12,915,686 (15.7)
Co-operative	140,000 (0.4)	232,000 (0.9)	809,000 (2.3)	413,000 (1.0)	140,000 (0.9)	1,285,000 (9.5)	1,089,000 (1.2)	1,930,000 (2.3)
Commercial bank and co-operative	2,564,784 (6.6)	480,000 (1.8)	5,866,000 (17.1)	4,496,000 (10.6)	1,835,186 (12.5)	10,000 (0.1)	10,265,970 (11.6)	4,986,000 (6.1)
Sub total	9,159,796 (23.4)	7,430,000 (28.3)	11,648,000 (33.9)	7,734,002 (18.2)	3,135,186 (21.3)	4,667,684 (34.5)	23,942,982 (27.2)	19,831,686 (24.1)
Non-institutional sources								
Commission agent	6,023,000 (15.4)	5,625,000 (21.4)	4,927,000 (14.3)	2,875,000 (6.8)	7,890,000 (53.7)	3,912,683 (28.9)	18,840,000 (21.4)	12,412,683 (15.1)
Relative	890,000 (2.3)	670,000 (2.5)	175,000 (0.5)	50,000 (0.1)	–	136,000 (1.0)	1,065,000 (1.2)	856,000 (1.0)
Commission agent and relative	992,506 (2.5)	190,000 (0.7)	210,000 (0.6)	1,466,000 (3.4)	–	–	1,202,506 (1.4)	1,656,000 (2.0)
Sub-total	7,905,506 (20.2)	6,485,000 (24.7)	5,312,000 (15.4)	4,391,000 (10.3)	7,890,000 (53.7)	4,048,683 (29.9)	21,107,506 (23.9)	14,924,683 (18.1)
Multiple sources								
Multiple sources	22,007,722 (56.3)	12,348,087 (47.0)	17,420,005 (50.7)	30,310,326 (71.4)	3,670,372 (25.0)	4,818,000 (35.6)	43,098,099 (48.9)	47,476,413 (57.7)
Grand total	39,073,024 (100)	26,263,087 (100)	34,380,005 (100)	42,435,328 (100)	14,695,558 (100)	13,534,367 (100)	88,148,587 (100)	82,232,782 (100)

Source: Field survey.

Note: Figures in parenthesis are percentages.

TABLE 6.7 Source–wise distribution of amount of outstanding debt against agricultural labourers (rupees)

District	Sangrur		Bathinda		Mansa		Overall	
Source	Deceased	Control group	Deceased	Control group	Deceased	Control group	Deceased	Control group
Commercial bank	655,000 (20.4)	402,000 (13.4)	212,000 (14.6)	6,000 (0.7)	348,000 (14.7)	35,000 (2.8)	1,215,000 (17.3)	443,000 (8.6)
Co-operative	–	–	55,000 (3.8)	–	–	–	55,000 (0.7)	–
Commission agent	170,000 (5.3)	35,000 (1.2)	65,000 (4.5)	20,000 (2.2)	195,000 (8.2)	61,000 (4.9)	430,000 (6.1)	116,000 (2.2)
Farmers	1,465,000 (45.7)	1,794,000 (59.6)	668,000 (46.2)	765,000 (86.0)	1,051,000 (44.3)	845,000 (67.5)	3,184,000 (45.3)	3,404,000 (66.1)
Relative	259,000 (8.1)	204,000 (6.8)	302,000 (20.9)	73,000 (8.2)	233,000 (9.8)	40,000 (3.2)	794,000 (11.3)	317,000 (6.1)
Others	655,000 (20.0)	575,000 (19.1)	145,000 (10.0)	25,000 (2.8)	544,000 (22.9)	270,000 (21.6)	1,344,000 (19.1)	870,000 (16.9)
Total	3,204,000 (100)	3,010,000 (100)	1,447,000 (100)	889,000 (100)	2,371,000 (100)	1,251,000 (100)	7,022,000 (100)	5,150,000 (100)

Source: Field survey.

Note: Figures in parenthesis are percentages.

TABLE 6.8 Distribution of number of agricultural labourers according to source-wise outstanding debt (numbers)

Districts	Sangrur		Bathinda		Mansa		Overall	
Category	Deceased	Control group	Deceased	Control group	Deceased	Control group	Deceased	Control group
Commercial bank	3 (7.3)	5 (11.6)	2 (5.3)	2 (6.4)	4 (9.8)	2 (6.7)	9 (7.5)	9 (8.6)
Co-operative	–	–	1 (2.6)	–	–	–	1 (0.8)	–
Commission agent	2 (4.9)	1 (2.3)	4 (10.5)	1 (3.2)	3 (7.3)	4 (13.3)	9 (7.5)	6 (5.8)
Farmers	26 (63.4)	23 (53.5)	22 (57.9)	24 (77.4)	15 (36.6)	15 (50.0)	63 (52.5)	62 (59.6)
Relatives	3 (7.3)	4 (9.3)	3 (7.9)	2 (6.4)	14 (34.1)	1 (3.3)	20 (16.7)	7 (6.7)
Others	7 (17.1)	10 (23.3)	6 (15.8)	2 (6.4)	5 (12.2)	8 (26.7)	18 (15.0)	20 (19.2)
Total	41 (100)	43 (100)	38 (100)	31 (100)	41 (100)	30 (100)	120 (100)	104 (100)

Source: Field survey.

Note: Figures in parenthesis are percentages.

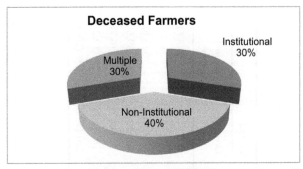

FIGURE 6.3 Source-wise distribution of outstanding debt against farmers

Source: Authors.

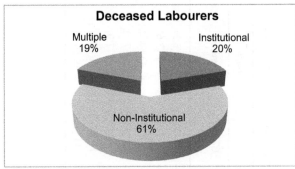

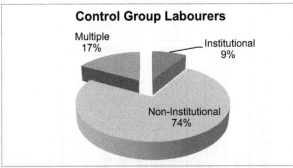

FIGURE 6.4 Source-wise percentage distribution of outstanding debt against agricultural labourers

Source: Authors.

their productive as well as non-productive needs. The share of institutional sources was about 27 per cent in the case of deceased farmers and 24 per cent in the case of control group farmers. The share of non-institutional sources like commission agents and relatives stands at 24 per cent in the case of deceased farmers and 18 per cent in the case of control group farmers. Analysis in this regard clearly indicates that both categories of farmers preferred multiple sources of finance.

Outstanding debt against farmers: sources

At the overall level about 30 per cent of the deceased farmers were indebted towards institutional sources, 40 per cent of them to non-institutional sources, mainly commission agents, and the remaining 30 per cent towards multiple sources. However, about 40 per cent of the control group farmers were indebted to institutional sources, about 34 per cent towards non-institutional sources and 26 per cent towards multiple sources.

Source-wise outstanding debt against deceased group of farmers of the three districts reveals that about 23 per cent of Sangrur, 28 per cent of Bathinda and 41 per cent of farm households of Mansa district were indebted to institutional source. In Sangrur, Bathinda and Mansa districts, 53 per cent, 48 per cent and 34 per cent, respectively, of control group farmers were indebted to the formal institutions. Distribution of deceased farmers' indebtedness to non-institutional sources reveals that it was 56.4 per cent in Sangrur district, 44.3 per cent in Bathinda district and 12.9 per cent in Mansa district. In the case of control group of farmers, 39.6 per of Sangrur district, 29.6 per cent of Bathinda district and 47.5 per cent of Mansa district were indebted to non-institutional sources. The high degree of indebtedness among the farmers of both deceased and control group belongs to the informal money lenders called commission agents.

Another serious and dangerous aspect of indebtedness of both categories of farmers across the three districts and at overall level was that they were indebted to multiple sources, especially deceased farmers. Analysis suggests greater indebtedness of deceased farmers towards non-institutional and multiple sources, which indicates that economic distress faced by them may be the cause for suicides.

Outstanding debt against agricultural labourers: sources

About 18 per of the deceased agricultural labourers at the overall level were indebted to institutional sources, and the remaining 82 per cent, mainly to the farmers, were indebted towards non-institutional sources. However, in the case of control group of agricultural labourers, about 89 per cent were indebted to non-institutional sources, such as farmers, relatives and commission agents. Analysis of outstanding debt across the districts against deceased as well as control group agricultural labourers reveals that they are also facing similar situation so far as the sources of indebtedness are concerned (Table 6.7). The high proportion of indebtedness from informal sources means that the labour households have been facing the situation of tied labour. This in fact is tantamount to undervaluing the labour, and also it shows signs of exploitative nature of working conditions. Thus, it is emerging from the analysis that high indebtedness of agricultural labourers of both the categories towards exploitive non-institutional sources is a worrisome feature. Therefore, it is urgent to look into the conditions of the agriculture labourers, and timely measures are required so that this class of labourers on the brink can be saved.

Analysis of percentage source-wise distribution of number of agricultural labourers of Sangrur, Bathinda, Mansa and at overall level shows that a large majority of the agricultural labourers were indebted to farmers of the same villages and villages of the area. The percentage distribution shows that about 63 per cent of deceased farmers of Sangrur, 58 per cent of Bathinda, 37 per cent of Mansa and 53 per cent at overall level were indebted to farmers. Again, about 54 per cent of farmers from control group of Sangrur, 77 per cent of Bathinda, 50 per cent of Mansa and 60 per cent at overall level were indebted to farmers. Analysis also shows that many agricultural labourers of the three districts and at overall level were also indebted towards commercial banks, commission agents, relatives and other sources.

Non-repayment of loan and indebtedness: perceptions

Undoubtedly farmers in Punjab are driven to a debt trap not only because of imprudent heavy borrowing from high-cost informal sources and for non-productive purposes but also because of fall in net farm incomes far below expectations (Shergill 1998; Bhangoo 2005). During liberalization and globalization policies era, prices of wheat and rice at home remained stagnant but continuously declined in the international market, hitting hard agriculture and making it unviable and non-competitive. Agricultural input prices have increased by 25 to 45 per cent, but the increase in agricultural output prices is only 9 to 9.5 per cent since 1967 (IDC 2006). The cost of cultivation of rice increased by 5 per cent from 44 per cent to 49 per cent during 2000–01 to 2005–06 over 1995–96 to 2000–01 and for wheat it increased by 8 per cent during the same period. The gross income was reduced by 33 per cent for rice and almost by 100 per cent for wheat from 1995–96 to 2000–01 to 2000–01 to 2005–06, respectively (IDC 2006). The cost of cotton cultivation increased 17 times and the income from cotton only 11 times during 1975–76 and 2001–02 (Narayanamoorthy 2006), and its continuous failure almost for a decade due to attack of American bollworm and water logging (Rangi and Sidhu 2000) has negatively affected the incomes of cotton growers. Punjab farmers have borrowed heavily for farm machinery, for digging/deepening tube wells and replacing old bore wells with submersible pumps and for cultivating input-intensive high-value crops in the expectation of high yield and prices. One-third of the old tube wells have already been replaced by submersible pumps in Punjab due to deepening of water table (Gill 2005). Non-realization of these expectations has been identified as the major cause of indebtedness by the experts and studies conducted earlier.

Analysis of Table 6.9 suggests that low-income earnings,[1] crop failure/damage[2] and indebtedness were the three major perceptions identified by the deceased and

TABLE 6.9 Distribution of farmers and agricultural labourers according to perceptions and causes for non-repayment of loan and indebtedness

District	Category perceptions	Deceased farmers	Control group farmers	Deceased labour	Control group labour
Sangrur	Low income	108 (54.27)	99 (49.75)	33 (47.83)	40 (57.97)
	Crop failure	52 (26.13)	40 (20.10)	–	–
	Indebtedness	39 (19.60)	60 (30.15)	36 (52.17)	29 (42.03)
	Sangrur sub-total	199 (100)	199 (100)	69 (100)	69 (100)
Bathinda	Low income	73 (42.44)	64 (37.21)	48 (80.00)	52 (86.67)
	Crop failure	99 (57.56)	95 (55.23)	–	–
	Indebtedness	–	13 (7.56)	12 (20.00)	8 (13.33)
	Bathinda sub-total	172 (100)	172 (100)	60 (100)	60 (100)
Mansa	Low income	64 (46.03)	76 (54.68)	35 (61.40)	40 (70.18)
	Crop failure	35 (25.18)	25 (17.99)	–	–
	Indebtedness	40 (28.78)	38 (27.34)	22 (38.60)	17 (29.82)
	Mansa sub-total	139 (100)	139 (100)	57 (100)	57 (100)
Overall	Low income	245 (48.00)	239 (46.90)	116 (62.40)	132 (71.00)
	Crop failure	186 (36.50)	160 (31.40)	–	–
	Indebtedness	79 (15.50)	111 (21.80)	70 (37.60)	54 (29.00)
Overall total		510 (100)	510 (100)	186 (100)	186 (100)

Source: Field survey.

Note: Figures in parenthesis are percentages.

control group of farmers and low-income earnings and indebtedness by agricultural labourers. At the overall level deceased and control group farmers equally identified low income and crop failure as the leading reasons for non-payment of instalments of outstanding loans, while deceased and control group labourers blamed low income and indebtedness for non-payment of outstanding loans. Almost deceased and control group farmers across the three districts perceived low-income earnings, crop failure/damage and indebtedness with minor differences as the causes for the non-payment of outstanding loans. Further, the deceased and control group agricultural labourers in the three selected districts identified low income and indebtedness as the causes of failure to repay the debt. Analysis of causes for the non-payment of outstanding loans by the deceased and control group farmers and agricultural labourers reveals that low incomes from agriculture, crop failure/damage due to many reasons and widespread indebtedness among this strata of population in rural Punjab were the real culprits for the prevailing situation in the agrarian sector of the state economy. The predominant factors that had played an important role in creating the heap of indebtedness among the farmers and

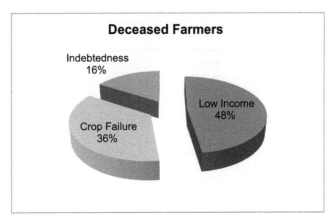

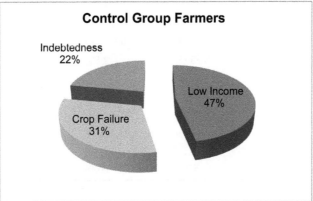

FIGURE 6.5 Distribution of farmers according to perceptions and causes for non-repayment of loan and indebtedness

Source: Authors.

agricultural labourers are beyond their control. Either they are man-made or they are related to vagaries of nature. These factors have turned the investment made in agriculture-related productive economic activities topsy turvy, and this non-remunerative work derailed their household economy.

Perceptions and causes for non-payment of outstanding loans: block-level analysis

Though agrarian distress has been the expression of multiple causes, indebtedness and indebtedness-related factors were considered the most vital manifestation of rural distress and precursor of farmers' and agricultural labourers' suicides in Punjab (Iyer and Manick 2000; Bhangoo 2005). In such a situation, it is of paramount

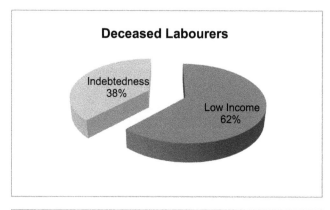

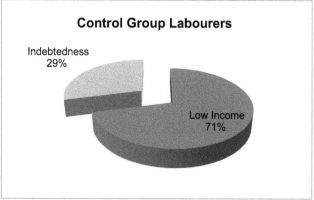

FIGURE 6.6 Distribution of agricultural labourers according to perceptions and causes for non-repayment of loan and indebtedness

Source: Authors.

importance to understand and grasp the nitty-gritty and ground realities of unabated rural and agrarian distress prevailing in Punjab. In this section, an attempt has been made to analyse the important indicators, such as causes and perceptions of the respondents of both the groups of farmers and agricultural labourers for the non-payment of outstanding loans/debt at the development block level.

In this light in the first place, the perceived causes for the non-payment of outstanding loans and increasing debt by both the groups of farmers and agricultural labourers have been discussed, and the developmental block-wise and district-wise information of the same has been given in Tables 6.10, 6.11 and 6.12. For convenience and clarity the perceptions of farmers and labourers have been clubbed into three categories as they also emerged from the responses of the farmers and agricultural labourers. These were low income from farm produce due to various reasons, especially small farm size, high farm input costs and non-remunerative farm produce prices and farm labour; crop failure/damage on many counts and indebtedness

TABLE 6.10 Percentage distribution of farmers and agricultural labourers according to perceptions and causes of non-repayment of loans and indebtedness of Bathinda district

Block	Category / perceptions	Farmers				Labourers			
		Deceased		Control group		Deceased		Control group	
		Number	Per cent	Number	Per cent	Number	Per cent	Number	Per cent
Bathinda	Low income	12	41.4	15	51.7	3	42.9	2	28.6
	Crop failure	10	34.5	4	13.8	–	–	–	–
	Indebtedness	7	24.1	10	34.5	4	57.1	5	71.4
	Sub-total	29	100	29	100	7	100	7	100
Sangat	Low income	3	20.0	5	33.3	7	58.3	4	33.3
	Crop failure	4	26.7	7	46.7	–	–	–	–
	Indebtedness	8	53.3	3	20.0	5	41.7	8	66.7
	Sub-total	15	100	15	100	12	100	12	100
Nathana	Low income	5	35.7	9	64.3	2	33.3	1	16.7
	Crop failure	2	14.3	3	21.4	–	–	–	–
	Indebtedness	7	50.0	2	14.3	4	66.7	5	83.3
	Sub-total	14	100	14	100	6	100	6	100
Bhaga Bhai Ka	Low income	3	21.4	3	21.4	1	25.0	2	50.0
	Crop failure	8	57.2	5	35.7	–	–	–	–
	Indebtedness	3	21.4	6	42.9	3	75.0	2	50.0
	Sub-total	14	100	14	100	4	100	4	100
Phool	Low income	8	44.4	10	55.6	1	16.7	3	50.0
	Crop failure	3	16.7	2	11.1	–	–	–	–
	Indebtedness	7	38.9	6	33.3	5	83.3	3	50.0
	Sub-total	18	100	18	100	6	100	6	100

Talwandi Sabo	Low income	10	58.8	7	41.2	4	33.3	7	58.3
	Crop failure	3	17.7	3	17.6	–	–	–	–
	Indebtedness	4	23.5	7	41.2	8	66.7	5	41.7
	Sub-total	17	100	17	100	12	100	12	100
Maur	Low income	8	32.0	14	56.0	1	25.0	3	75.0
	Crop failure	10	40.0	7	28.0	–	–	–	–
	Indebtedness	7	28.0	4	16.0	3	75.0	1	25.0
	Sub-total	25	100	25	100	4	100	4	100
Rampura	Low income	17	42.5	21	52.5	2	22.2	4	44.4
	Crop failure	9	22.5	11	27.5	–	–	–	–
	Indebtedness	14	35.0	8	20.0	7	77.8	5	55.6
	Sub-total	40	100	40	100	9	100	9	100
Overall	Low income	66	38.4	84	48.8	21	35.0	26	43.3
	Crop failure	49	28.5	42	24.4	–	–	–	–
	Indebtedness	57	33.1	46	26.8	39	65.0	34	56.7
Grand total		172	100	172	100	60	100	60	100

Source: Field survey.

TABLE 6.11 Distribution of farmers and agricultural labourers according to perceptions and causes of non-repayment of loan and indebtedness of Mansa district

Block	Category/ perceptions	Farmers				Labourers			
		Deceased		Control group		Deceased		Control group	
		Number	Per cent	Number	Per cent	Number	Per cent	Number	Per cent
Bhikhi	Low income	8	57.1	3	21.4	3	33.3	4	44.4
	Crop failure	2	14.3	6	42.9	–	–	–	–
	Indebtedness	4	28.6	5	35.7	6	66.7	5	55.6
	Sub-total	14	100	14	100	9	100	9	100
Mansa	Low income	11	45.8	9	37.5	4	44.4	2	22.2
	Crop failure	3	12.5	4	16.7	–	–	–	–
	Indebtedness	10	41.7	11	45.8	5	55.6	7	77.8
	Sub-total	24	100	24	100	9	100	9	100
Sardulgarh	Low income	7	33.3	6	28.6	3	37.5	5	62.5
	Crop failure	5	23.8	3	14.3	–	–	–	–
	Indebtedness	9	42.9	12	57.1	5	62.5	3	37.5
	Sub-total	21	100	21	100	8	100	8	100
Junir	Low income	15	51.7	8	27.6	2	18.2	7	63.6
	Crop failure	6	20.7	3	10.3	–	–	–	–
	Indebtedness	8	27.6	18	62.1	9	81.8	4	36.4
	Sub-total	29	100	29	100	11	100	11	100

Budhladha	Low income	19	37.3	16	31.4	12	60.0	15	75.0
	Crop failure	7	13.7	11	21.6	–	–	–	–
	Indebtedness	25	49.0	24	47.0	8	40.0	5	25.0
	Sub-total	51	100	51	100	20	100	20	100
Overall	Low income	60	43.2	42	30.2	24	42.1	33	57.9
	Crop failure	23	16.5	27	19.4	–	–	–	–
	Indebtedness	56	40.3	70	50.4	33	57.9	24	42.1
Grand total		139	100	139	100	57	100	57	100

Source: Field survey.

TABLE 6.12 Distribution of farmers and agricultural labourers according to perceptions and causes of non-repayment of loan and indebtedness of Sangrur district

Block	Category/ perceptions	Farmers				Labourers			
		Deceased		Control group		Deceased		Control group	
		Number	Per cent	Number	Per cent	Number	Per cent	Number	Per cent
Sunam	Low income	16	42.1	8	21.1	3	25.0	5	41.7
	Crop failure	10	26.3	14	36.8	–	–	–	–
	Indebtedness	12	31.6	16	42.1	9	75.0	7	58.3
	Sub-total	38	100	38	100	12	100	12	100
Malerkotla I	Low income	11	61.1	5	27.8	3	37.5	6	75.0
	Crop failure	4	22.2	8	44.4	–	–	–	–
	Indebtedness	3	16.7	5	27.8	5	62.5	2	25.0
	Sub-total	18	100	18	100	8	100	8	100
Malerkotla II	Low income	7	50.0	5	35.7	1	25.0	2	50.0
	Crop failure	2	14.3	4	28.6	–	–	–	–
	Indebtedness	5	35.7	5	35.7	3	75.0	2	50.0
	Sub-total	14	100	14	100	4	100	4	100
Sherpur	Low income	9	52.9	4	23.5	4	66.7	5	83.3
	Crop failure	3	17.7	8	47.1	–	–	–	–
	Indebtedness	5	29.4	5	29.4	2	33.3	1	16.7
	Sub-total	17	100	17	100	6	100	6	100
Dhuri	Low income	7	58.3	3	25.0	1	16.7	3	50.0
	Crop failure	2	16.7	7	58.3	–	–	–	–
	Indebtedness	3	25.0	2	16.7	5	83.3	3	50.0
	Sub-total	12	100	12	100	6	100	6	100

Bhawanigarh	Low income	8	38.0	12	57.1	2	40.0	4	80.0
	Crop failure	6	28.6	5	23.8	–	–	–	–
	Indebtedness	7	33.3	4	19.1	3	60.0	1	20.0
	Sub-total	21	100	21	100	5	100	5	100
Andana	Low income	6	26.1	15	65.2	5	55.6	3	33.3
	Crop failure	5	21.7	3	13.1	–	–	–	–
	Indebtedness	12	52.2	5	21.7	4	44.4	6	66.7
	Sub-total	23	100	23	100	9	100	9	100
Lehragaga	Low income	14	30.4	18	39.1	6	37.5	7	43.7
	Crop failure	12	36.1	6	13.1	–	–	–	–
	Indebtedness	20	43.5	22	47.8	10	62.5	9	56.3
	Sub-total	46	100	46	100	16	100	16	100
Sangrur	Low income	6	60.0	3	30.0	1	33.3	–	–
	Crop failure	3	30.0	2	20.0	–	–	–	–
	Indebtedness	1	10.0	5	50.0	2	66.7	3	–
	Sub-total	10	100	10	100	3	100	3	100
Overall	Low income	84	42.2	73	36.7	26	37.7	35	50.7
	Crop failure	47	23.6	57	28.6	–	–	–	–
	Indebtedness	68	34.2	69	34.7	43	62.3	34	49.3
Grand total		199	100	199	100	69	100	69	100

Source: Field survey.

due to many factors, specifically exorbitant rate of interest and problems with credit delivery system, were the three major causes for the non-payment of outstanding loans and increasing burden of debt.

The number and percentage distribution of perceived causes of non-payment of loans and indebtedness by farmers and agricultural labourers of developmental blocks of Bathinda district have been depicted in Table 6.10. Analysis shows that at overall level and in almost all the blocks of Bathinda district, deceased farmers identified indebtedness as the leading cause of non-payment of outstanding loans and burden of debt, followed by low income and crop failure and damage. However, in the case of control group farmers, low farm income has been perceived as the leading factor for non-payment of loans and debt followed by indebtedness and crop failure/damage in almost all the blocks. So far deceased agricultural labourers as well as control group have perceived that the most important cause of high indebtedness is low level of wage income. This is the cause of non-payment of loans and debt in the various blocks of Bathinda district.

The number and percentage distribution of perceived causes of non-payment of outstanding loans and increasing indebtedness by farmers and agricultural labourers of developmental blocks of Mansa district have been depicted in Table 6.11. Analysis reveals that at overall level and in almost all the blocks of Mansa district both the groups of farmers have identified indebtedness as the leading cause of non-payment of outstanding loans and burden of debt, followed by low income and crop failure and damage. The deceased as well as control group agricultural labourers at overall level and in almost all the blocks of Mansa district have perceived indebtedness followed by low labour income as the leading causes of non-payment of loans and debt. Analysis clearly shows that perceptions of both groups of farmers as well as agricultural labourers of Mansa district regarding non-payment of outstanding loans and debt are similar to those of Bathinda district.

Information regarding the distribution of perceived causes of non-payment of outstanding loans and increasing indebtedness by farmers and agricultural labourers of developmental blocks of Sangrur district has been depicted in Table 6.12. Analysis shows that deceased and control group farmers of different development blocks of Sangrur district have identified indebtedness as the major cause of non-payment of outstanding loans and debt followed by low farm income and successive crop failure/damage. In some blocks of Sangrur district more farmers have identified crop failure/damage as the reason behind non-payment of outstanding loans and debt as compared to blocks of Mansa and Bathinda districts. This may be due to crop failure/damage due to floods of Ghaggar River and shortage of irrigation water at the tail end of the canals' farms of the blocks along Haryana border.

It emerged from the block-wise analysis of three districts that almost similar situation prevailed regarding the causes of non-payment of loans and debt in the case of both groups of farmers and agricultural labourers. Therefore, urgent remedial steps should be initiated to increase the farm income and farm labour income, to minimize the crop damage/loss and to reduce the burden of debt. For this, reduction in farm input costs, ensuring remunerative prices of farm produce, raising incomes of farmers by adopting allied farm activities and diversification of agriculture in favour of cash crops, crop insurance and other steps should be taken to tame Ghaggar River and water logging; institutional support by the state, regulation of interest rates and other malpractices of both formal and informal credit agencies and improvements in credit delivery system and indebtedness reforms may be suggested for consideration of policymakers and the state.

Mode of suicides

The information and data regarding the different modes of suicides adopted by farmers and agricultural labourers has been shown in Table 6.13 and Figure 6.7.

Modes of committing suicide by farmers and agricultural labourers across the three districts and at overall level clearly relate it to farm operations as most commonly used method of suicides. Consumption of insecticides/pesticides was the major method adopted to commit suicide as these are easily available in the farm or in the households. The highest proportion of deceased farmers, that is 59.9 per cent in Bathinda district, consumed pesticides to commit suicides followed by 57.3 per cent in Sangrur district and 54 per cent in the Mansa district. Similarly, the deceased agricultural labourers have also consumed pesticides to commit suicides. It is important to note that the proportion of agricultural labourers of Mansa district was the highest, that is 47.4 per cent for using pesticides as a medium to commit suicides. It was followed by Sangrur district (where 44.9 per cent of agricultural labourers consumed pesticides) and Bathinda district (41.7 per cent of agricultural labourers consumed pesticides). Among the known medium of committing suicides, self-hanging emerged as the next important mode of committing suicides by the farmers and labourers. Mansa district emerged as the most dominant in terms of using self-hanging mode for suicides compared with the other two districts under examination. The other methods adopted for committing suicides were jumping before a running train and jumping into water either in the nearby river or bore well.

Mode of suicides: block-level analysis

Suicides among farmers and agricultural labourers may occur on many counts (economic, social, psychological, etc.) but are disturbing when the reported common cause is the indebtedness-driven economic distress and related problems. Earlier studies also analysed the mode of suicides adopted by farmers and agricultural labourers; here an attempt has been made to ascertain the mode of suicides at the block level, and related information has been presented in Tables 6.14 to 6.16.

Information of mode of suicides of different blocks of Bathinda district has been depicted in Table 6.14. A large majority of farmers of Nathana, Bhagta Bhai Ka and Maur have consumed insecticides/pesticides/poison to commit suicide as these are easily available in the farm or in households. Deceased agricultural labourers of all the blocks of Bathinda district have also consumed insecticides/pesticides/poison to commit suicide. The other modes adopted for

TABLE 6.13 Distribution of farmers and agricultural labourers according to mode of suicides

Mode	District							
	Sangrur		Bathinda		Mansa		Overall	
	Farmers	Labourers	Farmers	Labourers	Farmers	Labourers	Farmers	Labourers
Pesticides/poison	114 (57.3)	31 (44.9)	103 (59.9)	25 (41.7)	75 (54.0)	27 (47.4)	292 (57.3)	83 (44.6)
Hanging	7 (3.5)	6 (8.7)	17 (9.9)	8 (13.3)	25 (18.0)	11 (19.3)	49 (9.6)	25 (13.4)
Jumping into canal/well	2 (1.0)	–	2 (1.2)	2 (3.3)	10 (7.2)	3 (5.3)	14 (2.8)	5 (2.7)
Jumping under train	1 (0.5)	–	13 (7.6)	7 (11.3)	10 (7.2)	4 (7.0)	24 (4.7)	11 (5.9)
Electrocution	3 (1.5)	3 (4.4)	2 (1.2)	–	4 (2.9)	1 (1.8)	9 (1.8)	4 (2.2)
Exactly not known	17 (8.5)	3 (4.4)	4 (2.3)	8 (13.3)	6 (4.3)	2 (3.5)	27 (5.3)	13 (7.0)
Any other	55 (27.6)	26 (37.7)	31 (18.0)	10 (16.7)	9 (6.5)	9 (15.8)	95 (18.6)	45 (24.2)
Total	199 (100)	69 (100)	172 (100)	60 (100)	139 (100)	57 (100)	510 (100)	186 (100)

Source: Field survey.

Note: Figures in parenthesis are percentages.

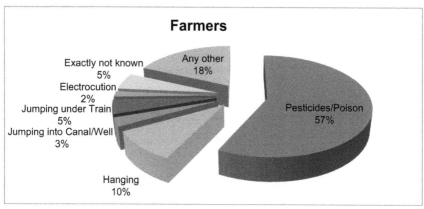

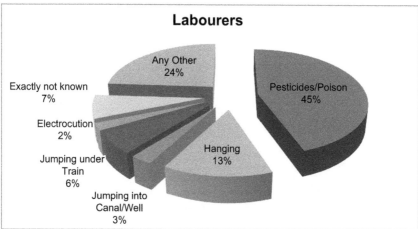

FIGURE 6.7 Distribution of farmers and agricultural labourers according to mode of suicides

Source: Authors.

committing suicides by farmers and agricultural labourers of Bathinda district blocks were jumping before running trains, jumping into canals/wells, hanging and self-immolation.

Distribution of deceased farmers and agricultural labourers regarding adopted mode of suicides of all the blocks of Mansa district has been shown in Table 6.15. A large majority of farmers and agricultural labourers have consumed insecticides/pesticides/poison to commit suicide. Deceased agricultural labourers of all the blocks of Mansa district have also consumed insecticides/pesticides/poison to commit suicide. The other modes adopted for committing suicides by farmers and agricultural labourers of Mansa district blocks were jumping before running trains, jumping into canals/wells, hanging and self-immolation.

TABLE 6.14 Percentage distribution of farmers and labourers according to mode of suicides of Bathinda district

Block	Category	Pesticides / poison	Hanging	Jumping into canal/well	Jumping under train	Others	Total
Bathinda	Farmers	13 (44.8)	4 (13.8)	–	1 (3.5)	11 (37.9)	29 (100)
	Labourers	2 (28.6)	–	–	3 (42.8)	2 (28.6)	7 (100)
Sangat	Farmers	9 (60.0)	2 (13.3)	1 (6.7)	2 (13.3)	1 (6.7)	15 (100)
	Labourers	4 (33.4)	1 (8.3)	1 (8.3)	–	6 (50.0)	12 (100)
Nathana	Farmers	9 (64.3)	2 (14.3)	–	1 (7.1)	2 (14.3)	14 (100)
	Labourers	4 (66.6)	1 (16.7)	–	–	1 (16.7)	6 (100)
Bhagta Bhai Ka	Farmers	10 (71.4)	1 (7.2)	–	–	3 (21.4)	14 (100)
	Labourers	3 (75.0)	–	1 (25.0)	–	–	4 (100)
Phool	Farmers	9 (50.0)	2 (11.1)	–	–	7 (38.9)	18 (100)
	Labourers	2 (33.3)	1 (16.7)	–	–	3 (50.0)	6 (100)
Talwandi Sabo	Farmers	10 (58.8)	3 (17.7)	–	–	4 (23.5)	17 (100)
	Labourers	3 (25.0)	5 (41.7)	–	1 (8.3)	3 (25.0)	12 (100)
Maur	Farmers	13 (52.0)	–	–	6 (24.0)	6 (24.0)	25 (100)
	Labourers	2 (50.0)	–	–	1 (25.0)	1 (25.0)	4 (100)
Rampura	Farmers	30 (75.0)	3 (7.5)	1 (2.5)	3 (7.5)	3 (7.5)	40 (100)
	Labourers	5 (55.6)	–	–	2 (22.2)	2 (22.2)	9 (100)
Overall	Farmers	103 (59.9)	17 (9.9)	2 (1.2)	13 (7.5)	37 (21.5)	172 (100)
	Labourers	25 (41.7)	8 (13.3)	2 (3.3)	7 (11.7)	18 (30.0)	60 (100)

Source: Field survey.

Note: Figures in parenthesis are percentages.

TABLE 6.15 Block-wise percentage distribution of farmers and labourers according to mode of suicides in Mansa district

Block	Category	Pesticides/poison	Hanging	Jumping into canal/well	Jumping under train	Others	Total
Bhikhi	Farmers	11 (78.6)	2 (14.3)	–	–	1 (7.1)	14 (100)
	Labourers	6 (66.7)	2 (22.2)	1 (11.1)	–	–	9 (100)
Mansa	Farmers	13 (54.2)	3 (12.5)	2 (8.3)	2 (8.3)	4 (16.7)	24 (100)
	Labourers	6 (66.7)	1 (11.1)	–	–	2 (22.2)	9 (100)
Sardulgarh	Farmers	11 (52.4)	2 (9.5)	1 (4.8)	3 (14.3)	4 (19.0)	21 (100)
	Labourers	2 (25.0)	1 (12.5)	1 (12.5)	–	4 (50.0)	8 (100)
Jhunir	Farmers	9 (31.0)	14 (48.3)	2 (6.9)	–	4 (13.8)	29 (100)
	Labourers	3 (27.3)	5 (45.4)	1 (9.1)	–	2 (18.2)	11 (100)
Budhladha	Farmers	31 (60.8)	6 (11.8)	3 (5.9)	5 (9.8)	6 (11.7)	51 (100)
	Labourers	10 (50.0)	2 (10.0)	–	4 (20.0)	4 (20.0)	20 (100)
Overall	Farmers	75 (53.9)	27 (19.4)	8 (5.8)	10 (7.2)	19 (13.7)	139 (100)
	Labourers	27 (47.4)	11 (19.3)	3 (5.3)	4 (7.0)	12 (21.0)	57 (100)

Source: Field survey.

Note: Figures in parenthesis are percentages.

TABLE 6.16 Block-wise percentage distribution of farmers and labourers according to mode of suicides in Sangrur district

Block	Category	Pesticides/poison	Hanging	Jumping into canal/well	Jumping under train	Others	Total
Sunam	Farmers	32 (84.2)	4 (10.5)	–	–	2 (5.3)	38 (100)
	Labourers	6 (50.0)	4 (33.3)	–	–	2 (16.7)	12 (100)
Malerkotla I–	Farmers	15 (83.3)	–	–	–	3 (16.7)	18 (100)
	Labourers	2 (25.0)	1 (12.5)	–	–	5 (62.5)	8 (100)
Malerkotla II–	Farmers	8 (57.1)	–	–	–	5 (42.9)	14 (100)
	Labourers	1 (25.0)	–	–	–	3 (75.0)	4 (100)
Sherpur	Farmers	9 (52.9)	–	–	–	8 (47.1)	17 (100)
	Labourers	1 (16.7)	–	–	–	5 (83.3)	6 (100)
Dhuri	Farmers	5 (41.7)	–	–	–	7 (58.3)	12 (100)
	Labourers	2 (33.3)	–	–	–	4 (66.7)	6 (100)
Bhawanigarh	Farmers	5 (23.8)	–	–	–	16 (76.2)	21 (100)
	Labourers	–	–	–	–	5 (100)	5 (100)
Andana	Farmers	19 (82.6)	–	1 (4.4)	–	3 (13.0)	23 (100)
	Labourers	7 (77.8)	–	–	–	2 (22.2)	9 (100)
Leharagaga	Farmers	25 (54.4)	3 (6.5)	–	3 (6.5)	15 (32.6)	46 (100)
	Labourers	9 (56.3)	1 (6.2)	–	–	6 (37.5)	16 (100)
Sangrur	Farmers	4 (40.0)	–	–	–	6 (60.0)	10 (100)
	Labourers	3 (100)	–	–	–	–	3 (100)
Overall	Farmers	122 (61.3)	7 (3.5)	1 (0.5)	3 (1.5)	66 (33.2)	199 (100)
	Labourers	31 (44.9)	6 (8.7)	–	–	32 (46.4)	69 (100)

Source: Field survey.

Note: Figures in parenthesis are percentages.

Distribution of deceased farmers and agricultural labourers regarding adopted mode of suicides of all the blocks of Sangrur district has been shown in Table 6.16. A majority of farmers and agricultural labourers have consumed insecticides/pesticides/poison to commit suicide. Deceased agricultural labourers of all the blocks of Sangrur district have also consumed insecticides/pesticides/poison to commit suicide. The other modes adopted for committing suicides by farmers and agricultural labourers of Sangrur district blocks were jumping before running trains, jumping into canals/wells, hanging and self-immolation.

Analysis of modes of committing suicide at block level in Punjab clearly relates it to farm operations, as the most commonly used method of suicides was consumption of insecticides/pesticides as these are easily available in the farm or in households. The deceased also adopted hanging, jumping into canals and other ways as modes of committing suicide. It emerged from the analysis that there is an urgent need for strong intervention by the state for rehabilitation of the families of suicide victims, such as adequate compensation in cash, pension for elder people, employment for family members, free skill and job-oriented education for children. Further, rationalization and scaling down of interest rate and waiving off entire loan in the case of sole earner are also required. Urgently any type of harassment of indebted farmers and labourers must be immediately banned and the guilty should be penalized.

Causes for suicides

Suicides among the farming community and agricultural labourers of Punjab, especially in the cotton belt of Malwa region, have been hitting the headlines for the past couple of years. This frightening and shocking phenomenon continues without any sign of abatement and reveals the plight of the deceased farmers and agricultural labourers and also of the control group farmers and agricultural labourers who are alive but whose condition resembles that of the victims. Suicides may occur on many counts (economic, social, psychological, etc.) but are worrisome and disturbing that the reported common cause of farmers' suicides in a prosperous state like Punjab is indebtedness. The emergence of suicide phenomenon has become a subject of debate, analysis and evaluation among all concerned. The information and data regarding the main causes reported and immediate provocation for farmers' and agricultural labourers' suicides has been presented in Table 6.17 and Figure 6.8.

The analysis of farmers' and agricultural labourers' suicides and contributing/provoking factors generally suggests that economic distress-led indebtedness and indebtedness-led humiliation due to harassment/threats are the driving forces of suicides. Almost a similar situation and trends have been witnessed across the three districts and at the overall level in this regard. But in reality, particularly, agrarian crisis manifestation in economic distress, social and cultural issues and inadequacies and shortcomings of credit set-up of the state are the root causes of indebtedness. Further, indebtedness-linked problems (family feud, alcohol and drug abuse,

TABLE 6.17 Causes for suicides of deceased farmers and agricultural labourers (numbers)

District	Sangrur		Bathinda		Mansa		Overall	
Causes	Farmers	Labourers	Farmers	Labourers	Farmers	Labourers	Farmers	Labourers
Economic distress	54 (27.1)	27 (39.1)	30 (17.4)	10 (16.7)	60 (43.2)	23 (40.4)	144 (28.2)	60 (32.3)
Indebtedness	54 (27.1)	10 (14.5)	53 (30.8)	19 (31.0)	56 (40.3)	23 (40.4)	163 (31.9)	52 (27.9)
Consecutive crop failure/damage	21 (10.6)	2 (2.9)	12 (6.9)	17 (28.3)	6 (4.3)	2 (3.5)	39 (7.7)	21 (11.3)
Drug addiction	28 (14.1)	11 (15.9)	9 (5.2)	3 (5.0)	8 (5.8)	2 (3.5)	45 (8.8)	16 (8.6)
Indebtedness and crop failure	2 (1.0)	–	32 (18.6)	3 (5.0)	8 (5.8)	5 (8.8)	42 (8.2)	8 (4.3)
Economic distress, indebtedness and crop failure	36 (18.1)	19 (27.5)	29 (16.9)	5 (8.3)	–	–	65 (12.7)	24 (12.9)
Any other	4 (2.0)	–	7 (4.1)	3 (5.0)	1 (0.7)	2 (3.5)	12 (2.4)	5 (2.7)
Total	199 (100)	69 (100)	172 (100)	60 (100)	139 (100)	57 (100)	510 (100)	186 (100)

Source: Field survey.

Note: Figures in parenthesis are percentages.

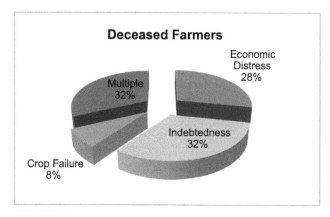

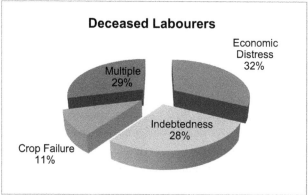

FIGURE 6.8 Causes for suicides of deceased farmers and agricultural labourers

Source: Authors.

conflict with others, court cases and notices, harassment/threats/humiliation in public, etc.) and resultant suicides have also been reported by the respondents during the survey. Therefore, in addition to economic solutions of the problem, some concrete measures on the social and cultural level must be initiated.

Causes for suicides among farmers and agricultural labourers: block-level analysis

Due to the prolonged prevailing agrarian distress, the unabated suicides among farmers and agricultural labourers are the most striking and horrible expression of the desperation among the farming community, that is farmers and agricultural labourers of Punjab (IDC 2006). Suicides may occur on many counts (economic, social, psychological, etc.) but are disturbing when the reported common cause of farmer suicides is indebtedness-driven economic distress (Mohanakumar and Sharma 2006). Earlier studies and this study concluded that family members of the deceased farmers and agricultural labourers have identified indebtedness as the leading cause of suicides among farmers, followed by economic distress, indebtedness and crop failure, consecutive crop failure/damage and others.[3] Here, an attempt has been made to ascertain the causes of suicides among the farmers and agricultural labourers at the block level, and the information related to this has been presented in Tables 6.18 to 6.20.

Distribution of perceived and identified causes for suicides among farmers and agricultural labourers of different blocks of Bathinda district has been depicted in Table 6.18. About 45 per cent family members of the deceased farmers of Bathinda block have identified indebtedness as the leading cause of suicides among farmers followed by economic distress, indebtedness and crop failure, consecutive crop failure/damage and others. Almost similar causes have been identified by the family members of the deceased farmers of the other blocks of Sangrur district. Similarly, the family members of the deceased agricultural labourers have identified indebtedness and consecutive crop failure/damage as the leading causes of suicides followed by economic distress, indebtedness and crop failure, consecutive crop failure/damage and others.

Information of identified causes and provocative factors for suicides among farmers and agricultural labourers of different blocks of Mansa district has been shown in Table 6.19. Respondent members of deceased farmers as well as agricultural labourers of all blocks of Mansa district largely have pinpointed indebtedness and economic distress as the leading causes of suicides followed by indebtedness and crop failure, consecutive crop failure/damage and others.

Information regarding the distribution of perceived and identified causes for suicides among farmers and agricultural labourers of different blocks of Sangrur district has been depicted in Table 6.20. A large majority of the family members of the deceased farmers of all blocks of Sangrur district have identified indebtedness and indebtedness-led economic distress as the leading causes of suicides among farmers followed by indebtedness and crop failure, consecutive crop failure/damage and others. In the case of deceased agricultural labourers, majority of their kin have identified indebtedness and economic distress as the leading causes of suicides followed by drug addiction.

Analysis of causes of suicides among farmers and agricultural labourers of Punjab suggests that indebtedness and indebtedness-led economic distress and crop failure/damage-related factors are the major leading issues. Therefore, policy initiatives should be undertaken by the state and state agencies to mitigate the agrarian distress; regulation of interest rates and other malpractices of both formal and informal credit agencies and improvements in credit delivery system and indebtedness reforms may be suggested for consideration of policymakers and the state. Further, measures should be directed to develop rural physical and social infrastructure. Extension of formal credit institutions, fulfilment of required credit needs of small and marginal farmers at low rates of interest and modernizing and refurbishing the canal irrigation systems along with social infrastructure of health and education, especially rural education, require proper attention.

TABLE 6.18 Block-wise distribution of causes for suicides among deceased farmers and agricultural labourers of Bathinda district (numbers)

Block	Category	ED	ID	CCF/D	DA	ID and CF/D	ED, ID and CF/D	Others	Total
Bathinda	Farmers	–	13 (44.8)	3 (10.3)	2 (6.9)	4 (13.8)	6 (20.7)	1 (3.5)	29 (100)
	Labourers	–	1 (14.3)	5 (71.4)	–	–	–	1 (14.3)	7 (100)
Sangat	Farmers	–	6 (40.0)	2 (13.3)	–	3 (20.0)	4 (26.7)	–	15 (100)
	Labourers	3 (25.0)	5 (41.7)	3 (25.0)	–	–	1 (8.3)	–	12 (100)
Nathana	Farmers	1 (7.1)	4 (28.6)	–	1 (7.1)	2 (14.3)	4 (28.6)	2 (14.3)	14 (100)
	Labourers	4 (66.6)	–	1 (16.7)	–	–	–	1 (16.7)	6 (100)
Bhagta Bhai Ka	Farmers	5 (35.7)	2 (14.4)	–	1 (7.1)	5 (35.7)	1 (7.1)	–	14 (100)
	Labourers	–	3 (75.0)	1 (25.0)	–	–	–	–	4 (100)
Phool	Farmers	9 (50.0)	5 (27.7)	1 (5.6)	2 (11.1)	1 (5.6)	–	–	18 (100)
	Labourers	1 (16.7)	1 (16.7)	2 (33.3)	–	2 (33.3)	–	–	6 (100)
Talwandi Sabo	Farmers	4 (23.5)	4 (23.5)	1 (5.9)	–	2 (11.8)	5 (29.4)	1 (5.9)	17 (100)
	Labourers	1 (8.3)	4 (33.3)	–	2 (16.8)	1 (8.3)	4 (33.3)	–	12 (100)
Maur	Farmers	3 (12.0)	9 (36.0)	3 (12.0)	2 (8.0)	3 (12.0)	4 (16.0)	1 (4.0)	25 (100)
	Labourers	–	–	1 (25.0)	1 (25.0)	–	1 (25.0)	1 (25.0)	4 (100)
Rampura	Farmers	8 (20.0)	10 (25.0)	2 (5.0)	1 (2.5)	13 (32.5)	5 (12.5)	1 (2.5)	40 (100)
	Labourers	1 (11.1)	5 (55.6)	3 (33.3)	–	–	–	–	9 (100)
Overall	Farmers	30 (17.4)	53 (30.8)	12 (7.0)	9 (5.2)	33 (19.2)	29 (16.9)	6 (3.5)	172 (100)
	Labourers	10 (16.6)	19 (31.7)	16 (26.7)	3 (5.0)	3 (5.0)	6 (10.0)	3 (5.0)	60 (100)

Source: Field survey.

Notes: 1. ED – economic distress, ID – indebtedness, CCF/D – consecutive crop failure/damage, DA – drug addicted, ID and CF/D – indebtedness and crop failure/damage, ED, ID and CF/D – economic distress, indebtedness and crop failure/damage.

2. Figures in parenthesis are percentages.

TABLE 6.19 Block-wise distribution of causes for suicides among deceased farmers and agricultural labourers of Mansa district (numbers)

Block	Category	ED	ID	CCF/D	DA	ID and CF/D	ED, ID and CF/D	Others	Total
Bhikhi	Farmers	1 (7.1)	7 (50.0)	2 (14.3)	–	4 (28.6)	–	–	14 (100)
	Labourers	2 (22.2)	5 (55.6)	1 (11.1)	1 (11.1)	–	–	–	9 (100)
Mansa	Farmers	11 (45.8)	12 (50.0)	1 (4.2)	–	–	–	–	24 (100)
	Labourers	4 (44.4)	5 (55.6)	–	–	–	–	–	9 (100)
Sardulgarh	Farmers	13 (61.8)	6 (28.6)	–	1 (4.8)	1 (4.8)	–	–	21 (100)
	Labourers	2 (25.0)	2 (25.0)	1 (12.5)	1 (12.5)	2 (25.0)	–	–	8 (100)
Jhunir	Farmers	15 (51.7)	7 (24.1)	–	3 (10.3)	3 (10.3)	–	1 (3.5)	29 (100)
	Labourers	7 (63.6)	1 (9.1)	–	3 (10.3)	3 (27.3)	–	–	11 (100)
Budhladha	Farmers	20 (39.2)	24 (47.1)	3 (5.9)	4 (7.8)	–	–	–	51 (100)
	Labourers	8 (40.0)	10 (50.0)	–	–	–	–	2 (10.0)	20 (100)
Overall	Farmers	60 (43.2)	56 (40.3)	6 (4.2)	8 (5.8)	8 (5.8)	–	1 (0.7)	139 (100)
	Labourers	23 (40.4)	23 (40.4)	2 (3.5)	2 (3.5)	5 (8.7)	–	2 (3.5)	57 (100)

Source: Field survey.

Notes: 1. ED – economic distress, ID – indebtedness, CCF/D – consecutive crop failure/damage, DA – drug addicted, ID and CF/D – indebtedness and crop failure/damage, ED, ID and CF/D – economic distress, indebtedness and crop failure/damage.
2. Figures in parenthesis are percentages.

TABLE 6.20 Block–wise distribution of causes for suicides among deceased farmers and agricultural labourers of Sangrur district (numbers)

Block	Category	ED	ID	CCF/D	DA	ID and CF/D	ED, ID and CF/D	Others	Total
Sunam	Farmers	14 (36.8)	10 (26.4)	8 (21.1)	3 (7.9)	1 (2.6)	1 (2.6)	1 (2.6)	38 (100)
	Labourers	10 (83.4)	1 (8.3)	–	–	–	1 (8.3)	–	12 (100)
Malerkotla-I	Farmers	1 (5.6)	7 (38.9)	–	4 (22.2)	–	6 (33.3)	–	18 (100)
	Labourers	1 (12.5)	–	–	3 (37.5)	–	4 (50.0)	–	8 (100)
Malerkotla-II	Farmers	2 (14.3)	3 (21.4)	2 (14.3)	2 (14.3)	–	5 (35.7)	–	14 (100)
	Labourers	2 (50.0)	1 (25.0)	–	–	–	1 (25.0)	–	4 (100)
Sherpur	Farmers	5 (29.4)	5 (29.4)	2 (11.8)	3 (17.6)	–	2 (11.8)	–	17 (100)
	Labourers	1 (16.7)	3 (50.0)	–	–	–	2 (33.3)	–	6 (100)
Dhuri	Farmers	2 (16.6)	1 (8.3)	1 (8.3)	3 (25.0)	–	5 (41.7)	–	12 (100)
	Labourers	–	1 (16.7)	–	2 (33.3)	–	3 (50.0)	–	6 (100)
Bhawanigarh	Farmers	1 (4.8)	6 (28.6)	3 (14.3)	–	–	11 (52.4)	–	21 (100)
	Labourers	–	1 (20.0)	–	1 (20.0)	–	3 (60.0)	–	5 (100)
Andana	Farmers	9 (39.1)	7 (30.4)	–	4 (17.4)	1 (4.4)	2 (8.7)	–	23 (100)
	Labourers	4 (44.5)	2 (22.2)	–	2 (22.2)	–	1 (11.1)	–	9 (100)
Leharagaga	Farmers	19 (41.3)	14 (30.4)	4 (8.7)	5 (10.9)	–	3 (6.5)	1 (2.2)	46 (100)
	Labourers	7 (43.9)	3 (18.7)	–	3 (18.7)	–	3 (18.7)	–	16 (100)
Sangrur	Farmers	1 (10.0)	1 (10.0)	1 (10.0)	4 (40.0)	–	1 (10.0)	2 (20.0)	10 (100)
	Labourers	–	2 (66.7)	–	–	–	1 (33.3)	–	3 (100)
Overall	Farmers	54 (27.1)	54 (27.1)	21 (10.6)	28 (14.1)	2 (1.0)	36 (18.1)	4 (2.0)	199 (100)
	Labourers	25 (36.3)	14 (20.3)	–	11 (15.9)	–	19 (27.5)	–	69 (100)

Source: Field survey.

Notes: 1. ED – economic distress, ID – indebtedness, CCF/D – consecutive crop failure/damage, DA – drug addicted, ID and CF/D – indebtedness and crop failure/damage, ED, ID and CF/D – economic distress, indebtedness and crop failure/damage.

2. Figures in parenthesis are percentages.

Land sold, bought, mortgaged in and mortgaged out: after suicides

An attempt has been made to analyse the details of land sold, bought, mortgaged in and mortgaged out by the deceased farmers and agricultural labourers before and after suicides, so that implications and repercussions of suicides could be gauged on respective households. The information in this regard has been shown in Table 6.21.

At the overall level 51 deceased farmers' households sold 105.5 acres, and 6.5 acres of land has been mortgaged to pay the debt. In Sangrur district, 14 deceased farmers' households sold 47.5 acres and one household mortgaged 2.5 acres of land; in Bathinda district, 22 farmers' households sold 38 acres and two households mortgaged two acres; and in Mansa district, 15 deceased farmers' households sold 18 acres and two households mortgaged two acres. Many deceased farmers' households

TABLE 6.21 Details of land sold, bought, mortgaged in and mortgaged out of deceased

District	Category Details	Farmers Number	Land (acres)	Labourers Number	Land (acres)
Sangrur	Land sold	14	47.5	–	–
	Land bought	1	0.5	–	–
	Land mortgaged in	2	0.5	–	–
	Land mortgaged out	1	2.5	–	–
	Sub-total	18	51	–	–
Bathinda	Land sold	22	38	–	–
	Land bought	–	–	–	–
	Land mortgaged in	1	2	–	–
	Land mortgaged out	2	2	2	1.5
	Sub-total	25	42	2	1.5
Mansa	Land sold	15	20	–	–
	Land bought	–	–	–	–
	Land mortgaged in	–	–	–	–
	Land mortgaged out	2	2	–	–
	Sub-total	17	22	–	–
Overall	Land sold	51	105.5	–	–
	Land bought	1	0.5	–	–
	Land mortgaged in	3	2.5	–	–
	Land mortgaged out	5	6.5	2	1.5
	Grand total	60	115	2	1.5

Source: Field survey.

have also leased out land after suicides to pay the debt and left agriculture due to sole earner's death. The noteworthy fact here is that no farmer household bought land after suicide in the family. This shows that suicides hit hard the economy of the deceased farmers and agricultural households across the three districts. In fact, they have disposed of the asset, that is land, which is the only source of livelihood.

Conclusions

Earlier discussion and analysis pertaining to various aspects of the magnitude and manifestations of agrarian distress suggests that marginalization of agriculture and prevailing agrarian crisis has been attributed to the economic crisis. Un-remunerative prices of farm products, low and stagnated yields, fall in net farm incomes, successive crop failure and high and increasing costs of cultivation have landed the small and marginal farmers in a debt trap and suicides. In this study, deceased and control group small and marginal farmers were heavily indebted as their share in the debt was 75 per cent. Interestingly, a negligible burden of debt has been reported in the case of medium and large farmers' category of both the groups of deceased and control group farmers. This undoubtedly shows that small and marginal farmers of both the groups in the state have been under great distress and committing suicides.

The indicator of average outstanding loan per deceased and control group farmers' and agricultural labourers' households suggests that they were heavily indebted. Source-wise analysis of indebtedness suggests that comparatively greater indebtedness of deceased farmers towards non-institutional and multiple sources indicates economic distress faced by them may be the cause for suicides. It emerged from the analysis that high indebtedness of deceased and control group agricultural labourers towards exploitative non-institutional sources seems to have been reached to the worrisome level.

Analysis of causes for the non-payment of outstanding loans by the deceased and control group of farmers and agricultural labourers revealed that low income from agriculture, crop failure/damage due to many reasons and widespread indebtedness among this strata of population in rural Punjab were the real culprits for the prevailing situation in the agrarian sector of the state economy. Therefore, it is suggested that efforts should be made to mitigate these problems of the rural masses with appropriate policy initiatives.

Modes of committing suicide by farmers and agricultural labourers across the three districts and at overall level clearly relate it to farm operations, as the most commonly used method of suicides was consumption of insecticides/pesticides which are easily available in the farm or in the households.

The analysis of contributing/provoking factors for suicides of farmers and agricultural labourers suggests that economic distress-led indebtedness and indebtedness-led humiliation were the driving forces of suicides. Almost a similar situation and trends have been witnessed across the three districts and at the overall level in this regard.

Many deceased farmers' households have sold, mortgaged and leased out land after suicides to pay the debt and left agriculture due to sole earner's death. This shows that suicides hit hard the economy of the deceased farmers and agricultural farmers across the three districts.

Notes

1 The respondent farmers reported that low farm income earnings were low due to, first, high input costs, especially diesel, chemical fertilizers, seeds, pesticides and operational costs; and second due to non-remunerative prices of farm products in the market and distress sale of farm produce during peak harvesting seasons. However, the respondent agricultural labourers perceived low wages and dearth of alternative employment avenues for them in the rural areas.
2 During survey of the villages, it was reported that crop failure and damage may be due to natural and man-made factors. Floods, drought, water logging, untimely rain and hail-storms were the major natural factors for crop failure and damage. Supply of spurious fertilizers, pesticides, seeds and crop confiscated by the lender to recover loans were the man-made factors reported by the respondents.
3 It was noticed and observed that family members and kin of deceased and control group farmers as well as agricultural labourers strongly perceived the burden of indebtedness as the major cause of suicides. Also, the respondents perceived that other reported causes such as drug addiction, family feuds, social problems, crop failure/damage and unproductive use of credit were the outcome of indebtedness.

7

A VILLAGE ON SALE

Microscopic analysis of rural distress

Agrarian distress widely differs across households, villages and districts in Punjab. Some villages have displayed severe impact of agrarian distress due to some extraordinary factors related to that village and area. These factors can be successive crop failure,[1] shortage of water for irrigation, erratic and limited supply of electricity, crop damage due to pest attacks, price volatility and high indebtedness. There are several villages in the three severely distressed districts under scrutiny that have been facing high degree of agrarian distress. This is precisely because of the extraordinary circumstances that led to unbearable distress and disruption of normal life.

An extraordinary situation faced by Harkishanpura village of Bathinda district led the village panchayat and elders of the village to put up, in front of the village, a notice board 'Village on Sale' in January 2001 (Sharma 2008).[2] This was the consequence of the long-standing agrarian distress, which remained unattended and unheard by the state government and local administration. A resolution was passed by the village panchayat, prodding the chief minister of Punjab to purchase the village land and allow them to work as labourers so that they can eke out a living. The burden of debt is rising, and due to crop failure they had been unable to repay the loans. However, the Akali Dal–BJP coalition government for five years (1997–2002) at the helm of affairs has completely neglected the crisis faced by the village in particular and agrarian crisis in general (Jaura, Narpinder and Rishi 2002). During the assembly election of 2002, the Congress party was elected to power and replaced the Akali Dal–BJP government. Then agriculture minister of the Congress-led state government, Ms. Rajinder Kaur Bhathal, visited the village on 21 July 2002, and announced several initiatives with a promise to help the village to remove distressing factors.[3] During the field visit, the minister has announced to establish manufacturing industries where the villagers will be able to get remunerative employment (TNS 2002). The promises made by the minister to the villagers as usual remained empty promises without any follow-up action on the ground. This has dampened the faith of the villagers in the state's political leadership and high hopes from the government.

Despite the efforts of the villagers to escape from the death trap, they continue to face the debt trap, and as it turned unbearable, suicide was the only answer. It is significant to point out here that 15 suicides were committed by the villagers due to unabated distress faced by them. The details of source, name of the person and the year in which the suicide was committed are recorded in Table 7.1. This is sufficient ground to examine this village as a case study for gauging the severity of the agrarian situation and neglect of the state and local administrations for providing any long-lasting solution. Therefore, a village study approach is adopted to examine the village as a social unit for possible solution for removing the agrarian distress through adopting an alternative village development strategy.

In theory, the study of a village, as unit of social science research, rests on its being close to the people, their life, livelihood and culture, and on its role as a focal point of reference for individual prestige and identification (Dasgupta 1978). Indian villages are perceived to be micro-units of society, production, identity and administration, and as such often form the structure on which analyses of rural life are based (Rigg 1994). Further, villages have survived hundreds of years of wars, making and breaking up of empires, famines, floods and other natural disasters as the principal social and administrative unit. But the rural social and economic structure based on class

TABLE 7.1 List of deceased farmers of Harkishanpura

S. No.	Source	Name	Father's/spouse's name	Year of suicide
1	BKU	Hari Singh	Bakhtaur Singh	14 March 1990
2	BKU	Sakhia Singh	Bhag Singh	29 March 1997
3	BKU	Nasib Kaur	Bawa Singh	18 September 1997
4	BKU	Jivan Singh	Sher Singh	7 February 1999
5	BKU	Nazar Singh	Chhota Singh	1 January 2000
6	BKU	Darshan Singh	Gaza Singh	13 November 2004
7	GoP	Sewak Singh	Mukhtiar Singh	2002
8	GoP	Gurjant Singh	Gurdial Singh	2002
9	GoP	Gurjant Singh	Gurdial Singh	2001
10	GoP	Tej Kaur	Harnek Singh	2007
11	GoP	Sukhdev Ram	Bant Ram	2001
12	GoP	Joginder Singh	Sapuran Singh	2003
13	GoP	Rashem Singh	Harnek Singh	2001
14	GoP	Balwinder Singh	Ajaib Singh	2004
15	GoP	Gursewak Singh	Shingara Singh	2003

Sources: 1. Bharatiya Kisan Union (BKU), Ugrahan, Bathinda. 2. Government of Punjab (GoP), 2009, Farmers' and Agricultural Labourers' Suicides Due to Indebtedness in the Punjab State, Department of Economics and Sociology, Punjab Agricultural University, Ludhiana.

and caste hierarchy in India and Punjab has positioned certain members of the village community in a better position to make use of the ever-expanding economic and social development opportunities in the wake of accelerated commercialization, privatization and globalization. Therefore, it is of paramount importance to look into the various socioeconomic issues of rural life with the intention to suggest some concrete policy initiatives for the betterment of the rural areas of Punjab.

This chapter analyses and documents the available natural, human, socioeconomic and environmental resources; the limitations and needs for development are also assessed for the rural and marginalized areas of Punjab. In addition, the study aims at preparing strategic developmental programmes and activities to mitigate the impact of the prevailing agrarian distress and economic instability with the focus on the agricultural sector. Therefore, in this chapter an attempt has been made to capture a microscopic view of the prevailing agrarian crisis. For this purpose, village Harkishanpura of Rampura tehsil ('tehsil' means subdivision of a district ['tehsil' means sub-district]), district Bathinda, Punjab, has been selected.

Harkishanpura: the sale story

Harkishanpura a sleepy village of Rampura tehsil of Bathinda district of Punjab, which was in the news during the late 1990s and early 2000s due to unprecedented agrarian crisis and distress. Because, in January 2001, of the negligent attitude of the state government and its agencies, the village panchayat in a meeting decided to put the entire village on sale, and for this purpose sale boards were put on all entry roads to the village, to register their protest against the non-responsive attitude of the administration. This was mainly done to draw the attention of the state and its agencies towards the prevailing and deepening agrarian distress. After this, there were many instances of other villages, which also put billboards in front of the village 'Village on Sale', in Punjab and other parts of the country due to agrarian distress. This act of the village leaders was to attract the attention of the state, national and local government agencies towards the extraordinary and unbearable distressful situation faced by the whole village. This was a rare act of solidarity of the whole village in a highly individualized capitalist-based household economy of the farmers and rural labour.

Harkishanpura village is composed of 126 households, out of which 64 households were farmers and 62 households were labourers. Total land area available was 500 hectares; out of this 474 hectares, that is 95 per cent, was net sown area, and 466 hectares, that is 98.3 per cent, of the net sown area was net irrigated area. But, during the survey, the farmers of the village reported shortage of canal irrigation water since their village was located at the tail end of the canal. The ground water of the village is of poor quality, which is unfit for irrigation. Harkishanpura village resembles other villages of the state, but mounting indebtedness due to agrarian distress and an indifferent attitude of the state pushed not only this village but several others into deep distress and socioeconomic crisis. Agrarian crisis and distress continue to multiply and deepen, but the state remained clueless about the reasons of the crisis; even efforts of agricultural scientists, economists and other experts fell short of expectations, and the disgraceful scar remained on the face of the prosperous state of the Indian Union. Other reasons for the decision to sell the village were the topography of the village land, location at the tail end of the canal irrigation system and successive failure/damage of cotton crop for several years during the 1990s due to man-made and natural factors, which resulted in piling of debt due to non-payment of loans. Though many farmers committed suicide in the village since 1990, in this analysis we include only four cases of deceased farmers and four of control group farmers from the village because the cases before 2000 are not included in the census survey conducted by Punjab Agriculture University on behalf of Punjab government on the basis of which the sample was drawn.

However, after 2005 some positive changes started appearing on the agrarian scene of the village. Notably, due to distress some of the villagers sold their land to outside rich and big farmers who installed deep bore wells to discover if there was any potable water available in the aquifer. This risk-bearing capacity of the rich farmers came handy in overcoming the irrigation water shortage due to discovery of good-quality water. Also some pressure on the government was generated to improve the canal water supply for the villages that are at the tail end of the canal. The improved water supply for irrigation, improved variety of the cotton seeds due to the arrival of Bt. cotton seeds and replacement of desi cotton were some factors that slightly reduced the impact of distress. Despite the efforts, the village is still suffering from a high degree of agrarian distress. Therefore, there is dire need to undertake concrete steps/efforts so that agrarian distress can be mitigated in the near future.

Location

Harkishanpura is a village in Rampura tehsil, Bathinda district, located two kilometres from Chandigarh-Mansa-Bathinda road in southern-west part of Punjab, India. The village has been connected by all weather road with subdivision headquarter city of Rampura and district headquarter city of Bathinda.

Land area

Land area and other sources available and optimal utilization of the same have important implications for the agricultural and economic development of the particular village/region. The information regarding the land area, irrigation and sources of irrigation of Harkishanpura village is presented in Table 7.2 and Figure 7.1.

In Harkishanpura, during 2010–11, the total land area available was 500 hectares; out of this 474 hectares, that is 95 per cent, was net sown area, and 466 hectares, that is 98.3 per cent, of the net sown area was net irrigated area. However, the gross sown area was 918 hectares, and out of these 902 hectares, that is 98.3 per cent, was gross irrigated area. The analysis of Table 7.1 suggests that gross and net area sown and area irrigated of Harkishanpura was somewhat similar to that of the overall situation

TABLE 7.2 Land area, irrigation and sources of irrigation in Harkishanpura, 2009–10

Total land area (ha)	500
Net sown area (ha)	474
Gross sown area (ha)	918
Net irrigated area (ha)	466
Gross irrigated area (ha)	902
Water table for drinking (feet)	70
Water table for irrigation (feet)	160

Source: ESO, Village Directory, Punjab, 2010–11.

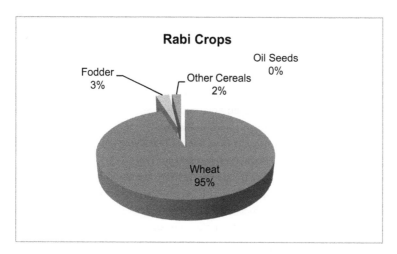

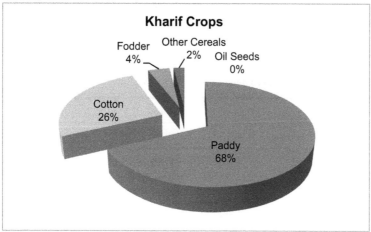

FIGURE 7.1 Distribution of gross sown area of Harkishanpura, 2010

Source: Authors.

of Punjab. But during primary survey, it has been reported that canal-irrigated areas faced problems of water shortage due to the location of the village at the tail end of the canal. It is important to note that the politically influential farmers whose farms are located upstream of the canal have been drawing more water from the canal though with illegal means. Precisely because of this reason the water supply decreases for villages located towards the tail end of the canal. Despite bringing this issue to the notice of the local administration, the local administration was paralysed by the politically influential farmers, and thus, the complaints of the downstream villages remained unheard. The non-availability of canal water limits the farmers to make use of tube well water because the farmers mix canal water with the tube well water to reduce the toxicity of ground water. The water-mixing strategy allows them at least to grow crops. The lack of canal water for irrigation resulted in low productivity of crops and often damage to crops.

Cropping pattern

A particular cropping pattern is determined by a number of factors like soil depth, soil quality, irrigation facilities, institutional framework and agriculture policy of the state. The marketing arrangements and infrastructure facilities also play an important role in determining the cropping pattern. Thus, it is determined by a combination of factors and is path dependent. The details of the existing cropping pattern of Harkishanpura village are presented in Table 7.3.

Analysis of the cropping pattern reveals that almost all the net sown area has been double cropped during Rabi and Kharif seasons. During Rabi 94.5 per cent area was under wheat and 5.5 per cent area was under other cereals, fodder and oil seeds. During the Kharif season, 68.1 per cent of the area was under paddy crop and 25.6 per cent was under cotton crop. Only 6.3 per cent area was under other cereals, fodder and oil seeds. Almost same cropping pattern has been prevailing in Malwa/cotton belt of the state. Unfortunately, sugarcane, pulses, oil seeds, other

TABLE 7.3 Rabi and Kharif cropping pattern of Harkishanpura, 2010

Rabi			*Kharif*		
Crop	*Area (ha)*	*Percentage*	*Crop*	*Area (ha)*	*Percentage*
Wheat	432	94.5	Paddy	314	68.1
Fodder	14	3.1	Cotton	118	25.6
Other cereals	10	2.2	Fodder	18	3.9
Oil seeds	1	0.2	Other cereals	10	2.2
Total	457	100	Oil seeds	1	0.2
			Total	461	100

Source: Compiled from ESO, Village Directory, Punjab, 2010–11.

cereals and vegetables have been neglected by the farmers of the village, as no area or very small area was under cultivation of these crops in the village during both Rabi and Kharif seasons. Therefore, there is the possibility and need to shift some area from the existing crops to sugarcane, pulses, oil seeds, other cereals and vegetables. The mono-culture of wheat–paddy rotation has been impinging on reduction of soil fertility. Paddy crop requires higher doses of water and generates high degree of humidity, which is adversely affecting the cotton crop. In fact, the cotton crop requires dry weather and when humidity level rises due to paddy crop, the pest attacks on the cotton crop increase. This increases pesticide use on the cotton crop, and even pesticides were unable to save the cotton crop from pest attacks. Consequently, the farmers were incurring excessive expenditure without receiving any returns. This is one important cause of growing distress among the farmers of the village.

Basic facilities and institutions

Basic facilities and institutions play an important role in the overall economic and social development of rural people. The details of existing basic facilities and institutions in Harkishanpura village are shown in Table 7.4 and Figure 7.2.

During the survey, it was reported that only one primary school and a community building/*dharmsala* were located in the village and all other basic and desired institutions were away from the village, due to which villagers were facing numerous problems. For instance, the health sub-centre and dispensary were located three kilometres from the village and the primary health centre and community health centre were ten kilometres from the village. The high school, where boys and girls

TABLE 7.4 Distance of educational, health and other institutions from Harkishanpura, 2010

Institution	Distance in kilometres
Middle school	3
High/higher secondary school	3
ITI boys/girls	27
Degree/polytechnic college	27
Health sub-centre	3
Dispensary	3
Primary health centre	10
Community health centre	10
25-bedded hospital	10
Bank	7
Focal point	3

Source: ESO, Village Directory, Punjab, 2010–11.

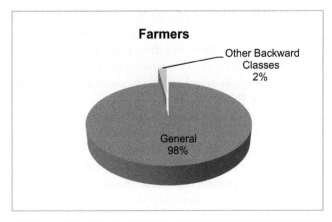

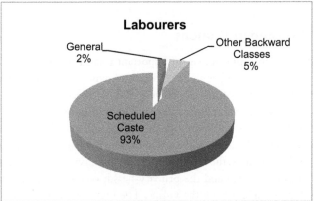

FIGURE 7.2 Distribution of households according to social category of Harkishanpura

Source: Authors.

from the village can attend school, is three kilometres from the village. It is important to understand that the skill formation technology institute and polytechnic
college were 27 kilometres from the village. However, for the ordinary degree college, the wards of the villagers need either to travel 27 kilometres one way or to stay
in or around the college. This adds huge cost to the household budget. Precisely
this may be the reason for the lack of education among the villagers and the high
dependence on agriculture for a livelihood. Analysis in this regard clearly brings
out the fact that Harkishanpura village was lacking basic facilities and institutions of
education, health and economic development.

Social categories and occupational distribution

Occupational distribution/pattern of population refers to the proportion of total
working population engaged in different economic activities: first, in primary sector

TABLE 7.5 Social category-wise distribution of households of Harkishanpura

Social category	Farmers	Labourers*	Total
General	63 (98.44)	1 (1.61)	64 (50.79)
Scheduled castes	–	58 (93.55)	58 (46.03)
Other backward classes	1 (1.56)	3 (4.83)	3 (2.38)
Total	64 (100)	62 (100)	126 (100)

Source: Field survey.

Notes: 1. * indicates agricultural and non-agricultural labourers.
2. Figures in parenthesis are percentages.

which includes agriculture, mining, fishing, animal husbandry and forestry; second, in secondary sector which consists of manufacturing, construction and electricity; and third, in tertiary/services sector which consists of trade, transport, communications, banking, insurance and personal services in an economy. Generally, economic progress and overall development are associated with changes in occupational distribution, means of production and shift of working population from primary activities to secondary, further to tertiary activities. In the present case, households' occupational distribution has been considered even though members of the households engaged in tertiary activities. Information regarding social category-wise distribution and occupational distribution of households of Harkishanpura village is shown in Table 7.5.

There were 126 households in the village; out of them 64 were farmers and 62 labourers. Further, about 98 per cent farmers' households belonged to Jat Sikhs, a general category considered an upper caste in Punjab, and around 2 per cent to other backward classes (OBCs). As far as labourers were concerned, about 94 per cent of the households belonged to scheduled castes (SCs), 5 per cent to OBCs and 2 per cent to general category. On the whole, about 51 per cent households of the village belonged to general category and 49 per cent to SCs and OBCs. Due to lack of location of institutions in the vicinity of the village, the opportunities to diversify in terms of occupational choice are scarce.

Housing conditions

Type of house and conditions of housing are important determinants of living standards and health and are also major public health issues, especially in rural areas. Poor and pitiable housing conditions are associated with a wide range of health ailments and conditions, including respiratory infections and mental health. Therefore, it is of paramount importance to look into the housing conditions of farmers and agricultural labourers of Harkishanpura village. The information regarding distribution of respondent farmers and agricultural labourer households according to type of house is presented in Table 7.6 and Figure 7.3.

TABLE 7.6 Distribution of farmers and labourers according to type of house of Harkishanpura

Type of house	Farmers	Labourers	Total
Pakka	28 (43.75)	3 (5.08)	31 (24.60)
Semi pakka	36 (56.25)	59 (95.16)	95 (75.40)
Kaccha	–	–	–
Total	64 (100)	62 (100)	126 (100)

Source: Field survey.

Note: Figures in parenthesis are percentages.

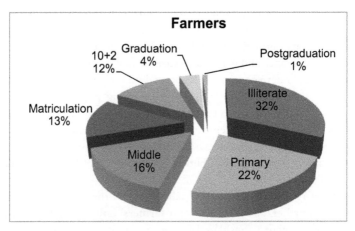

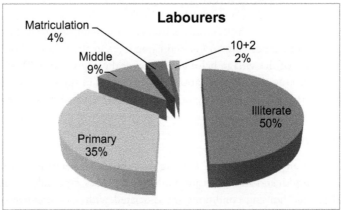

FIGURE 7.3 Distribution of farmers' and labourers' households of Harkishanpura according to level of education

Source: Authors.

Analysis of housing conditions reveals that around 75 per cent village houses were semi-*pakka* and 25 per cent were *pakka* houses. Further, housing conditions of agricultural labourers were worse as compared to farmers, as 95 per cent of the labourer households and around 56 per cent farmers had semi-*pakka* houses in the village. It can be safely concluded that housing conditions of the residents of Harkishanpura village were not satisfactory as compared with the state average and other better villages of Punjab. It needs to be mentioned here that housing and living conditions were drastically changed after the advent of the green revolution. However, the agrarian distress halted that process. Therefore, housing conditions deteriorated contrary to expected improvements.

Literacy and education level

Empirically, there is a positive and significant relationship between literacy and economic progress, and it benefits both the individuals and the communities over the period of time. Further, it is also believed and evident that literacy and education among farmers and agricultural labourers positively influence the level of agricultural productivity and its growth. It is also suggested that education among farmers and farm workers results in cost-cutting and yield-raising techniques and expansion and promotion of agricultural institutions such as co-operative marketing and banking. Education also improves wages and conditions of employment for agricultural labourers (Chaudhri 1979). In this light, an attempt has been made to examine the literacy and level of education among farmers and farm workers of Harkishanpura village; information regarding this is presented in Table 7.7 and Figure 7.4.

Level of education among the residents of Harkishanpura village showed that only six persons, that is 0.6 per cent of the population, members of farmers' households, were postgraduates. It is significant to note that as expected no member from the labourers' households reached the level of postgraduation. Further, about 41 per cent of the residents of Harkishanpura were illiterate, 28 per cent primary, 13 per cent middle, 9 per cent matriculate, 8 per cent plus two and 2 per cent graduates. An important fact that emerges from the analysis of Table 7.7 is that the female illiteracy is very high but education proportions compared with males are very low.

Analysis of education level among farmers' households and labourers' households reveals that comparatively educational achievements among labourers' households were very poor. The high share in illiteracy and low level of education among the labourers' households clearly shows the low human capital in comparison with the farm households. Another aspect of education level suggests that there are significant differences in male–female literacy and education level among farmers' and labourers' households. Therefore, analysis based on field survey in this regard amply shows that the education level in the village was very low and displays the neglect of the village by the state in terms of locating adequate facilities.

TABLE 7.7 Distribution of farmers and labourers of Harkishanpura according to level of education (persons)

Category	Farmers			Labourers			Gross total
Level	Male	Female	Total	Male	Female	Total	
Illiterate	78 (27.9)	98 (36.0)	176 (31.9)	130 (54.0)	115 (47.1)	245 (50.1)	421 (40.6)
Primary	58 (20.7)	64 (23.5)	122 (22.1)	73 (30.2)	95 (38.9)	168 (34.6)	290 (27.9)
Middle	54 (19.3)	36 (13.2)	90 (16.3)	21 (8.7)	22 (9.0)	43 (8.8)	133 (12.8)
Matriculation	38 (13.6)	34 (12.5)	72 (13.0)	10 (4.1)	8 (3.3)	18 (3.7)	90 (8.7)
10+2	36 (12.9)	30 (11.0)	66 (12.0)	8 (3.3)	4 (1.6)	12 (2.5)	78 (7.5)
Graduation	14 (5.0)	6 (2.2)	20 (3.6)	–	–	–	20 (1.9)
Postgraduation	2 (0.7)	4 (1.5)	6 (1.1)	–	–	–	6 (0.6)
Total	280 (100)	272 (100)	552 (100)	242 (100)	244 (100)	486 (100)	1,038 (100)

Source: Field survey.

Note: Figures in parenthesis are percentages.

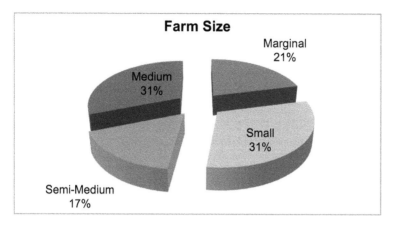

FIGURE 7.4 Distribution of farmers according to land-size category of Harkishanpura

Source: Authors.

Farm size, owned and leased land

Size of the landholding is an important determinant of agricultural development. Fragmentation of ownership landholdings in India is a major challenge and problem before Indian and Punjab agriculture, as the majority of the farmers are small and marginal. This leads to the conclusion that majority of landholdings in India are too small to be economically viable to promote modern agricultural development. Farmers, especially marginal, small and semi-medium, leased in land of others to survive in agriculture, which makes their operational landholdings viable to some extent. An attempt has been made to study the size-wise distribution of farmers of Harkishanpura, their owned and leased in land; information regarding this has been presented in Table 7.8 and Figure 7.5.

Farm size-wise distribution of farmers of Harkishanpura shows that there was not a single large farm household having more than ten hectares of farm in the village. The distribution of farmers in this regard reveals that around 20 per cent farmers were marginal, 31 per cent small, 17 per cent semi-medium and 31 per cent medium farmers in the village. Analysis also reveals that a very big chunk of the village land has been owned by medium category of farmers. This compelled the small, marginal and semi-medium farmer categories to look for land to lease in to make their operational landholding viable as the maximum land on lease in the village was with these categories of the farmers. Therefore, analysis depicts that small and marginal farmers were dominant category in this village. Small and marginal farmers cannot achieve and realize the desired level of economies of scale of operation. Keeping in view the market conditions and required level of mechanization, the small and marginal categories of farming turned non-viable. Precisely due to this very fact, the village has been facing severe agrarian distress compared to other villages.

TABLE 7.8 Farm size-wise, ownership and leased in landholdings-wise distribution of farmers of Harkishanpura village

Farm category holding type	Number	Ownership (ha)	Leased in (ha)
Marginal (<1 ha)	13 (20.31)	10.13 (5.36)	1.62 (9.52)
Small (1–2 ha)	20 (31.25)	24.91 (13.18)	6.08 (35.72)
Semi-medium (2–4 ha)	11 (17.19)	31.19 (16.51)	7.70 (45.24)
Medium (4–10 ha)	20 (31.25)	122.72 (64.95)	1.62 (9.52)
Total	64 (100)	188.95 (100)	17.02 (100)

Source: Field survey.

Note: Figures in parenthesis are percentages.

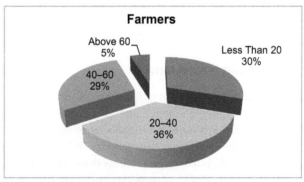

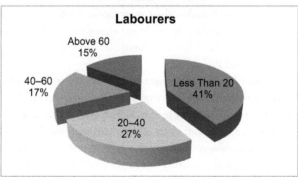

FIGURE 7.5 Distribution of farmers and labourers according to age in years of Harkishanpura

Age-wise distribution

Age is one of the important personal factors that influence and determine the other variables of economic progress. Therefore, it is helpful and required to study the age-wise analysis of the respondents. In this study, an attempt has been made to capture

TABLE 7.9 Age-wise and sex-wise distribution of farmers' and labourers' population of Harkishanpura

Age (Years)	Farmers			Labourers			Total		Gross total
	Male	Female	Total	Male	Female	Total	Male	Female	
Less than 20	98	84	182	116	106	222	214	190	404
	(31.4)	(28.2)	(29.8)	(43.9)	(38.7)	(41.3)	(37.2)	(33.2)	(35.2)
20–40	108	111	219	76	66	142	184	177	361
	(34.6)	(37.3)	(35.9)	(28.8)	(24.1)	(26.4)	(31.9)	(30.9)	(31.5)
40–60	95	81	176	35	58	93	130	140	269
	(30.5)	(27.2)	(28.9)	(13.3)	(21.1)	(17.3)	(22.6)	(24.5)	(23.4)
Above 60	11	22	33	37	44	81	48	66	114
	(3.5)	(7.4)	(5.4)	(14.0)	(16.1)	(15.1)	(8.3)	(11.5)	(9.9)
Total	312	298	610	264	274	538	576	572	1,148
	(100)	(100)	(100)	(100)	(100)	(100)	(100)	(100)	(100)

Source: Field survey.

Note: Figures in parenthesis are percentages.

these variables of the farmers and agricultural labourers of Harkishanpura village. The information and data regarding age-wise distribution of respondents are presented in Table 7.9.

Total population of the village was 1,148 persons; out of it 610 belonged to farmers' households and 538 persons to labourers' households and 576 were males and 572 females. Age-wise distribution shows that 35.2 per cent population was below the age of 20 years, 31.5 per cent between 20 and 40 years, 23.4 per cent between 40 and 60 years and 9.9 per cent above 60 years of age. It is significant to notice that the younger age group of population is predominant in the village, which is tantamount to 'demographic dividend'. Age-wise and sex-wise analysis of population of the village reveals that there were no differences in age-wise distribution of farmers' and labourers' households, but sex ratio of labourers' households seems to be balanced as compared to farmers' households. On the whole, the sex ratio in general and age-specific sex ratios in particular were almost balanced.

Agricultural implements

General agricultural practices and farming techniques have been changed and evolved over the period of time as various agricultural implements and machines are being used for ploughing, seeding and harvesting purposes. Modern agricultural implements and machinery have made farm operations easier and fast and have helped farmers in their farm work minimize the use of manual workforce and

TABLE 7.10 Agricultural machinery in Harkishanpura

Machinery	Number
Tractors	22
Harvest combine	1
Electric-operated tube wells	70
Diesel-operated tube wells	15

Source: Field survey.

also have immensely improved the production and productivity. In this light, here an attempt has been made to look at the use of agricultural machinery and implements in Harkishanpura village; details of agricultural machinery and implements are shown in Table 7.10.

On the whole, there were 22 tractors with farmers of Harkishanpura, one harvesting combine, 70 electric-operated tube wells and 15 diesel-operated tube wells. Mechanization of agriculture of the village seems to be in line with Punjab agriculture.

Consumption pattern and expenditure

Consumption pattern and consumption expenditure of households are vital and key indicators of household member's well-being, which includes expenditure on housing, energy, education, health, social ceremonies, transport and food, and it accounts for a greater part, that is roughly more than 50 per cent of the household's income. In this analysis consumption expenditure is decomposed into three parts, namely expenditures on durable goods, expenditures on non-durable goods and expenditures on services. Information and details of consumption expenditure of farmers' and labourers' households of Harkishanpura village are presented in Table 7.11.

The consumption expenditure is classified into three sub-categories of consumption expenditure on non-durables, services and durables. Residents of the village incurred around 75 per cent expenditure on consumer non-durable items, about 22 per cent on services and the remaining around 4 per cent on durable goods. Furthermore, in the non-durable consumption expenditure, cereals, grocery and milk were the dominant items, and these were accounted for more than 50 per cent of the annual average consumption expenditure. Under the category of services expenditure, the major items were education, health and travel and transport. As far as the annual average expenditure and consumption pattern of farmers and labourers were concerned, no significant differences could be ascertained. Almost similar consumption pattern has been seen among the labourers' and farmers' households of the village. Therefore,

TABLE 7.11 Annual average consumption expenditure of farmers' and labourers' households of Harkishanpura (rupees)

Type of expenditure	Consumption items	Farmers	Labourers	All
Non-durable	Cereals	18,590.63 (21.1)	13,524.19 (22.1)	16,097.1 (20.3)
	Milk and milk products	10,192.19 (11.5)	6,955.48 (11.4)	8,599.5 (10.8)
	Grocery	18,043.75 (20.4)	17,122.58 (28.0)	17,590.5 (22.2)
	Cloths	4,390.63 (4.9)	2,398.39 (3.9)	3,410.3 (4.3)
	Vegetables	7,290.63 (8.3)	5,054.03 (8.3)	6,190.1 (7.8)
	Ceremonies/marriages	5,103.14 (5.8)	9,838.71 (1.6)	7,433.3 (9.4)
	Sub-total	63,610.97 (72.0)	54,893.38 (75.2)	59,320.8 (74.8)
Services	Education	5,935.94 (6.7)	1,440.48 (2.4)	3,723.9 (4.7)
	Health	6,842.22 (7.7)	3,582.90 (5.9)	5,238.4 (6.6)
	Transport and travel	2,410.94 (2.7)	2,834.68 (4.6)	2,619.4 (3.3)
	Telephone	1,618.75 (1.8)	872.58 (1.4)	1,251.6 (1.6)
	Home electricity	5,009.38 (5.7)	3,503.06 (5.7)	4,268.2 (5.4)
	Sub-total	21,817.23 (24.7)	12,233,70 (20.0)	17,101.5 (21.6)
Durable	Durable	2,875.00 (3.3)	2,908.06 (4.8)	2,891.3 (3.6)
Grand total		88,303.20 (100)	70,035.16 (100)	79,313.8 (100)

Source: Field survey.

Note: Figures in parenthesis are percentages.

analysis suggests that residents of the village had simple subsistence consumption pattern.

Capital expenditure

Capital expenditure means expenditure on upgrading, purchasing and investing in assets and fixed assets which generate income and benefit in the future. From the viewpoint of agricultural investment, the purchase of land, land improvements, installation of bore wells and purchase of agricultural machinery are the major capital expenditures. Capital expenditure positively and significantly contributes to the agrarian economy and economy of the farmers. Therefore, ideally it is important to look into the capital expenditure incurred by the farmers and agricultural labourers of Harkishanpura. Information and data regarding capital expenditure of various types are compiled and presented in Table 7.12.

The capital expenditure incurred by the farmers during 2010–12 has been classified into three categories: expenditure on inputs, fixed assets and others. Analysis suggests that distribution of average annual capital expenditure was 85 per cent on agricultural inputs, 8 per cent on machinery and 7 per cent on others, including loan repayment. Under capital expenditure on inputs, expenditure on labour,

TABLE 7.12 Annual average capital expenditure of farmers of Harkishanpura, 2010

Expenditure	Items	Expenditure (rupees)	Percentage
Inputs	Labour (all types)	16,046.86	24.44
	Diesel/lubricants	9,476.56	14.43
	Fertilizers	12,156.25	18.52
	Pesticides	12,640.63	19.26
	Seeds	5,173.44	7.88
	Electricity for agriculture	–	–
Fixed assets	Machinery	5,887.50	8.21
Others	Transport and travel	3,893.75	5.93
	Loan repayment	828.13	1.26
	Any other	31.25	0.05
Total		65,634.38	100

Source: Field survey.

pesticides, fertilizers, diesel and lubricants and seeds were the major items. Further, little expenditure has been incurred on fixed assets and machinery and other expenses like loan repayments and travel and transport costs. This may be due to low level of income of the farmers and higher level of debt accumulation and indebtedness of the farmers. Therefore, it is urgently required that the incomes of the farmers may be supplemented so that the farmers on the brink may be saved and the deceased would suitably be rehabilitated.

Outstanding loan against farmers and agricultural labourers: extent and sources

In this section, an attempt has been made to examine the important indicators of indebtedness among farmers and agricultural labourers of Harkishanpura village. The selected indicators are farm size-category-wise distribution of total debt, per farm household debt, per acre debt and sources of indebtedness. The information relating to these indicators of farmers and agricultural labourers has been presented in Tables 7.13 to 7.15.

Analysis of total debt against different farm categories shows that the share of marginal farmers was 10.5 per cent, small farmers 22 per cent, semi-medium 14.8 per cent and medium farmers 52.7 per cent in the village. It is important to note that average per acre debt was highest in the case of marginal farmers, that is Rs 58,213, Rs 46,118 against small farmers, Rs 24,634 against semi-medium farmers and Rs 27,483 against medium farmers. As far as per farmer household average debt is concerned, it was Rs 253,453 against the farm households of the village. Analysis shows that it was highest in the case of medium farmers and lowest in the case of

TABLE 7.13 Farm size-category-wise distribution of amount of indebtedness among Harkishan-pura farmers (rupees)

Category	Total debt	Per acre debt	Per farmer debt
Marginal (up to 2.5 acres)	1,710,000 (10.5)	58,213	131,538
Small (2.5–5 acres)	3,573,000 (22.0)	46,118	178,650
Semi-medium (5–10 acres)	2,395,000 (14.8)	24,634	217,727
Medium (10–25 acres)	8,543,000 (52.7)	27,483	427,150
Total	16,221,000 (100)	31,502	253,453

Source: Field survey.

Note: Figures in parenthesis are percentages.

TABLE 7.14 Source-wise distribution of outstanding debt against farmers of Harkishanpura (rupees)

Institutional (only)	
Commercial bank	820,000 (5.1)
Co-operatives	–
Commercial bank and co-operatives	673,000 (4.1)
Sub-total	1,493,000 (9.2)
Non-institutional (only)	
Commission agent	615,000 (3.8)
Relative	–
Commission agent and relative	400,000 (2.5)
Sub-total	1,015,000 (6.3)
Multiple sources	
Multiple sources	13,713,000 (84.5)
Grand total	16,221,000 (100)

Source: Field survey.

Note: Figures in parenthesis are percentages.

marginal farmers. It can be concluded that the farmers of the village across size categories and classes were indebted.

Analysis of source-wise distribution of outstanding debt against farmers of Harkishanpura clearly shows that maximum amount has been borrowed from multiple sources, that is institutional and non-institutional. The survey results reveal that 84.5 per cent amount of outstanding debt against farmers was from multiple sources and mainly from informal lenders. However, the share of institutional sources was

TABLE 7.15 Source-wise distribution of outstanding amount of debt against agricultural labourers of Harkishanpura

Sources	Debt
Commercial bank	110,000 (7.7)
Co-operatives	–
Commission agent	–
Farmers	900,000 (62.8)
Relatives	79,000 (5.5)
Others	344,000 (24.0)
Total	1,433,000 (100)

Source: Field survey.

Note: Figures in parenthesis are percentages.

9.2 per cent of the total debt and 6.3 per cent of non-institutional sources. It can be concluded that for borrowing funds, the farmers of all the farm categories prefer multiple sources of loan.

An attempt has also been made to look into the source-wise distribution of outstanding amount of debt against agricultural labourers of the village. The analysis of the survey results clearly brings out the fact that farmers were the leading source of outstanding debt against agricultural labourers, followed by others, commercial banks and relatives. The share of farmers in total outstanding amount of debt against agricultural labourers was 62.8 per cent, others 24 per cent, commercial banks 7.7 per cent and relatives 5.5 per cent. This clearly shows that agricultural labourers of the village were indebted mainly to farmers of the village.

Plight of deceased and control group farmers of Harkishanpura

To investigate ground realities and gravity of the agrarian distress, this study recounts the plight of the deceased and control group farmers as explained by farmers and nearest relatives. It is important and desirable to look into the individual cases of both the group of famers to gauge the ground realities and situation in the country side. Here, in this light, an attempt in this section is made to present some selected severely distressed cases of deceased.

Deceased farmers

1   Jivan Singh, son of Sher Singh, committed suicide in 2000. His father reported that indebtedness and economic distress were the main causes of suicide of his son. He was indebted to multiple sources, that is commercial bank (Rs 3 lakhs) and commission agent (Rs 4.5 lakhs). The family has sold 3.5 acres of land,

out of which 1.5 acres to big farmers and two acres to a commission agent for repayment of debt. Recently, eight-acre land has been mortgaged to a bank. The economic condition of family was miserable.

2   Balbir Kaur, wife of Gurcharan Singh, committed suicide on 6 June 2001. Her son said that indebtedness and pressure exerted by lenders for repayment of debt were the cause of suicide. Family has indebted Rs 1.80 lakhs towards commercial banks, 45,000 towards co-operatives and Rs 276,000 towards commission agent. The family has been compelled to sell one acre of land for repayment of debt. Now the household was cultivating eight acres of land.

3   Malkeet Kaur, wife of Gurjant Singh, committed suicide in 2002. Her husband reported indebtedness and pressure by the lenders as the cause of suicide. The family was indebted to multiple sources: Rs 2.25 lakhs to commercial banks, Rs 40,000 to co-operatives, Rs 80,000 to commission agents and Rs 30,000 to relatives. The family had sold 2.5 acres of land and now has only three acres of land to cultivate. The family's economic condition is very appalling, and they were thinking of selling the remaining land to clear the debt.

4   Shavia Singh, son of Bhag Singh, committed suicide in 2002. The family had Rs 1.11 lakh debt owned to the commercial bank. His brother reported that indebtedness and economic distress were the main causes of suicide of his brother. The family has only two acres of land, and the economic condition of the family was precarious.

Control group farmers

1   Makhan Singh, wife of Gurchet Singh, has five acres land, out of which 2.5 acres of land was mortgaged out to a big farmer of the village. The remaining 2.5 acres of land is at the tail end of canal and has been facing the problem of shortage of water for irrigation. The family was indebted Rs 2.25 lakhs to commercial bank and Rs 2 lakhs to a commission agent. The economic condition of the family was very poor and shocking.

2   Bishaka Singh, son of Gurmukh Singh, has two acres of land. The family has been indebted Rs 1 lakh to a commercial bank, Rs 32,000 to co-operatives and Rs 4 lakhs to a commission agent. The economic condition of the family was in bad shape and planning to abandon cultivation.

3   Gurmeet Singh, son of Bhag Singh, has five acres of land, out of which two acres is draught-prone land, so he has been incurring a loss of Rs 70,000 annually from this land. The family owes Rs 1.4 lakhs to a commercial bank, Rs 35,000 to co-operatives, Rs 1.5 lakhs to a commission agent and Rs 1 lakh to relatives. The economic condition of the family was miserable.

4   Roop Singh, son of Puran Singh, of Harkishanpura village has only two acres of land, and this land is at the tail end of canal; consequently, the family has been facing the problem of shortage of water for irrigation. The family is indebted Rs 1.25 lakhs to a commercial bank, Rs 25,000 to co-operatives and Rs 15,000 to a commission agent. The economic condition of the family was precarious.

Understanding sale story of the village

When India adopted liberalization and globalization public policy in July 1991, Punjab was facing social turmoil. During the decade and a half period of turmoil, the governance institutional system in Punjab turned dysfunctional. The institutional support to the agricultural sector was jeopardized, and public capital formation collapsed. With increasing liberalization and privatization, there emerged the instability of prices, especially of cotton crop input, and consequently, input cost increased multiple times. Furthermore, institutional credit support was relatively dried up and informal private lenders increased. As a consequence, the surplus of the farmers declined along with increasing cost of living due to high cost of services (education and health) used by the population. The repeated cotton crop failure due to pest attacks by the American bollworm and non-availability of canal water as the village is located at the tail end of the canal added fuel to the fire. This has resulted into borrowings from all possible sources irrespective of the cost of credit. In the absence of the capacity and capability to repaying the borrowed money, the farmers and agricultural labourers were into a debt trap. Even the whole village borrowed very costly money from HOUSEFED, a Punjab government society, at 16 per cent interest. This loan amount was meant for the construction of houses, but none of the villagers constructed houses but used this money either to repay the money to the informal lenders or the institutional loan due to pressure of these agencies for recovery of loans. The estimated burden of debt when the village panchayat put the notice in front of the village 'Village on Sale' was of the order of Rs 89 lakhs (Rangi, Sidhu and Sachdeva 2005).

The intensity of the debt burden on the small and marginal farmers was much higher compared with the large-sized category of farmers of the village. On an average, the marginal farmers were having Rs 151,645 debt per operated hectare. The small farmers were having Rs 121,964 debt per operated hectare. Thus, there is an inverse relationship between farm size and debt burden, that is large-sized farmers having lower debt burden and small-sized farmers having heavy debt burden. The source-wise borrowings reveal the fact that nearly 48 per cent of the credit advanced to Harkishanpura was by the informal lenders popularly known as 'Commission Agents', in the local language 'Arthiyas'. This share of debt for marginal and small farmers was 45.86 per cent and 48.68 per cent, respectively (Rangi, Sidhu and Sachdeva 2005).

During our field survey visits and interaction with the villagers, it was revealed that the farmers and the labourers had tried every best possible way to return the loans raised. Repeated crop failure, low yields and volatility in the output prices reduced their income/returns from farming. In the absence of repayable capacity, some of the farmers sold out their only prized possession, that is 'land'. Despite the fact that they sold out 600 acres of land, this was not sufficient to get out of the debt trap. Since the individual farmers and their strategy to get out of the debt trap did not succeed, they continuously faced threat from the informal lenders and government agencies to auction their land. This has forced the villagers to unite themselves and fight to save their only source of livelihood, that is land. The village panchayat not only put in the outskirts of the village the billboard that the village was on sale but resisted attempts of the lenders to auction the land. Instead, the villagers unitedly brought their distress to the notice of the government at the helm of affairs as well as to the general public that distress is man-made and other villages will also follow suite and put before the villages notices displaying village on sale. While showing unity in the difficult circumstances, the villagers decided to lose their prized posses-sion in exchange of some alternative remunerative future arrangements of their livelihood. However, temporarily they remained successful in not allowing the agricultural land to be auctioned by the creditors. Then there comes new seed of Bt-cotton which replaced the highly pest-prone desi/indigenous variety of cotton as well as the discovery of potable groundwater from the deeper aquifer around 400 feet. This temporarily changed the fortune of the villagers along with union governments' loan waiver, reduction of interest rates and increased inflow of agriculture credit. Despite all this, the indebtedness situation of the villagers has been deepening due to lack of alternative employment opportunities and supplementary occupations. The political leadership has been preoccupied in privatization mode to use state power to establish and secure its business, instead of working towards the solution of the problems faced by the people in the countryside. The ruling elite changed their character from gentlemen politi-cians to business tycoons that have left the masses to fend for themselves in the growing onslaught of the market-oriented economy. The deepening agrarian distress and growing economic difficulties for the poor and the destitute in fact is the opportunity for the rich and the political influential class to grab land. This has started the process of depeasantization at a much fast rate. As a result of it iniquities in every sphere have increased at a scale which is unprecedented compared with the era of state-led economic development.

Conclusions

The village on sale story shows the intensity of the agrarian distress prevailing in the rural areas of Punjab. The agrarian distress is very much rooted in the very structure of the economic activities in which the economic agents of production are engaged in. The analysis of sources of irrigation of land area suggests that gross and net areas sown and irrigated were similar to that of Punjab, but during primary survey it has been reported that canal-irrigated area faced problems of water short-age due to the location of the village on the tail end of the canal, which resulted in low productivity and damage to crops in the village. Wheat, paddy and cotton were the dominating crops of the village. Almost same cropping pattern prevailed in Malwa/cotton belt of the state. Unfortunately, sugarcane, pulses, oil seeds, other cereals and vegetables have been neglected by the farmers of the village as no area or very small area was under cultivation of these crops in the village. Mechanization of agriculture of the village seems to be in line with Punjab agriculture. About 98 per cent farmers' households belonged to Jat Sikhs, a general category considered upper caste in Punjab, and around 2 per cent to OBCs. As far as labourers were concerned, about 94 per cent belonged to SCs, 5 per cent to OBCs and 2 per cent to general category. On the whole, about 51 per cent of the households of the village belong to general category and 49 per cent to SCs and OBCs. It can be safely concluded that housing conditions of the residents of Harkishanpura village are not satisfactory and thus needs better houses to reside. Age-wise and sex-wise analysis of population of the village reveals that there were no differences in age-wise distribution of farmers' and labourers' households, but sex ratio of labourers' households seems to be balanced as compared to farmers' households. On the whole, sex ratio in general and age-specific sex ratios in particular were almost balanced.

Primary school and community building/*dharmsala* were located in the village and all other basic and desired institutions were away from the village, due to which villagers were facing numerous problems. Analysis in this regard clearly manifests that Harkishanpura was lacking basic facilities and institutions of education, health and economic development. As far as the annual average expenditure and consumption pattern of farmers and labourers were concerned, no significant differences have been reported. Almost a similar consumption pattern has been seen among the labourers' and farmers' households of the village. Therefore, analysis suggests that residents of the village have simple subsistence consumption pattern. Further, little expenditure has been incurred on fixed assets and machinery and other expenses like loan repayments and travel and transport costs. This may be due to low level of income of the farmers, which results in debt accumulation and indebtedness of the farmers. Therefore, it is urgently required that the incomes of the farmers may be supplemented so that the farmers on the brink may be saved and deceased would suitably be rehabilitated.

Notes

1 During the survey and visits to the village Harkishanpura, the survey team has been apprised of availability of spurious seeds, fertilizers and pesticides in the market as the main causes of cotton crop failure in the cotton belt of Punjab.
2 The panchayat of the village made efforts to bring to the notice of the political leadership the deep-rooted distress due to repeated failure of crops due to non-availability of canal water and American bollworm on cotton crop. However, the government remained complacent towards the demand of the village regarding attending to their problems. The village panchayat and elders of the village came out with a solution to put up a notice at the entry points of the village as well as inside the village 'Village on Sale'. This, in fact, drew the attention of various organizations such as Punjab Agriculture University, Ludhiana, newspapers and others concerned. The village distress came to the notice of state- and national-level agencies (for a detailed account for this, see TNS 2002; Rangi, Sidhu and Sachdeva 2005).

3 It is pertinent to note that the visit of the minister to the village ignited hope for possible solution to the suffering villagers. The village leaders made a plea before the minister – Ms. Rajinder Kaur Bhattal, minister for agriculture and rural development – to set up industry while taking over the land of the village. Each village member demanded a secured employment in the proposed factory for earning livelihood which will save them from the increasing debt burden. The minister promised to establish industry and accord special status to the village, apart from several improvements in terms of better supply of canal irrigation, water and electricity and upgrading the village school. However, when we visited the village nearly after a decade the promises were made, nothing had happened on the ground.

8

SUMMARY, CONCLUSIONS AND POLICY SUGGESTIONS

Agrarian distress has been the result of multiple causes, but indebtedness and indebtedness-related factors were identified to be the most vital factor of rural distress and the precursor of farmer and agricultural labourer suicides. Indian agriculture has undergone some major structural changes during 2001–13 that have enhanced the market-induced vulnerability of farmers, especially small and marginal ones. As a consequence, agriculture has been progressively acquiring the small farm character, which affected the income and expenditure of the cultivators. Also, agricultural labourers mainly derive their livelihood from wage employment in agriculture. Economically, socially and politically, they are the marginalized, overworked, underprivileged and underpaid section of the Indian population but indispensable to agricultural operations.

Agrarian distress is stressful behaviour arising out of social, economic and psychological factors, and overwhelmingly, a common result of this stress has been the indebtedness-led economic distress and farm suicides across the country. Other contributing factors to agrarian crisis and farmer and agricultural labourer distress have been identified: crop collapse on many counts, consistently lower prices for agricultural produce disproportionate to the prices of farm inputs, unavailability and inferior quality of inputs, failure of research and extension services, mounting indebtedness from both institutional and non-institutional sources that resulted in a debt trap, and the exploitation of farmers (especially small and marginal ones) by informal lenders. And interlocked input–output product markets have deepened the misery and distress of farmers and caused severe agony and economic stress.

This book has looked into the causes of such persistent agrarian distress and farmer and agricultural labourer suicides, and it suggests policy initiatives to alleviate rural distress. The study described here was conducted to ascertain the causes of prevailing agrarian crisis in Punjab agriculture and distress among farmers and agricultural labourers. Further, the study was done to examine the purpose and use pattern of agricultural credit, to identify factors precipitating indebtedness and suicides in the state and to identify the socioeconomic profile of the deceased farmers and agricultural labourers and the control group of farmers and agricultural labourers. The study also attempted to gauge the intensity of the agrarian crisis over space and time by analysing a unique data set, covering the period 2000 to 2013, of Punjab based on a census survey. Finally, the study was performed to assess the main causes of suicides among agricultural labourers and farmers, to draw comparisons between the deceased and the on-the-brink/control group on various counts and to suggest relevant policy implications and policy changes that would mitigate these serious problems.

A discussion, a review of studies and an analysis of agrarian distress and rural suicides revealed that the agrarian distress is deep rooted and complex and demands a detailed and deeper investigation. Evidently, the collapse of public investment in agriculture, along with public institutions catering to farmers and farming, aggravated the problem. Further, the changing agrarian political economy demonstrates that agriculture is facing a severe crisis and a heavy and unbearable burden of debt against farmers and agricultural labourers, especially small and marginal ones, from informal sources of credit, and it leads in increasing the incidence of suicides among farmers and agricultural labourers. The literature has also discussed and shed light on the issues of economic distress, the agrarian crisis, the causes and magnitude of indebtedness and of suicides and finally possible remedial measures. Solutions suggested for agrarian distress include access and equity in irrigation, access to institutional credit, especially to small and marginal farmers, delinking input–output product markets, strengthening of research and extension services in agriculture, providing inputs at affordable prices and diversifying the economy, especially for Punjab's rural areas. Due to divergent estimates and conclusions, a precise and concrete idea and solution regarding the crisis remains lacking. Further, most of the studies on the subject have ignored and neglected agricultural labourers, who are an important section of rural Punjab and indispensable to agriculture. Reports suggest that agricultural labourers were also under great distress due to the prolonged and prevailing agrarian crisis, and many of them have died by suicide in the past couple decades. At the same time, some gaps in the research remain, and some studies have been found to be incoherent. Thus, in this study, an attempt has been made to overcome the shortcomings and fulfil the gaps that emerged from the literature survey.

A comparative state-level picture of farm suicides shows that major agricultural states of India are facing the severe agrarian distress and the problem of farm suicides. Further, the comparative per one lakh rates of suicides among the general population and among all cultivators and main cultivators show that the main cultivators and all cultivators of India were under agrarian distress, due to which they resorted to suicide. Recently, the agriculturally advanced states of Punjab, specifically Haryana, Gujarat and Karnataka, having large irrigation facilities and high agricultural production and yield levels, witnessed a surge in farm suicides.

For the purpose of the analysis in this book, Punjab has been divided into two parts. First, the highly agrarian–distressed districts mainly cover the Malwa region and, second, the less agrarian-distressed districts of the Shiwalik foothills, Doaba and Majha. All indicators of the extent of farm suicides in Punjab reveal that farmers and agricultural labourers of the state are facing a severe crisis and dying by suicide due to the crisis. Punjab's Malwa region is highly distressed and prone to farm suicide, the main reason for which seems to be the high dependence of small and marginal farmers on agriculture without supplementing their income with farm-related and non-farm-related activities. Thus, the suicide-prone small and marginal farmers of these districts have their main stay in agriculture and rely less on non-farm-related activities.

The overriding reason for the farm suicides identified in this research was debt: a large majority of the farm suicides occurred for this reason. In Punjab, small and marginal farmers have been facing severe and cruel agrarian distress, and they deserve supportive, remedial measures.

Further, the deceased farmers who have died by suicide due to reasons other than debt were small and marginal farmers who belonged to highly agrarian-distressed districts, and only a small number of them belonged to less-agrarian-distressed districts. The real reason behind the farmer suicides may be related to the agricultural sector of the economy, in that these farmers fall into distressed areas of the state and distressed sections of the farming community. The trend of farm labour suicides was found to be similar to that of farmer suicides in that the leading cause in both cases was debt. It can be concluded that, on the whole, the agrarian sector of Punjab is in the grip of agrarian crisis.

This study was undertaken to investigate why some of the farmers and agricultural labourers died by suicide and why others are still surviving. This study, based on a primary survey covering 1392 rural households from three districts of the Malwa region of Punjab, has examined why farmers and agricultural labourers have died by suicide. This study is unique and the first of its kind to examine the factors that have allowed some to survive and others to die by suicide. The policy lessons that have emerged from this study are useful both for Punjab and for the other agrarian-distressed states in India.

The socioeconomic profile of the deceased group and the control group of farmers and agricultural labourers suggests that all the developmental blocks of the three districts have received/required representation in the sample. Further, highly distressed villages of all the blocks of the three districts have also been given adequate representation in the sample. We can conclude that the sample drawn was a representative sample and that findings based on this sample may be generalized.

As far as the age distribution of the deceased group of farmers and agricultural labourers was concerned, a large number were below age 35, which is young group. This group of farmers was found to be highly distressed: this age group had the highest number of suicides. Similar trends have been noticed in the case of control group farmers and agricultural labourers in age distribution across the developmental blocks of the three districts. This demonstrates the emerging stress and hardships faced by young and middle-aged farmers in tolerating and enduring the agrarian crisis. This analysis shows that the distress engulfed also the women of the households of farmers and agricultural labourers, as some women also died by suicide due to economic distress.

The high incidence of suicides among Jat Sikh farmers indicates that they did not seem to compromise over social values and loss of social status, and also those economic factors are not sparing Jat Sikh farmers, irrespective of their caste hierarchy. Analysis of the deceased farmers and agricultural labourers suggests that a large majority of them belonged to the Sikh religion. In the case of control group farmers and agricultural labourers in all the developmental blocks, a similar age distribution has been reported. It emerged from the incidence of suicides among Sikh farmers and agricultural labourers that agrarian distress undermined their existing religious values. Lack of education among deceased farmers and agricultural labourers and control group farmers and agricultural labourers was evident: none of the respondents was a postgraduate or professionally qualified, and only a few were graduates. This not only limits the occupational choices of the farmers but also results in farmers failing to grasp the nitty-gritty of modern agriculture and increases their dependency on non-viable traditional agriculture and on costly non-institutional (informal) sources of credit. The comparatively higher percentage of unmarried farmers and agricultural labourers among the deceased group may be due to an absence of support from spouses during this crisis.

The analysis of the farm-size distribution of operational landholdings of deceased and control group farmers reveals that the concentration of small and marginal farmers does not generate enough income to buy modern agricultural implements and farm inputs and to make heavy investments in agriculture. Having only a small or marginal-size farm, accompanied with the fragmentation of landholdings, also prevents farmers using new farm machinery and other costly farm inputs, and any attempt to buy such inputs leads to debt. An analysis of the average size of landholdings of deceased and control group farmers suggests that there was no difference, and similar landholding sizes have been reported for these farmers at the overall level and at the district levels. Further, the average landholding size reported in this study has also been similar to those prevailing in Punjab.

The finding from the field survey reveals that the deceased and control group of small and marginal farmers were heavily indebted: their (small and marginal farmers) share in the total debt of the sampled households was 75 per cent. Interestingly, a negligible burden of debt has been reported in the case of the medium and large farmers category of the deceased and the control groups. Thus, there is an inverse relationship between farm size and burden of debt; as farm size increases, the burden of debt decreases. This undoubtedly shows that small and marginal farmers of both groups have been under great distress and dying by suicide. The indicators of average outstanding loan per deceased and control group farmer and agricultural labourer households suggest that they were heavily indebted. A source-based analysis of indebtedness suggests comparatively greater indebtedness among deceased farmers who borrowed money from non-institutional sources and multiple sources, which indicates that economic distress they faced may be the cause of their suicides.

An analysis of the causes for the deceased and control group of farmers and agricultural labourers not paying their outstanding loans reveals that low incomes from agriculture, crop failures, crop damage and widespread indebtedness among these strata of population in rural Punjab were the real culprits for the prevailing situation in the agrarian sector of the state economy. This level of agrarian distress suggests that the marginalization of agriculture and the prevailing agrarian crisis should be attributed to the economic crisis in Punjab. Incommensurate prices for farm products, low and stagnated yields, decreases in net farm incomes, successive crop failures and high and increasing costs of cultivation have landed the small and marginal farmers in a debt trap and led to suicides.

Modes farmer and agricultural labourer suicides across the blocks of the three districts and at the overall level clearly relate to farm operations. The most commonly used method of suicide was consumption of insecticides/pesticides since they are easily available in the farms or in the households.

The analysis of contributing/provoking factors for farmer and agricultural labourer suicides suggests that economic distress–led indebtedness and indebtedness-led humiliation were the driving force of suicides. A similar situation and similar trends have been witnessed across the blocks of the three districts and at the overall level in this regard.

Many deceased farmers' households have sold, mortgaged and leased out land after the suicides to pay debts and then left agriculture due to the death of the farmer as the sole household earner. This phenomenon has been observed and reported across the developmental blocks of the three districts and at the overall level. This shows that suicides hit hard the economy of the deceased farmers and agricultural farmers across the three districts. Therefore, it is urgently suggested that the rehabilition of the families of the deceased farmers and agricultural farmers be prioritized by the state.

A microscopic analysis of Harkishanpura village suggests that gross and net areas sown and irrigated were comparatively similar to that of Punjab, but during the primary survey, it has been reported that canal-irrigated areas faced water shortages due to the location of the village at the tail end of the canal, which resulted in low productivity and damaged crops in the village. The cropping pattern of the village under investigation was highly concentrated. It was mainly wheat, paddy and cotton crops, which used a similar cropping pattern to the one prevailing in Malwa/ the cotton belt of the state. Unfortunately, sugarcane, pulses, oil seeds, other cereals and vegetables have been neglected by the farmers of the village in that no area or negligible area was reported as cultivating these crops in the village.

The village farming community was dominated by Jat Sikhs, a general category considered to be upper caste in Punjab, as a few farmers' households belonged to OBCs. So far as the labourers were concerned, this section of the village population was dominated by SCs. On the basis of a social category distribution of village households, it was evident that an almost equal number of households belong to a Jat Sikh category and to both SCs and OBCs category. The study shows that the status and conditions of housing in the village were not satisfactory and that housing required a substantial amount of improvement. A somewhat similar situation regarding age and sex demographics among the village population was reported during the period of survey. However, the sex ratio among the labourers' households seems to be slightly better as compared to farm households. For the village as a whole, the sex ratio in general and age-specific sex ratios in particular were found to be balanced.

Primary school and community building/*dharmsala* were located in the village, and all other basic and desired institutions were away from the village, due to which villagers faced numerous problems. An analysis of these factors revealed that Harkishanpura was lacking basic facilities and institutions for education, health and economic development. As far as the annual average expenditure and consumption pattern of farmers and labourers was concerned, no significant differences were reported. A similar consumption pattern was seen among the labourers' and farmers' households in the village. Therefore, the analysis suggests that residents of the village have a simple subsistence consumption pattern. Furthermore, little money has been spent on fixed assets and machinery and other expenses like loan repayments and travel and transport costs. This may be due to low level of income of the farmers, which results in debt accumulation and the indebtedness of the farmers. Therefore, the incomes of the farmers must be supplemented so that the farmers on the brink may be saved and the would-be deceased instead rehabilitated.

The agricultural sector is the engine of growth in the Punjab economy: it still substantially contributes to the income of the state. The agricultural sector has been a facing multi-pronged crisis after the recent liberalization policy. Analysis pointed out that the rising costs, dipping income and increasing incidence of indebtedness among the small and marginal farmers led to a spate of suicides. The agrarian crisis in the Punjab economy is deep rooted and needs new policy initiatives, both short term and long term. As a short-term measure, farmers should be freed from the tyranny of intermediaries by reforming the rent-seeking, anti-farmer commission agents/arthiya system.

The interlocking of credit and output markets is a major factor behind the crisis of indebtedness leading to suicides. The first step towards saving farmers from these suicides is breaking the credit–crop nexus. This can be dismantled by changing the present system, in which farmers make payments through arthiyas/commission agents. The state machinery should realize that the Agricultural Produce Marketing Committee Act was formulated back in 1961, when it was essential to provide farmers who were new to commercial crops with an assured market and save them from being fleeced by cartels of private buyers. The Act has now become a facilitator for arthiyas to recover their dues from farmers rather than help the farmers. Further, interlinked credit contracts and the Act forbid their selling produce directly to procuring agencies. The state government should ensure that the system of making payments to farmers through commission agents be immediately replaced by direct payments. Further, another option with the government in the case farmers who do not have bank accounts is to involve Primary Agriculture Credit Societies in the sale of grains, and payments can be made to farmers through these societies.

The state government and its agencies can also provide greater storage facilities in the mandis (grain markets) so that the distress sale of crops can be stopped during peak harvesting season. This task should not be left to the centre or procuring agencies alone. Appropriate godowns, shelters and basic amenities in mandis would also go a long way to protecting the interests of farmers, who can then wait for a better price to sell their output. The commission to arthiyas has increased steadily, but they have not been asked to provide any amenity to farmers. The arthiyas should be compelled to spend a certain percentage of their *arht* (commission) on providing these amenities to their client farmers.

The results of our study amply established the fact that small and marginal farmers and agricultural labourers are under great distress and had the highest number of suicides. The families of the deceased farmers and agricultural labourers are undergoing social and economic trauma. There is an urgent need to save these families, on humanitarian grounds. Therefore, it is suggested that Rs 10 lakhs, as immediate compensation, be given as one-time grants to the victimized families of the farmers and agricultural labourers, respectively. Waiving the whole institutional and non-institutional debt of deceased families would also be a step in the right direction. Placing a moratorium on debt held by all the categories of farmers and agricultural labourers with the commission agents/informal money lenders is desired to stop suicides in rural Punjab. Furthermore, it is suggested that suitable and gainful government employment to the victims' kin be provided. The government should bear the cost of educating the children of the family of the deceased farmers and labourers.

The highest number of farmers who died by suicide, measured by regions, belonged to Malwa. The lack of irrigation at the tail end of the canal area and floods in the Ghaggar belt have been reported as important factors for crop failure/crop damage. So, immediately modernizing that refurbishing the old canal system of the state and preventing floods while taming the Ghaggar River are urgently required.

For a long-term solution to agrarian distress, it is suggested that the Punjab government step up efforts to pull rural people out of agriculture by giving agroprocessing industry a policy push. The subsidies and tax concessions that have been offered and provided to the corporate sector/mega projects should be given to rural entrepreneurs who are willing to start new manufacturing firms that will process local raw materials and employ rural labour. It is suggested that the Punjab government encourage next-generation, member-based cooperatives.

The rural economic transformation of the Punjab economy is a desired longrun goal for economic development. This transformation is possible if primary producers are integrated with both manufacturing and marketing activities to reap the surpluses generated by them. Therefore, it is suggested that the Punjab government extend necessary infrastructure facilities and ensure that farming becomes a *part-time* occupation.

The future of the Punjab agricultural progress will depend on crop diversification, especially of paddy. This will not only save groundwater resources but also help harmonize agricultural development. Alternative remunerative crops are available, which can viably replace paddy cultivation, provided that a guaranteed market and price support system is put in place by the state government. It is suggested that the Punjab government develop a cargo airport to transport the outputs of these alternative crops to international markets. Furthermore, to reap the benefits of the rise in agricultural productivity, the Punjab government should harness the biotechnological revolution while investing in generating adequate skills at three levels by imparting training (1) to scientists working in universities, (2) to scientists involved in agricultural research and extension services and, of course, (3) to farmers. Public capital formation to support agriculture and rural development needs to be stepped up.

Agricultural production and agricultural productivity are subject to changes in weather conditions, and Punjab state is especially prone to untimely rains because of western disturbances (untimely rains caused by western winds). Therefore, reaping the benefits of the crops sown by the farmers may be difficult. Thus, it is suggested that the Punjab government provide universal agriculture insurance to the farmers. In this scenario, the available satellite technology and information technology need to be harnessed to make timely assessments of the losses occurring due to untimely rains. This will reduce the time between the assessment of the losses and reimbursement payments in lieu of crop losses. This step can reduce the uncertainty of the farmers and reduce distress and suicides.

Marketing and brand creations are highly specialized activities. Market intelligence is required for the successful functioning of economic activities. Punjab state is deficient on this count. Therefore, it is suggested that the Punjab government announce that it is establishing a market intelligence cell. There is an urgent need to establish the International Institute of Trade and Marketing as an autonomous body. This institute would fill the gap of information needed for searching for domestic and international markets and would also provide essential marketing skills at the doorstep of rural people.

Agricultural research and the extension system in Punjab are in shambles and need to be revived. Individual farmers do not have the capacity to invest in research and development. The research and development expenditure involves externalities due to the public good of research, development and extension services. Thus, individual farmers shy away from incurring research and development expenditure. Therefore, it is suggested that government take up this responsibility to provide these services. The Punjab government has dragged its feet in fulfilling this responsibility. Agricultural research and the extension system need to be modernized. Therefore, it is suggested that the state government spend at least 2 per cent of the agricultural net state domestic product on agricultural research and development.

Appendices

APPENDIX I

I   Interview schedule for victim farmers

1. Village name: ....   2. Block ....

3. Tehsil ....   4. District ....

A. Respondent Profile

    A.1 Name ....

    A.2 Relation with victim ....

    A.3 Education qualification ....   A.4 Male/female ....

    A.5 Age ....   A.6 Phone no...............................

    A.7 Type of house ....

B. Personal Profile

    B.1 Name ....   B.2 Father's name ....

    B.3 Male/female ....   B.4 Age ....

    B.5 Caste ....   B.6 Occupation ....

    B.7 Educational qualifications ....

    B.8 Marital status ....

    B.9 Family background/status: Sarpanch ☐   Panch ☐
                                       Zaildar ☐   Others ☐

A.10 Family Details:

S. no.	Name	Age	Educational qualification	Occupation	Relation with victim	Remarks
1						
2						
3						
4						
5						
6						
7						
8						
9						
10						

C. Land Details (Acres)

C.1 (i) Ownership .... (ii) Leased in ....

(iii) Leased out .... (iv) Total ....

C.2 (i) Irrigated .... (ii) Unirrigated ....

C.3 If irrigated, then what is the source?

(i) Canal .... (ii) Tube well ....

C.4 Sources of irrigation

(i) Own .... (ii) Hired .... (iii) Others ....

C.5 Land bought/sold after 2000

(i) Bought .... from whom ....

(ii) Sold .... to whom ....

C.6 Land mortgaged after 2000

(i) Mortgaged out .... to whom ....

(ii) Mortgaged in .... from whom ....

C.7 Whether your land is flood prone   Yes/No

If yes, extent of damage annually (rupees) ....

C.8 Whether your land is draught prone   Yes/No

If yes, extent of damage annually (rupees) ....

D. Agriculture Machinery

    D.1 (i) Tractor (Hrs. power) ……………….. (ii) Trolley ……...………….....…

        (iii) Plough …...........…………. (iv) Harvesting combine ……...………..

        (v) Reaper………………....………..... (vi)others……..………............……

    D.2 Number of tube wells …………….......

        (i) Electric (power) ………....….…....   (ii) Diesel …………...….…

    D.3 Details of canal irrigation (acres) …………………………….......……

    D.4 Problems of canal irrigation

        (a) …………………. (b) …………………. (c) ………………….

E. Details of Allied Activities

    E.1 Dairying

        (i) Buffaloes …………………….. (ii) Cows ……………………..

        (iii) Milk production ……………… (iv) Annual ale …………………

    E.2 Poultry

        (i) Birds …………… (ii) Annual production …………… (iii) Sale ……………

    E.3 Bee keeping

        (i) Number (Box) …………… (ii) Production …………… (iii) Sale ……………

    E.4 Others

        (i) Number ……………… (ii) Production ……………… (iii) Sale ………………

F. Crop Details (during suicide year and one year before suicide)
    F.1 Details of crops, yield and estimated income

Crop	Acres		Yield per acre		Estimated per acre income		Remarks
	Suicide year	Before	Suicide year	Before	Suicide year	Before	
Wheat							
Paddy							
Cotton							
Sugarcane							
Oil seeds							
Fodder							
Vegetables							
Others							

F.2 Details of crop sold
- (a) To whom
  - (i) Same commission agent ☐
  - (ii) Each year to new commission agent ☐
- (b) Payment method
  - (i) One month ☐ (ii) Two months ☐
  - (iii) More than 3 months ☐
- (c) Interest paid by commission agent   Yes/No

  If yes, how much interest (rupees) ....

F.3 Are you forced by bought material from commission agent   Yes/No

F.4 Details of material bought from commission agent

(a) .... (b) .... (c) ....

G. Income Details
G.1 Sources of income (rupees)

Sources	Income		Remarks
	Suicide year	Before	
Agriculture			
Total			

H. Debt/Indebtedness Details
H.1 Amount, purpose, date of contract, rate of interest, repaid and balance of debt.

Sources	Amount	Year	Rate percentage	Purpose	Use of loan amount	Repaid	Balance
Commercial banks							
Co-operatives							
Commission agents							
Relatives							
Others							
Total							

H.2 Whether loan instalments paid on time

(i) Yes .... (ii) No................................

If no, what were the causes?

(a) ....
(b) ....
(c) ....
(d) ....

I. Suicide Details

I.1 Date and year........................... Place........................

Method

(i) Pesticide/Poison ☐ (ii) Hanging ☐
(iii) Jumping into river/well ☐ (iv) Under train ☐
(v) Electrocution ☐ (vi) Exactly not known ☐
(vii) Any other ☐

I.2 Views of the villagers regarding family and victim

a. Family
(i) Normal............................. (ii) Specific ....
b. Victim
(i) Normal...... .... (ii) Specific ....

I.3 Immediate provocation for suicide

(i) Family feud .... (ii) Outside feud ....
(iii) Bankers' pressure ....
(iv) Commission agents' pressure ....
(v) Humiliation/insult in public by lender..............................
(vi) Others specify ....

I.4 Rank the real causes for suicide

(i) Economic distress ☐ (ii) Indebtedness ☐
(iii) Consecutive crop failure/damage ☐
(iv) Drug addicted ☐
(v) Indebtedness and crop failure/damage ☐
(vi) Any other specify ☐
(vii) Economic distress, indebtedness and crop failure/damage ☐

I.5 Family feud/dispute Yes ☐ No ☐

If yes
(i) Kind/type...
(ii) Level... Court level/panchayat level
(iii) Causes/factors...

I.6 Feud/dispute/litigation out of family   Yes ☐   No ☐

If yes

(i)   Kind/type ....

(ii)   Level .... Court level/panchayat level

(iii) Causes/factors ....

I.7 Mental/physical status of the victim

(a)   Mentally sound   Yes ☐   No ☐

(b)   Mentally stressed   Yes ☐   No ☐

     if yes, the level, causes and treatment ....

(c)   Any disease (specify)   Yes ☐   No ☐

     if yes, the level, causes and treatment ....

I.8 Whether any member of the family committed suicide earlier   Yes ☐   No ☐

If yes, Name.............................. Relation with victim.......................

Date and year........................... Cause..

Place.. Method..

I.9 Economic impact of suicide...

(i)   Employment   Yes ☐   No ☐

     if yes, what..

(ii)   Land sold   Yes ☐   No ☐

     if yes, how much .... to whom.....................

(iii) Land bought   Yes ☐   No ☐

     if yes, how much .... from whom.....................

(iv) Land mortgaged   Yes ☐   No ☐

     if yes, how much .... to whom.....................

(v)   Land mortgaged in   Yes ☐   No ☐

     if yes, how much .... from whom.....................

(vi) Debt repaid   Yes ☐   No ☐

     if yes, how much .... to whom.....................

(vii) New loan   Yes ☐   No ☐

     if yes, how much .... from whom.....................

I.10 Social/other impact of suicide...

(i)   Wards education   Yes ☐   No ☐ if yes, how ....

(ii)   Status of family   Yes ☐   No ☐ if yes, what...........................

(iii) Any other   Yes ☐   No ☐ if yes, specify ....

I.11 General/specific reaction in village after suicide

J. Role of Farmer Unions/NGOs/Government/Others
 J.1 Support financial/others from

Organization	Yes	No	What	How much
Kisan unions				
NGOs				
Political parties				
Government state/centre				
Any other				

 J.2 Role of Panchyat
  Positive/supportive ☐ Negative ☐ No role ☐

 J.3 Role of police
  Positive/supportive ☐ Negative ☐ No role ☐

 J.4 Farmers' and labourers' suicides in the area
  Stopped   ☐ Continue ☐ Don't know ☐

K. Perceptions
 K.1 Regarding agrarian crisis (causes)
 K.2 Regarding indebtedness (causes)
 K.3 Regarding farmer suicides (causes)
 K.4 Regarding agrarian crisis (solution)
 K.5 Regarding indebtedness (solution)
 K.6 Regarding farmer suicides (solution)
 K.7 Would you like to continue in agriculture? Yes ☐ No ☐
   If no, your occupational preferences ....
 K.8 Regarding farmer–commission agent relationship (problems)
 K.9 Regarding farmer–commission agent relationship (solutions)
 K.10 Regarding canal irrigation (problems)
 K.11 Regarding canal irrigation (solutions)
 K.12 Regarding floods (problems)
 K.13 Regarding floods (solutions)
 K.14 Regarding drought (problems)
 K.15 Regarding drought (solutions)

L. Expenditure

L.1 Capital expenditure in rupees

Expenditure	Daily	Monthly	Yearly total	Remarks
Labour (all types)				
Diesel/lubricants				
Fertilizer				
Pesticides				
Seeds				
Machinery				
Transport and travel				
Loan repayments				
Electricity for agriculture				
Any other				

L.2 Consumption expenditure in rupees

Expenditure	Daily	Monthly	Yearly total	Remarks
Cereals				
Milk products				
Grocery				
Vegetables				
Education				
Health				
Transport and travel				
Telephone, etc.				
Home electricity				
Cloths				
Intoxicants				
Ceremonies a. b. c.				
Any other				

(Signature of Investigator)

II Interview schedule for non-victim farmers

1. Village name: .... 2. Block ....

3. Tehsil .... 4. District ....

A. Personal Profile
   A.1 Household head's name ....
   A.2 Father's name ....
   A.3 Male/female .... A.4 Ag ....
   A.5 Caste .... A.6 Occupation ....
   A.7 Educational qualifications..
   A.8 Marital status..
   A.9 Family background/status:
        Sarpanch ☐   Panch ☐   Zaildar ☐   Others ☐
   A.10 Phone no...................................... A.11 Type of house ....

A.12 Family Details:

S. no.	Name	Age	Educational qualification	Occupation	Relation with victim	Remarks
1						
2						
3						
4						
5						
6						
7						
8						
9						
10						

B. Land Details (Acres)
   B.1 (i)   Ownership .... (ii) Leased in...........................
        (iii) Leased out .... (iv) Total ....
   B.2 (i)   Irrigated..................................... (ii) Unirrigated.......................
   B.3 If irrigated, then what is the source
        (i)   Canal.. (ii) Tube well.............................
   B.4 Sources of irrigation
        (i) Own..................... (ii) Hired..................... (iii) Others...................

B.5 Land bought/sold after 2000
    (i) Bought from.................................. whom..
    (ii) Sold...............................……..... to whom......................................

B.6 Land mortgaged after 2000
    (i) Mortgaged out...........….......…........ to whom....................................
    (ii) Mortgaged in..........…........…........ from whom................................

B.7 Whether your land is flood prone Yes/No
    If yes, extent of damage annually (rupees) ....

B.8 Whether your land is draught prone Yes/No
    If yes, extent of damage annually (rupees) ....

C. Agriculture Machinery
    C.1 (i) Tractor (Hrs. power)...........…....... (ii) Trolley...................…......
        (iii) Plough.................................
        (iv) Harvesting combine...................... (v) Reaper................................
        (vi) Others............................…......

    C.2 Number of tube wells.........…............. (i) Electric (power)..................
        (ii) Diesel............….......................

    C.3 Details of canal irrigation (acres) ....

    C.4 Problems of canal irrigation...
        (a) .... (b)........................... (c) ....

D. Details of Allied Activities
    D.1 Dairying
        (i) Buffaloes .... (ii) Cows...........................
        (iii) Milk production .... (iv) Annual sale.................................

    D.2 Poultry
        (i) Birds...(ii) Annual production......................
        (iii) Sale.................................

    D.3 Bee keeping
        (i) Number (books)................
        (ii) Production..... .... (iii) Sale...............................

    D.4 Others
        (i) Number..
        (ii) Production ....(iii) Sale ....

E. Crop Details

E.1 Details of crops, yield and estimated income

Crop	Acres		Yield per acre		Estimated per acre income		Remarks
Wheat							
Paddy							
Cotton							
Sugarcane							
Oil seeds							
Fodder							
Vegetables							
Others							

E.2 Details of crop sold

(a) To whom
   (i) Same commission agent ☐
   (ii) Each year to new commission agent ☐

(b) Payment method
   (i) One month ☐   (ii) Two months ☐
   (iii) More than 3 months ☐

(c) Interest paid by commission agent   Yes/No
   If yes, how much interest (rupees) ……...………………….

E.3 Are you forced by bought material from commission agent   Yes/No

E.4 Details of material bought from commission agent

(a) …………………….. (b) ………………………. (c) ……………………………

F. Income Details

F.1 Sources of income (rupees)

Sources	Income		Remarks
Agriculture			
Total			

G. Debt/Indebtedness Details

G.1 Amount, purpose, date of contract, rate of interest, repaid and balance of debt.

Sources	Amount	Year	Rate percentage	Purpose	Use of loan amount	Repaid	Balance
Commercial banks							
Co-operatives							
Commission agents							
Relatives							
Others							
Total							

G.2 Whether loan instalments paid on time

(i) Yes...................... (ii) No......................

If no, what were the causes? (a) (b) (c) (d)

H. Role of Farmer Unions/NGOs/Government/Others

H.1 During any crisis/farm crisis, who is supporting and financing you?

Organization	Yes	No	What	How much
Kisan unions				
NGOs				
Political parties				
Government state/centre				
Village panchayat				
Any other				

H.2 Farmers' and labourers' suicides in the area......

Stopped ☐ Continue ☐ Don't know ☐

I. Perceptions
    I.1   Regarding agrarian crisis (causes)
    I.2   Regarding indebtedness (causes)
    I.3   Regarding farmer suicides (causes)
    I.4   Regarding agrarian crisis (solution)
    I.5   Regarding indebtedness (solution)
    I.6   Regarding farmer suicides (solution)
    I.7   Would you like to continue in agriculture? Yes ☐ No ☐
           If no, your occupational preferences ....
    I.8   Regarding farmer–commission agent relationship (problems)
    I.9   Regarding farmer–commission agent relationship (solutions)
    I.10 Regarding canal irrigation (problems)
    I.11 Regarding canal irrigation (solutions)
    I.12 Regarding floods (problems)
    I.13 Regarding floods (solutions)
    I.14 Regarding drought (problems)
    I.15 Regarding drought (solutions)

J. Expenditure
    J.1 Capital expenditure in rupees

Expenditure	Daily	Monthly	Yearly total	Remarks
Labour (all types)				
Diesel/lubricants				
Fertilizer				
Pesticides				
Seeds				
Machinery				
Transport and travel				
Loan repayments				
Electricity for agriculture				
Any other				

    J.2 Consumption expenditure in rupees

Expenditure	Daily	Monthly	Yearly total	Remarks
Cereals				
Milk products				
Grocery				
Vegetables				

Expenditure	Daily	Monthly	Yearly total	Remarks
Education				
Health				
Transport and travel				
Telephone, etc.				
Home electricity				
Cloths				
Intoxicants				
Ceremonies a. b. c.				

(Signature of Investigator)

III   Interview schedule for agriculture labour suicide victims

A.   Respondent Profile
  A.1   Name ....
  A.2   Relation with victim ....
  A.3   Education qualification ....
  A.4   Male/female ....
  A.5   Age ....
  A.6   Phone no ....

B.   Personal Profile
  B.1   Name .... B.2   Father's name ....
  B.3   Male/female........................... B.4   Age...
  B.5   Caste..................................... B.6   Occupation..................................
  B.7   Educational qualifications ....
  B.8   Marital status..... ....
  B.9   Family background/status:
        Sarpanch ☐   Panch ☐   Zaildar ☐   Others ☐
  B.10 Family details:

S. no.	Name	Age	Educational qualification	Occupation	Relation with victim	Remarks
1						
2						
3						
4						
5						

S. no.	Name	Age	Educational qualification	Occupation	Relation with victim	Remarks
6						
7						
8						
9						
10						

C. Employment and Economic Activities

    C.1 Engaged to a particular farmer   Yes ☐   No ☐

       If yes,   (i) Monthly/annual wages in rupees..

              (ii) Any other income from farmer in rupees ....

    C.2 Whether change farmer every year Yes ☐   No ☐

       If yes, why? .... If no, why?................................

    C.3 If not engaged to single farmer

       (i) Then, daily wages in rupees...

          Monthly.......................... wages......................... Yearly......................

       (ii) In a year how many days you find work?......................................

    C.4 Specify any other type of employment..

    C.5 Dairying

       (i)   Buffaloes................................... (ii) Cows......................................

       (iii) Milk production........................ (iv) Annual sale............................

    C.6 Poultry

       (i)   Birds.. (ii) Annual production.................

       (iii) Sale...

    C.7 Bee keeping

       (i) Number.................. (ii) Production..................... (iii) Sale................

    C.8 Others

       (i) Number.................. (ii) Production..................... (iii) Sale................

D. Income Details

    D.1 Sources of family income (rupees)

Sources	Income		Remarks
	Suicide year	One year before suicide	
Labour			
Others			
Any other			
Total			

E.   Debt/Indebtedness Details

E.1 Amount, purpose, date of contract, rate of interest, repaid and balance of debt

Sources	Amount	Year	Rate percentage	Purpose	Use of loan amount	Repaid	Balance
Commercial banks							
Co-operatives							
Commission agents							
Relatives							
Others							
Total							

E.2 Whether loan instalments paid on time

(i) Yes................................   (ii) No.......................

If no, what were the causes?   (a)   (b)   (c)   (d)

F.   Suicide Details

F.1   Date and year...................   Place...................

Method

(i)   Pesticide/poison   ☐   (ii) Hanging   ☐
(iii) Jumping into river/well ☐   (iv) Under train   ☐
(v)   Electrocution   ☐   (vi) Exactly not known   ☐
(vii) Any other   ☐

F.2 Views of the villagers regarding family and victim.............

(a) Family

(i) Normal........................ (ii) Specific........................

(b) Victim

(i) Normal........................ (ii) Specific........................

F.3 Immediate provocation for suicide
    (i)   Family feud ....(ii) Outside feud............................
    (iii) Bankers' pressure..
    (iv) Commission agents' pressure..
    (v) Humiliation/insult in public by lender..
    (vi) Others specify...

F.4 Rank the real causes for suicide......
    (i)   Economic distress ☐   (ii) Indebtedness ☐
    (iii) Consecutive crop failure/damage   ☐
    (iv) Drug addicted   ☐
    (v) Indebtedness and crop failure/damage ☐
    (vi) Any other specify ☐
    (vii) Economic distress, indebtedness and crop failure/damage ☐

F.5 Family feud/dispute Yes ☐ No ☐
If yes (i) Kind/type.....................
         (ii) Level........................... Court level/panchayat level
         (iii) Causes/factors...............

F.6 Feud/dispute/litigation out of family   Yes ☐ No ☐
If yes (i) Kind/type.....................
         (ii) Level........................... Court level/panchayat level
         (iii) Causes/factors...............

F.7 Mental/physical status of the victim
(a) Mentally sound   Yes ☐   No ☐
(b) Mentally stressed   Yes ☐   No ☐
    if yes, the level, causes and treatment.........................
(c) Any disease (specify) Yes ☐   No ☐
    if yes, the level, causes and treatment.........................

F.8 Whether any member of the family committed
    suicide earlier   Yes ☐   No ☐
    If yes, name.................. Relation with victim..............
    Date and year.............. Cause....................................
    Place........................... Method................................

F.9 Economic impact of suicide...
    (i)   Employment   Yes ☐ No ☐
         if yes, what...
    (ii) Land sold   Yes ☐ No ☐
         if yes, how much.......... to whom...........
    (iii) Land bought   Yes ☐ No ☐
         if yes, how much........... from whom........

    (iv) Land mortgaged   Yes ☐ No ☐
         if yes, how much............ to whom.........

    (v) Land mortgaged in   Yes ☐ No ☐
         if yes, how much............ from whom.....

    (vi) Debt repaid   Yes ☐ No ☐
         if yes, how much............ to whom.........

    (vii) New loan   Yes ☐ No ☐
         if yes, how much............ from whom....

F.10 Social/other impact of suicide...

    (i)   Wards' education   Yes ☐ No ☐ if yes, how...........

    (ii) Status of family   Yes ☐ No ☐ if yes, what...........

    (iii) Any other   Yes ☐ No ☐ if yes, specify........

F.11 General/specific reaction in village after suicide......

G.   Role of Labour Unions/NGOs/Government/Others

    G.1 Support financial/others from........................

Organization	Yes	No	What	How much
Agriculture labour unions				
NGOs				
Political parties				
Government state/centre				
Any other				

    G.2 Role of panchayat Positive/supportive ☐
         Negative ☐   No role ☐

    G.3 Role of police Positive/supportive ☐
         Negative ☐   No role ☐

    G.4 Farmers' and labourers' suicides in the area .... Stopped ☐
         Continue ☐   Don't know ☐

H.   Perceptions

    H.1   Regarding agrarian crisis and farm labour (causes)

    H.2   Regarding indebtedness of labourers (causes)

    H.3   Regarding labourers' suicides (causes)

    H.4   Regarding agrarian crisis and farm labourers (solution)

    H.5   Regarding indebtedness of labourers (solution)

    H.6   Regarding labourers' suicides (solution)

    H.7   Would you like to continue as a labourer in agriculture
          Yes ☐ No ☐

If no, your occupational preferences ....

I.   Expenditure

    I.1   Consumption expenditure in rupees

Expenditure	Daily	Monthly	Yearly total	Remarks
Cereals				
Milk products				
Grocery				
Vegetables				
Education				
Health				
Transport and travel				
Telephone, etc.				
Home Electricity				
Cloths				
Intoxicants				
Ceremonies a. b. c.				
Any other				

(Signature of Investigator)

IV   Interview schedule for agriculture non-victim labourers

1.   Village name: .... 2.   Block ....

3.   Tehsil .... 4.   District ....

A.   Personal Profile

    A.1   Household head's name ....

    A.2   Father's name ....

    A.3   Male/female .... A.4 Age .... A.5 Caste ....

    A.6   Occupation .... A.7 Educational qualifications ....

    A.8   Marital status ....

    A.9   Family background/status: Sarpanch ☐   Panch ☐
          Zaildar ☐   Others ☐

    A.10   Phone no ....

A.11 Family details:

S. no.	Name	Age	Educational qualification	Occupation	Relation with victim	Remarks
1						
2						
3						
4						
5						
6						
7						
8						
9						
10						

B. Employment and Economic Activities

B.1 Engaged to a particular farmer   Yes ☐   No ☐

If yes, (i) Monthly/annual wages in rupees ....

(ii) Any other income from farmer in rupees ....

B.2 Whether change farmer every year   Yes ☐   No ☐

If yes, why? .... If no, why?............................

B.3 If not engaged to single farmer

(i) Then, daily wages in rupees ....

Monthly wages .... Yearly ....

(ii) In a year how many days do you find work? ....

B.4 Any other type of employment specify ....

B.5 Dairying   (i) Buffaloes .... (ii) Cows ....

(iii) Milk production .... (iv) Annual sale ....

B.6 Poultry   (i) Birds .... (ii) Annual production ....

(iii) Sale ....……

B.7 Bee keeping (i) Number ....….. (ii) Production ....

(iii) Sale ....

B.8 Others   (i) Number .... (ii) Production ....

(iii) Sale ....

C. Income Details

C.1 Sources of family income (rupees)

Sources	Income		Remarks
Labour			
Others			
Any other			
Total			

D. Debt/Indebtedness Details

D.1 Amount, purpose, date of contract, rate of interest, repaid and balance of debt

Sources	Amount	Year	Rate percentage	Purpose	Use of loan amount	Repaid	Balance
Commercial banks							
Co-operatives							
Commission agents							
Relatives							
Others							
Total							

D.2 Whether loan instalments paid on time

(i) Yes .... (ii) No ....

If no, what were the causes? (a) .... (b) .... (c) .... d) ....

E. Role of Labour Unions/NGOs/Government/Others

   E.1 Details of crops, yield and estimated income

Organization	Yes	No	What	How much
Labour unions				
NGOs				
Political parties				
Government state/centre				
Village panchayat				
Any other				

   E.2 Farmers' and labourers' suicides in the area ....
   Stopped ☐   Continue ☐   Don't know ☐

F. Perceptions
   F.1 Regarding agrarian crisis (causes)
   F.2 Regarding indebtedness (causes)
   F.3 Regarding farmer suicides (causes)
   F.4 Regarding agrarian crisis (solution)
   F.5 Regarding indebtedness (solution)
   F.6 Regarding farmer suicides (solution)
   F.7 Would you like to continue as a labourer in agriculture
        Yes ☐   No ☐

        If no, your occupational preferences ....
        ....

G. Expenditure

   G.1 Consumption expenditure in rupees

Expenditure	Daily	Monthly	Yearly total	Remarks
Cereals				
Milk products				
Grocery				
Vegetables				
Education				
Health				
Transport and travel				
Telephone, etc.				

Home electricity				
Cloths				
Intoxicants				
Ceremonies a. b. c.				
Any other				

(Signature of Investigator)

V Village profile and interview schedule for sample farmers (village profile)

1. Name: .... 2. Block .... 3. Tehsil ....

4. Distance (km) from Mandi .... Block town ....

   Tehsil town .... District town ....

5. Level of school (a) Primary .... (b) High .... (c) +2 ....

6. Higher educational institutions (specify) ....

7. Total population .... Male .... Female ....

8. Literacy rate .... Male .... Female ....

9. Health facilities (a) PHC .... (b) CHC ....

   (c) Hospital .... (d) No ....

10. Stature of villagers in local politics as member/chairman:

    (i) Panchayat samiti ☐   (ii) Zila parishad ☐
    (iii) Director co-op. bank ☐   (iv) District committees ☐

11. Stature of villagers in state politics (i) MLA ☐   (ii) MP ☐
    (iii) Minister ☐   (iv) Chairman ☐   (v) Others ☐

12. Sources of irrigation (i) Canal ☐   (ii) Tube wells ☐
                            (iii) Others ☐
    In case of canals, weather the village is at the tail end   Yes ☐   No ☐
    Sufficient supply of water ☐   Shortage ☐   Acute shortage ☐
    In case of ground water, the quality of water, Good ☐
    Poor ☐   Unfit for irrigation ☐

A. Personal Profile

    A.1   Household head's name ....

    A.2   Father's name ....

    A.3   Male/female ....   A.4 Age ....

    A.5   Caste ....   A.6 Occupation ....

    A.7   Educational qualifications ....

    A.8   Marital status ....

    A.9   Family background/status: Sarpanch ☐   Panch ☐
                                   Zaildar ☐   Others ☐

    A.10   Phone no .... A.11 Type of house ....

    A.11   Family details:

S. no.	Name	Age	Educational qualification	Occupation	Relation with victim	Remarks
1						
2						
3						
4						
5						
6						
7						
8						
9						
10						

B. Land Details (Acres)

    B.1 (i) Ownership .... (ii) Leased in ....

       (iii) Leased out .... (iv) Total ....

    B.2 (i) Irrigated .... (ii) Unirrigated ....

    B.3 If irrigated, then what is the source?

       (i) Canal .... (ii) Tube well ....

    B.4 Sources of irrigation   (i) Own ....

       (ii) Hired .... (iii) Others ....

B.5 Land bought/sold after 2000

  (i) Bought .... from whom ....

  (ii) Sold .... to whom ....

B.6 Land mortgaged after 2000

  (i) Mortgaged out .... to whom ....

  (ii) Mortgaged in .... from whom ....

B.7 Whether your land is flood prone   Yes/No

  If yes, extent of damage annually (rupees) ....

B.8 Whether your land is draught prone   Yes/No

  If yes, extent of damage annually (rupees) ....

C. Agriculture Machinery

  C.1 (i) Tractor (Hrs. power .... (ii) Trolley ....

  (iii) Plough .... (iv) Harvesting combine ....

  (v) Reaper .... (vi) Others ....

  C.2 Number of tube wells ....

  (i) Electric (power) .... (ii) Diesel ....

  C.3 Details of canal irrigation (acres) ....

  C.4 Problems of canal irrigation

  (a) .... (b) .... (c) ....

D. Details of Allied Activities

  D.1 Dairying (i) Buffaloes .... (ii) Cows ....

  (iii) Milk production .... (iv) Annual sale ....

  D.2 Poultry (i) Birds ....

  (ii) Annual production .... (iii) Sale ....

  D.3 Bee keeping (i) Number (books) ....

  (ii) Production .... (iii) Sale ....

  D.4 Others (i) Number ....

  (ii) Production .... (iii) Sale ....

E.   Crop Details
  E.1 Details of crops, yield and estimated income

Crop	Acres		Yield per acre		Estimated per acre income		Remarks
Wheat							
Paddy							
Cotton							
Sugarcane							
Oil seeds							
Fodder							
Vegetables							
Others							

  E.2 Details of crop sold
    (a) To whom   (i) Same commission agent ☐
        (ii) Each year to new commission agent ☐
    (b) Payment method   (i) One month ☐
        (ii) Two months ☐   (iii) More than 3 months ☐
    (c) Interest paid by commission agent   Yes/No

        If yes, how much interest (rupees) ....
  E.3 Are you forced by bought material from commission agent   Yes/No
  E.4 Details of material bought from commission agent

    (a) .... (b) .... (c) ....

F.   Income Details
  F.1 Sources of income (rupees)

Sources	Income		Remarks
Agriculture			
Total			

G. Debt/Indebtedness Details
   G.1 Amount, purpose, date of contract, rate of interest, repaid and balance of debt

Sources	Amount	Year	Rate percentage	Purpose	Use of loan amount	Repaid	Balance
Commercial banks							
Co-operatives							
Commission agents							
Relatives							
Others							
Total							

   G.2 Whether loan instalments paid on time

   (i) Yes .... (ii) No ....

   If no, what were the causes? (a) .... (b) ....
   (c) .... (d) ....

H. Role of Farmer Unions/NGOs/Government/Others
   H.1 During any crisis/farm crisis, who is supporting and financing you?

Organization	Yes	No	What	How much
Kisan unions				
NGOs				
Political parties				
Government state/centre				
Village panchayat				
Any other				

H.2 Farmers' and labourers suicides in the area ....

Stopped ☐   Continue ☐   Don't know ☐

I.   Perceptions
    I.1   Regarding agrarian crisis (causes)
    I.2   Regarding indebtedness (causes)
    I.3   Regarding farmer suicides (causes)
    I.4   Regarding agrarian crisis (solution)
    I.5   Regarding indebtedness (solution)
    I.6   Regarding farmer suicides (solution)
    I.7   Would you like to continue in agriculture?   Yes ☐   No ☐

       If no, your occupational preferences ....
    I.8   Regarding farmer–commission agent relationship (problems)
    I.9   Regarding farmer–commission agent relationship (solutions)
    I.10   Regarding canal irrigation (problems)
    I.11   Regarding canal irrigation (solutions)
    I.12   Regarding floods (problems)
    I.13   Regarding floods (solutions)
    I.14   Regarding drought (problems)
    I.15   Regarding drought (solutions)

J.   Expenditure
    J.1   Capital expenditure in rupees

Expenditure	Daily	Monthly	Yearly total	Remarks
Labour (all types)				
Diesel/lubricants				
Fertilizer				
Pesticides				
Seeds				
Machinery				
Transport and travel				
Loan repayments				
Electricity for agriculture				
Any other				

J.2 Consumption expenditure in rupees

Expenditure	Daily	Monthly	Yearly total	Remarks
Cereals				
Milk products				
Grocery				
Vegetables				
Education				
Health				
Transport and travel				
Telephone, etc.				
Home electricity				
Cloths				
Intoxicants				
Ceremonies a. b. c.				

(Signature of Investigator)

APPENDIX II

District-, block- and village-wise number of farmers and agricultural labourers

Block	Village	Farmers			Labourers		
		Deceased	Control group	Total	Deceased	Control group	Total
District: Sangrur							
		199	199	398	69	69	138
Sunam	Kanakwal	6	6	12	2	2	4
	Khanal kalan	7	7	14	3	3	6
	Janal	3	3	6	2	2	4
	Sheron	4	4	8	1	1	2
	Tolawal	2	2	4	–	–	–
	Rogla	4	4	8	2	2	4
	Bir kalan	4	4	8	–	–	–
	Fatehgarh	4	4	8	–	–	–
	Chhanjli	4	4	8	–	–	–
	Kauhrian	–	–	–	2	2	4
	Total	38	38	76	12	12	24
Malerkotla-I	Hathan	7	7	14	3	3	6
	Kheri jattan	5	5	10	2	2	4
	Gwara	6	6	12	3	3	6
	Total	18	18	36	8	8	16
Malerkotla-II	Shergarh Cheema	6	6	12	2	2	4
	Sekhupur khurd	5	5	10	–	–	–
	Dehlej kalan	3	3	6	–	–	–
	Nathoheri	–	–	–	2	2	4
	Total	14	14	28	4	4	8

Block	Village	Farmers			Labourers		
		Deceased	Control group	Total	Deceased	Control group	Total
Sherpur	Badshahpur	4	4	8	1	1	2
	Bari	5	5	10	2	2	4
	Mullowal	3	3	6	1	1	2
	Khari Khurd	3	3	6	1	1	2
	Katron	2	2	4	1	1	2
	Total	17	17	34	6	6	12
Dhuri	Bugra	4	4	8	5	5	10
	Ladda	4	4	8	1	1	2
	Kanjli	4	4	8	–	–	–
	Total	12	12	24	6	6	12
Bhawanigarh	Fagguwala	11	11	22	3	3	6
	Bhatiwal Kalan	10	10	20	2	2	4
	Total	21	21	42	5	5	10
Andana	Andana	23	23	46	4	4	8
	Banga	–	–	–	5	5	10
	Total	23	23	46	9	9	18
Leheragaga	Lehal khurd	–	–	–	3	3	6
	Lehal kalan	8	8	16	2	2	4
	Dhindsa	7	7	14	2	2	4
	Ghorenab	8	8	16	–	–	–
	Bhutal kalan	17	17	34	1	1	2
	Balran	6	6	12	2	2	4
	Ladal	–	–	–	4	4	8
	Bhutal khurd	–	–	–	2	2	4
	Total	46	46	92	16	16	32
Sangrur	Ubhawal	5	5	10	1	1	2
	Chathe shekhwan	5	5	10	2	2	4
	Total	10	10	20	3	3	6
District: Bathinda							
		172	172	344	60	60	120
Sangat	Sangat	6	6	12	–	–	–
	Jai singh wala	6	6	12	3	3	6
	Chak ruldu singh wala	3	3	6	3	3	6
	GuruSar Senewal	–	–	–	2	2	4
	Mashana	–	–	–	4	4	8
	Total	15	15	30	12	12	24

(Continued)

Block	Village	Farmers			Labourers		
		Deceased	Control group	Total	Deceased	Control group	Total
Bathinda	Behman dewana	5	5	10	3	3	6
	Virk Khurd	8	8	16	1	1	2
	Virk Kalan	2	2	4	–	–	–
	Deon	3	3	6	–	–	–
	Kot Shamir	4	4	8	–	–	–
	Ganga	7	7	14	2	2	4
	Akalia	–	–	–	1	1	2
	Total	29	29	58	7	7	14
Nathana	Poohala	4	4	8	–	–	–
	Giddhar	4	4	8	1	1	2
	Dhelwian	3	3	6			
	Ganga	1	1	2	3	3	6
	Nathana	2	2	4	2	2	4
	Total	14	14	28	6	6	12
Bhagta Bhai Ka	Kotha Guru	5	5	10	2	2	4
	Gumti Kalan	3	3	6	–	–	–
	Dailpur Mirja	6	6	12	–	–	–
	Gurusar	–	–	–	2	2	4
	Total	14	14	28	4	4	8
Phul	Raiya	6	6	12	4	4	8
	Dhapali	12	12	24	–	–	–
	Bhi Roopa	–	–	–	2	2	4
	Total	18	18	36	6	6	12
Talwandi Sabo	Kalal Wala	7	7	14	–	–	–
	Raiya	4	4	8	–	–	–
	Jeon Singh Wala	1	1	2	5	5	10
	Lehari	3	3	6	–	–	–
	Ramtirath Jaga	1	1	2	1	1	2
	Lellewala	1	1	2	–	–	–
	Bhabivander	–	–	–	3	3	6
	Singo	–	–	–	3	3	6
	Total	17	17	34	12	12	24
Maur	Jodhpur Pakhar	8	8	16	2	2	4
	Bhai Bakhtaur	5	5	10	2	2	4
	Sandoha	4	4	8	–	–	–
	Mour Charrat Singh	3	3	6	–	–	–
	Maisar Khanna	5	5	10	–	–	–
	Total	25	25	50	4	4	8

Block	Village	Farmers			Labourers		
		Deceased	Control group	Total	Deceased	Control group	Total
Rampura	Chowke	11	11	22	–	–	–
	Pittho	6	6	12	4	4	8
	Jaidan	3	3	6	–	–	–
	Jeound	6	6	12	–	–	–
	Mandi Kalan	1	1	2	3	3	6
	Gill Kalan	5	5	10	–	–	–
	Pittho	4	4	8	–	–	–
	Harkishanpura	4	4	8	–	–	–
	Chowke	–	–	–	1	1	2
	Jathu Ka	–	–	–	1	1	2
	Total	40	40	80	9	9	18
District: Mansa							
		139	139	278	57	57	114
Bhikhi	Mati	5	5	10	5	5	10
	Aklia	4	4	8	–	–	–
	Hero Kalan	2	2	4	3	3	6
	Alisher Khurd	1	1	2	–	–	–
	Atla Kalan	2	2	4	1	1	2
	Total	14	14	28	9	9	18
Mansa	Tamkot	14	14	28	9	9	18
	Khokhar Kalan	10	10	20	–	–	–
	Total	24	24	48	9	9	18
Sardulgarh	Ranjitgarh Bander	6	6	12	–	–	–
	Jatana	3	3	6	–	–	–
	Mirpur Kalan	6	6	12	–	–	–
	Mirpur Khurd	6	6	12	8	8	16
	Total	21	21	42	8	8	16
Jhunir	Kore wala	9	9	18	2	2	4
	Tandian	5	5	10	3	3	6
	Baje wala	5	5	10	4	4	8
	Mofer	10	10	20	2	2	4
	Total	29	29	58	11	11	22
Budhladha	Tahlian	9	9	18	5	5	10
	Krishangarh	22	22	44	6	6	12
	Dialpura	20	20	40	9	9	18
	Total	51	51	102	20	20	40

REFERENCES

Acharya, S. S. (2000) 'Subsidies in Indian Agriculture and Their Beneficiaries', *Agricultural Situation in India*, 47(5): 251–260.

Acharya, S. S. and R. L. Jogi (2004) 'Farm Input Subsidies in Indian Agriculture', Working Paper, No. 140, Jaipur: Institute of Development Studies.

AFDR (2000) *Suicides in Rural Areas of Punjab: A Report (in Punjabi)*, Ludhiana, Punjab: Association for Democratic Rights.

Aleem, Irfan (1990) 'Imperfect Information, Screening, and the Costs of Informal Lending: A Study of a Rural Credit Market in Pakistan', *World Bank Economic Review*, 4(3): 329–349.

Balakrishnan, P., R. Golait and P. Kumar (2008) 'Agriculture Growth in India since 1991', *Study No. 27*, Mumbai: Reserve Bank of India.

Bell, Clive and T. N. Srinivasan (1989) 'Interlinked Transactions in Rural Markets: An Empirical Study of Andhra Pradesh, Bihar and Punjab', *Oxford Bulletin of Economics and Statistics*, 51(1): 73–83.

Bhaduri, Amit (1984) *The Economic Structure of Backward Agriculture in India*. London: Macmillan.

Bhalla, G. S. (1995) 'Agriculture Growth and Industrial Development in Punjab', in John W. Mellor (ed.), *Agriculture on the Road to Industrial Development*, Baltimore: The Johns Hopkins University Press.

Bhalla, G. S. and G. K. Chadha (1983) *The Green Revolution and the Small Peasant: A Study of Income Distribution among Punjab Cultivators*, New Delhi: Concept Publishers.

Bhangoo, K. S. (2005) 'Agrarian Crisis: Indebtedness and Farmers' Suicides in Punjab', *Journal of Agriculture Development and Policy*, 17(2): 43–60.

Bhangoo, K. S. (2006) 'Farmers' Suicides in Punjab: A Study of Bathinda District', *Journal of Agriculture Development and Policy*, 18(1 and 2): 13–32.

Bhangoo, K. S. (2014) 'Political Economy of Agrarian Distress in Punjab', in Inderjeet Singh, Sukhwinder Singh and Lakhwinder Singh (eds.), *Punjab's Economic Development in the Era of Globalisation*, Delhi: LG Publishers Distributors: 191–214.

Byres, T. J. (1986) 'The Agrarian Question, Forms of Capitalist Agrarian Transition and the State: An Essay with Reference to Asia', *Social Scientist*, 14(11/12): 3–67.

Chaba, A. A. (2019) "Watered Down Waiver, Lack of Reforms Has Farmers in a Bind", *Indian Express*, March 16, Chandigarh.

Chahal, T. S. (2005) *Forced Fall: A Case of Punjab Farmers*, Amritsar: ID&P.

Chand, R. (2009) 'Capital Formation in Indian Agriculture: National and State Level Analysis', in D. Narsimha Reddy and Srijit Mishra (eds.), *Agrarian Crisis in India*, New Delhi: Oxford University Press: 44–60.

Chang, Ha-Joon (2003) 'The Market, the State and Institutions in Economic Development', in Ha-Joon Chang (ed.), *Rethinking Development Economics*, London: Athens Press: 41–60.

Chaudhri, D. P. (1979) *Education, Innovations and Agricultural Development: A Study of North India (1961–72)*, London: Croom Helm.

CSO (2012) *Net State Domestic Product*, Ministry of Statistics and Programme Implementation, Central Statistical Organization, New Delhi: Government of India.

Darling, M. L. (1925) *The Punjab Peasant in Prosperity and Debt*, Oxford: Oxford University Press.

Dasgupta, Biplab (ed.) (1978) *Village Studies in the Third World*, Delhi: Hindustan Publishing Corporation.

Deshpande, R. S. (2002) 'Suicides by Farmers in Karnataka: Agrarian Distress and Possible Alleviatory Steps', *Economic and Political Weekly*, 37(25): 2601–2610.

Deshpande, R. S. (2009) 'Agrarian Transition and Farmers' Distress in Karnataka', in D. Narsimha Reddy and Srijit Mishra (eds.), *Agrarian Crisis in India*, New Delhi: Oxford University Press.

Deshpande, R. S. and Khalil Shah (2010) 'Globalisation, Agrarian Crisis and Farmers' Suicides: Illusion and Reality', in R. S. Deshpande and Saroj Arora (eds.), *Agrarian Crisis and Farmer Suicides*, New Delhi: Sage: 118–148.

Devi, Y. L., J. Singh and S. Kumar (2011) 'Decomposition Analysis of Temporal Changes in Human Labour Use in Punjab Agriculture' *Journal of Agricultural Development and Policy*, 21(1): 63–72.

Dhaliwal, S. (2014) 'Little Help, Suicide by Farmers Unabated', *The Tribune*, 2 July, Chandigarh.

Dhesi, A. S. and Gurmail Singh (2008) *Rural Development in Punjab: A Success Story Going Astray*, New Delhi: Routledge-Taylor and Francis Group.

Durkheim, Emile (1952) 'Suicide: A Study in Sociology', translated by John A. Spaulding and George Simpson, London: Routledge and Kegan Paul.

Faurè, Jean-Marc, Jippe Hoogeveen and Jelle Bruinsma (2013) 'The FAO Irrigated Area Forecast for 2030'. ftp://ftp.fao.org, accessed on 20 March 2013.

Galab, S., E. Rewathi and P. Prudhvikar Reddy (2009) 'Farmers' Suicides and Unfolding Agrarian Crisis in Andhra Pradesh', in D. Narsimha Reddy and Srijit Mishra (eds.), *Agrarian Crisis in India*, New Delhi: Oxford University Press: 164–198.

Ghuman, R. S. (2005) 'Rural Non-farm Employment Scenario', *Economic and Economic Weekly*, 40(41): 4473–4480.

Ghuman, R. S., Inderjeet Singh and Lakhwinder Singh (2007) *Status of Local Agricultural Labour in Punjab*, Mohali: Punjab State Farmers' Commission, Government of Punjab.

Gill, Anita (2004) 'Interlinked Agrarian Credit Markets: Case Study of Punjab', *Economic and Political Weekly*, 39(33): 3741–3751.

Gill, Anita (2006) 'The Punjab Peasant: He Too Dies in Debt', *Mainstream Weekly*, XIIV(26): 19–25.

Gill, Anita (2010) 'Punjab Peasantry: A Question of Life and Debt', in R. S. Deshpande and Saroj Arora (eds.), *Agrarian Crisis and Farmer Suicides,* New Delhi: Sage Publishers: 292–311.

Gill, Anita (2014) 'Agriculture Credit in Punjab: Have Policy Initiatives Made Indent in Informal Credit Market?', Paper presented at the International Conference on *Rejuvenation of Punjab Economy*, organized by Centre for Development Economics and Innovation Studies, Punjabi University, Patiala, March 21–23.

Gill, Anita and Lakhwinder Singh (2006) 'Farmers' Suicides and Response of Public Policy', *Economic and Political Weekly*, XLI(26): 2762–2768.

Gill, Sucha Singh (1988) 'Contradictions of Punjab Model of Growth and Search for Alternatives', *Economic and Political Weekly*, 23(42): 2167–2173.

Gill, Sucha Singh (2005) 'Economic Distress and Suicides in Rural Punjab', *Journal of Punjab
Studies*, 12(2): 219–238.

Gill, Sucha Singh (2010) 'Agrarian Transformation and Marginalization of the Poor Peasantry
in Punjab', in Chetan Singh (ed.), *Social Transformation in North-Western India during the 20th
Century*, New Delhi: Manohar.

Government of India (2005) 'Agriculture and Food Security', Mid-term Review of the Tenth
Five Year Plan, Part II, Chapter 5, New Delhi: Planning Commission.

Government of India (2007) 'Report of the Expert Group on Agricultural Indebtedness',
Ministry of Finance, New Delhi: Government of India.

Government of India (2011) *Census of India – Primary Census Abstract – Figures at a Glance*,
Punjab Series 4, Chandigarh: Director of Census Operations, Punjab, Ministry of Home
Affairs.

Government of India (2013) *Economic Survey*, Ministry of Finance, New Delhi: Government
of India.

Government of Punjab (2010) 'Survey Information', Chandigarh: Department of Rural
Development and Panchayat.

Government of Punjab (2012) *Statistical Abstract*, Chandigarh: Economic Adviser, Government of Punjab.

Government of Punjab (2013) *Agriculture at a Glance – Information Service*, Chandigarh: Department of Agriculture.

Gupta, M. and S. Choudhuri (1997) 'Formal Credit, Corruption and the Informal Credit
Market in Agriculture: A Theoretical Analysis', *Economica*, 64(254): 331–343.

Hindustan Times (2014) 'Two Debt-Ridden Farmers End Life in Bathinda', *Hindustan Times*,
23 May, 3, Chandigarh.

IDC (1998) *Suicides in Rural Punjab*, Chandigarh: Institute of Development and Communication.

IDC (2006) *Suicides in Rural Punjab*, Chandigarh: Institute of Development and Communication.

Iyer, K. Gopal and Saroj Arora (2010) 'Indebtedness and Farmers' Suicides', in R. S. Deshpande and Saroj Arora (eds.), *Agrarian Crisis and Farmer Suicides*, New Delhi: Sage Publishers: 264–291.

Iyer, K. G. and M. S. Manick (2000) *Indebtedness, Impoverishment and Suicides in Rural Punjab*,
New Delhi: Indian Publishers and Distributors.

Jaura, P., Narpinder and Gautam Rishi (2002) 'A Village for Sale: Plight of Harkishanpura
in Punjab', *People's Democracy*, 22 September, Accessed on 14 July 2014 from www.
people'sdemocracy.in.

Jodhka, Surinder S. (2006) 'Beyond "Crises": Rethinking Contemporary Punjab Agriculture', *Economic and Political Weekly*, 41(16): 1530–1537.

Johl, S. S. (1986) 'Diversification of Agriculture in Punjab', *Expert Committee Report*, Chandigarh: Government of Punjab.

Johl, S. S. (1986) Report of expert committee on diversification of agriculture in Punjab,
Government of Punjab, Chandigarh.

Kulkarni, H. and Mihir Shah (2013) 'Punjab Water Syndrome: Diagnostics and Prescrip-
tions', *Economic and Political Weekly*, 48(52): 64–73.

Kumar, Shiv (2014) 'Social Capital and Poverty: A Case Study of Household Welfare in Rural
Punjab' (unpublished Ph.D. Thesis), Patiala: Punjabi University.

Kuznets, S. (1966) *Modern Economic Growth: Rate, Structure and Spread*, New Haven: Yale University Press.

Lerche, Jens (2011) 'Agrarian Crisis and Agrarian Question in India', *Journal of Agrarian
Change*, 11(1): 104–118.

McGranahan, Donald V. (1971) 'Analysis of Socio-Economic Development through a System of Indicators', *Annals of the American Academy of Political and Social Sciences*, 393(1): 65–81.

Menon, Parvathi (2001) 'Round Up from States', *Frontline*, 18(2): January 20–February 2.

Mishra, Srijit (2007) 'Agrarian Crisis in Post-Reform India: A Story of Distress, Despair and Death', Working Paper, No. 1, Mumbai: Indira Gandhi Institute of Development Research.

Mohan, Rakesh (2006) 'Agricultural Credit in India: Status, Issues and Future Agenda', *Economic and Political Weekly*, 41(11): 1013–1021.

Mohanakumar, S. and R. K. Sharma (2006) 'Analysis of Farmer Suicides in Kerala', *Economic and Political Weekly*, 41(16): 1553–1558.

Mohanti, B. B. (2005) 'We Are Like the Living Dead: Farmer Suicides in Maharashtra, Western India', *Journal of Peasant Studies*, 32(2): 243–276.

Mohanty, B. B. (1999) 'Agricultural Modernization and Social Inequality: Case Study of Satara District', *Economic and Political Weekly*, 34(26): A50–A61.

Movement Against State Repression (MASR) (2001) *Representation to the Union Minister for Agriculture on Suicide Deaths in Punjab*, Chandigarh: Movement Against State Repression.

Mukherjee, S. (2018) "Big Rise in Farmer Suicides in Four States During 2016, Says NCRB Data", *Business Standard*, March 23, New Delhi.

Nagraj, K. (2008) 'Farmer Suicides in India: Magnitudes, Trends and Spatial Patterns', Madras Institute of Technology, *Macroscan*. http://www.macroscan.org/anl/mar08/pdf/Farmers_Suicides.pdf, accessed on 24 February 2015.

Nagaraj, K., P. Sainath, R. Rukmani, and R. Gopinath (2014) "Farmers' Suicides in India: Magnitudes, Trends, and Spatial Patterns, 1997–2012", *Tenth Anniversary Conference of the Foundation for Agrarian Studies, "On Agrarian Issues"*, January 9–12, Kochi.

Nair, K. N. and Aridam Banerjee (2011) 'Structural Changes in Land Distribution and Implications for Improving Access to Land', in D. Narayana and Raman Mahadeven (eds.), *Shaping India: Economic Change in Historical Perspective*, New Delhi: Routledge: 46–66.

Nair, K. N. and Vineetha Menon (2010) 'Distress, Debt, and Suicides among Farmer Households: Findings from Village Studies in Kerela', in D. Narsimha Reddy and Srijit Mishra (eds.), *Agrarian Crisis in India*, New Delhi: Oxford University Press: 230–260.

Nair, K. N. and Gurpreet Singh (2014) 'Some Issues Concerning the Role of Technological and Institutional Changes in the Growth and Transformation of Agriculture in Punjab', Paper presented at the International Conference on *Rejuvenation of Punjab Economy*, organized by the Centre for Development Economics and Innovation Studies, Punjabi University, Patiala, March 21–23.

Narayanamoorthy, A. (2006) 'Relief Package for Farmers: Can It Stop Suicides?' *Economic and Political Weekly*, XLI(31): 3353–3355.

National Commission on Farmers (NCF) (2006) 'Serving Farmers and Saving Farming – Towards Faster and More Inclusive Growth of Farmers' Welfare', Government of India, Ministry of Agriculture, New Delhi: National Commission on Farmers.

National Sample Survey Organization (NSSO) (1956) *All India Rural Credit Survey – 1951–52*, Mumbai: Reserve Bank of India, Government of India.

National Sample Survey Organization (NSSO) (2005a) 'All India Debt and Investment Survey – "Household Indebtedness in India as on 30.06.2002"', Ministry of Planning and Statistics Implementation, New Delhi: Government of India.

National Sample Survey Organization (NSSO) (2005b) 'Indebtedness of Farmer Households', 59th Round, Publication No. 498, New Delhi: Government of India.

North, D. C. (2003) 'The Role of Institutions in Economic Development', Discussion Paper Series No. 2003.2, Geneva: United Nations Economics Commission for Europe.

PAU (2009) 'Farmers' and Agricultural Labourers' Suicides Due to Indebtedness in the Punjab State: A Pilot Survey of Bathinda and Sangrur Districts', Ludhiana: Punjab Agriculture University.

Pavithra, S. and Kamal Vatta (2013) 'Role of Non-Farm Sector in Sustaining Rural Livelihoods in Punjab', *Agricultural Economics Research Review*, 26(2): 257–265.

Posani, Balamuralidhar (2009) 'Crisis in the Countryside: Farmer Suicides and the Political Economy of Agrarian Distress in India', Working Paper Series, No. 09-95, Development Studies Institute, London: London School of Economics and Political Science.

Pradhan, Narayan Chandra (2013) 'Persistence of Informal Credit in Rural India: Evidence from "All-India Debt and Investment Survey" and Beyond', WPS (DEPR):05/2013. RBI Working Paper Series, Mumbai: Reserve Bank of India.

Punjab State Farmers' Commission (PSFC, 2006) *Agricultural and Rural Development of Punjab: Transforming Crisis to Growth*, Chandigarh: Government of Punjab.

Punjab State Farmers' Commission (PSFC, 2007) *Flow of Funds to Farmers and Indebtedness in Punjab*, Mohali: Government of Punjab.

Rajeev, Meenakshi, B. P. Vani, and Manojit Bhattacgarjee (2011) 'Nature and Dimensions of Farmers' Indebtedness in India and Karnataka', Working Paper, No. 267, Bangalore: The Institute of Social and Economic Change.

Ramachandran, V. K. and M. S. Swaminathan (2005 eds.) *Financial Liberalisation and Rural Credit in India,* New Delhi: Tulika Books.

Rangi, P. S. and M. S. Sidhu (2000) 'A Study of Contract Farming of Tomato in Punjab', *Agricultural Marketing*, 42(4): 15–23.

Rangi, P. S., M. S. Sidhu and Jatinder Sachdeva (2005) 'Farm Indebtedness in Punjab: A Case Study of a Village in Distress', *Productivity*, 46(2–3): 230–239.

Rao, V. M. (2010) 'Farmers' Distress in a Modernizing Agriculture – The Tragedy of the Upwardly Mobile: An Overview', in D. Narsimha Reddy and Srijit Mishra (eds.), *Agrarian Crisis in India*, New Delhi: Oxford University Press: 109–125.

Reddy, D. Narasimha and Srijit Mishra (2009a) *Agrarian Crisis in India*, New Delhi: Oxford University Press.

Reddy, D. Narasimha and Srijit Mishra (2009b) 'Agriculture in the Reforms Regime', in D. Narasimha Reddy and Srijit Mishra (eds.), *Agrarian Crisis in India*, New Delhi: Oxford University Press: 1–43.

Rigg, Jonathan (1994) 'Redefining the Village and Rural Life: Lessons from South East Asia', *The Geographical Journal,* 160(2): 123–135.

Sahay, Gaurang R. (2011) 'Globalisation, Liberalisation and Agrarian Distress: A Study of Suicides among Farmers in India', Berlin: VI Global Labour University Conference.

Sanchita, Mukherjee (2009) 'Examining Farmer Suicides in India: A Study of Literature', *Munich Personal RePEc Archive*, Centre for Development Studies, Thiruvananthapuram, http://mpra.ub.uni-muenchen.de/35675/, accessed on 29 July 2012.

Satish, P. (2006) 'Institutional Credit, Indebtedness and Suicides in Punjab', *Economic and Political Weekly*, XLI(26): 2754–2761.

Schultz, T. P. (1988) 'Education Investments and Returns', in Hollis Chenery and T. N. Srinivasan (eds.), *Handbook of Development Economics*, Vol. 1, Amsterdam: North Holland: 543–632.

Sekhon, M. K., M. Kaur, M. S. Sidhu and A. K. Mahal (2011) 'Squeezing Size of Land Holdings and Sustainability to Farming in Punjab', in H. S. Shergill, S. S. Gill and Gurmail Singh (eds.), *Understanding North-West Indian Economy*, New Delhi: Serials Publications.

Shah, Mihir, Rangu Rao and P. S. Vijay Shankar (2007) 'Rural Credit in 20th Century India: Overview of History and Perspectives', *Economic and Political Weekly*, 42(15): 1351–1364.

Sharma, Devinder (2008) 'Indian Villages for Sale', *News Letter*, 13 February, Accessed on 14 July 2014 from www.countercurrent.org.

Shergill, H. S. (1998) *Rural Credit and Indebtedness in Punjab*, Chandigarh: Institute Development Communication.

Shergill, H. S. (2010) *Growth of Farm Debt in Punjab 1997 to 2008*, Chandigarh: Institute Development Communication.

Shergill, H. S. (2011) 'Globalisation and Growth of Farmer's Indebtedness in Punjab', in H. S. Shergill, S. S. Gill and Gurmail Singh (eds.), *Understanding North-West Indian Economy*, New Delhi: Serials Publications: 203–218.

Shergill, H. S. (2013) *Why Area under Rice Will Not Be Reduced in Punjab*, Chandigarh: Institute for Development and Communication (IDC).

Shetty, S. L. (2010) 'Agricultural Credit and Indebtedness', in D. Narsimha Reddy and Srijit Mishra (eds.), *Agrarian Crisis in India*, New Delhi: Oxford University Press.

Sidhu, Aman and Inderjit Singh Jaijee (2011) *Debt and Death in Rural India – The Story of Punjab*, New Delhi: Sage Publishers.

Sidhu, M. S. (2014) 'Marketing and Agricultural Development in Punjab', Paper presented at the International Conference on *Rejuvenation of Punjab Economy*, organized by the Centre for Development Economics and Innovation Studies, Punjabi University, Patiala, March 21–23.

Sidhu, M. S. and V. P. Singh (2011) 'Problems and Prospects of Agriculture in Punjab', in H. S. Shergill, S. S. Gill and Gurmail Singh (eds.), *Understanding North-West Indian Economy*, New Delhi: Serials.

Sidhu, R. S., A. S. Bhullar and A. S. Joshi (2005) 'Income, Employment and Productivity Growth in the Farming Sector of Punjab: Some Issues', *Journal of Indian School of Political Economy*, 17(1 and 2): 59–72.

Sidhu, R. S., Sukhpal Singh, A. Kaur and M. Goyal (2000) 'Loans Overdue and Indebtedness in Punjab Agriculture: A Case of Cotton Belt', NABARD Chair Unit, Ludhiana: Punjab Agricultural University.

Sidhu, R. S., Sukhpal Singh and A. S. Bhullar (2011) 'Farmer Suicides in Punjab: A Census Survey of the Two Most Affected Districts', *Economic and Political Weekly*, XLVI(26 and 27): 131–137.

Sidhu, R. S., K. Vatta and A. Kaur (2011) 'Instability in Crop Yields and Variability across Different Farm Size Categories in Punjab', *Journal of Agricultural Development and Policy*, 21(1): 9–20.

Singh, Dipinder (2011) 'Economic Development, Rural Non-Farm Employment and Public Policy: A Case Study of Punjab', Chapter 4: 56–82 (unpublished Ph.D. Thesis), Patiala: Punjabi University.

Singh, I. and P. Aggarwal (2010) 'Ecological Implications of Agriculture Development in Punjab', in S. S. Gill, Lakhwinder Singh and Reena Marwah (eds.), *Economic and Environmental Sustainability of the Asian Region*, New Delhi: Routledge: 183–200.

Singh, Inderjeet, Sukhwinder Singh and Lakhwinder Singh (2014) 'Economic Development in Punjab – An Introduction', in Inderjeet Singh, Sukhwinder Singh and Lakhwinder Singh (eds.), *Punjab's Economic Development in the Era of Globalisation*, Delhi: LG Publishers and Distributors: 11–39.

Singh, K., S. Singh and H. S. Kingra (2009) 'Agrarian Crisis and Depeasantisation in Punjab: Status of Small/Marginal Farmers Who Left Agriculture', *Indian Journal of Agriculture Economics*, 64(4): 585–603.

Singh, Karam (2009) 'Agrarian Crisis in Punjab: Indebtedness, Low Returns and Farmers' Suicides', in D. Narsimha Reddy and Srijit Mishra (eds.), *Agrarian Crisis in India*, New Delhi: Oxford University Press: 261–284.

216 References

Singh, Lakhwinder (2002) 'Restructuring Monetary and Fiscal Policies for the Indian Federation', in R. N. Pal (ed.), *Indian Constitution: A Review,* Chandigarh: CRRID Publications.

Singh, Lakhwinder and Sukhpal Singh (2002) 'Deceleration of Economic Growth in Punjab: Evidence, Explanation and a Way-Out', *Economic and Political Weekly*, 37(6): 579–586.

Singh, S. (2016) "Rethinking Diversification of Agriculture in the Indian Punjab: An Examination of Strategy and Mechanisms", in Lakhwinder Singh Nirvikar Singh (Eds.), *Economic Transformation of a Developing Economy: The Experience of Punjab, India.* Singapore: Springer Nature, 77–96.

Singh, S. and S. Bhogal (2014) 'Punjab's Small Peasantry: Thriving or Deteriorating?', *Economic and Political Weekly*, 49(26 and 27): 95–100.

Singh, S., H. S. Kingra and Sangeeta (2011) 'Agrarian Crisis, Indebtedness and Farmers' Suicides in Punjab', in H.S. Shergill, S. S. Gill and Gurmail Singh (eds.), *Understanding North-West Indian Economy*, New Delhi: Serials: 187–202.

Singh, Satjit (2008) 'Human Capital, Household Inequality and Public Policy: A Case Study of Rural Punjab' (unpublished Ph.D. Thesis), Patiala: Punjabi University.

Singh, Sukhpal and Sangeet (2014) 'Economic Conditions of Agricultural Labourers and Public Policies in Punjab', in Inderjit Singh, Sukhwinder Singh and Lakhwinder Singh (eds.), *Punjab's Economic Development in the Era of Globalisation*, New Delhi: LG Publishers: 215–228.

Singh, Sukhpal, Manjeet Kaur and H. S. Kingra (2008) 'Indebtedness among Farmers in Punjab', *Economic and Political Weekly*, 43(26/27): 130–136.

Sirohi, Samita and B. C. Barah (2011) 'Policy Imperatives for Addressing Agrarian Distress', in B. C. Barah and Samita Sirohi (eds.), *Agrarian Distress in India: Problems and Remedies*, New Delhi: Concept Publishing Company.

Sridhar, V. (2004) 'An Agrarian Tragedy', *Frontline*, 21(13): 4–29.

Suri, K. C. (2006) 'Political Economy of Agrarian Distress', *Economic and Political Weekly*, XLI(16): 1523–1529.

Swaminathan, M. S. (2006) 'Serving Farmers and Saving Farming – Towards Faster and More Inclusive Growth of Farmers' Welfare', Government of India, Ministry of Agriculture, New Delhi: National Commission on Farmers.

TNS (2002) 'Bhattal Promises Relief to Farmers', *The Tribune*, 22 July, Chandigarh.

The Tribune (2014) 'Farmers' Suicides: Hassanpur Brothers Had Lost Father to Same Old Debt', *The Tribune*, 12 May, 4, Chandigarh.

UNDP (2012) 'The Rise in the South-Human Progress in the Diverse World', *Human Development Report 2013*, New York: The United Nation Development Programme.

Vasavi, A. R. (2012) 'Shadow Spaces: Suicides and the Predicament of Rural India', Gurgaon: Three Essays Collective.

Vijayakumar, Lakshmi Jane Pirkis, Tran Thanh Huong, Paul Yip, Rohini De A. Seneviratne and Herbert Hendin (2012) 'Socio-Economic, Cultural and Religious Factors Affecting Suicide Prevention in Asia', www.who.int/mental_health, accessed on 23 July 2012.

Vyas, V.S. (2004) 'Agrarian Distress: Strategies to Protect Vulnerable Sections', *Economic and Political Weekly*, 39(52): 5576–5579 and 5581–5582.

INDEX

Note: Page numbers in *italic* indicate a figure and page numbers in **bold** indicate a table on the corresponding page.

For Product Safety Concerns and Information please contact our EU
representative GPSR@taylorandfrancis.com
Taylor & Francis Verlag GmbH, Kaufingerstraße 24, 80331 München, Germany

www.ingramcontent.com/pod-product-compliance
Ingram Content Group UK Ltd.
Pitfield, Milton Keynes, MK11 3LW, UK
UKHW021308290425
457818UK00043B/137